MASTERS OF THE COMIC BOOK UNIVERSE REVEALED!

ARIE KAPLAN

CHICAGO
REVIEW
PRESS

Library of Congress Cataloging-in-Publication Data

Kaplan, Arie.
  Masters of the comic book universe revealed! / Arie Kaplan.
      p. cm.
  Includes index.
  ISBN-13: 978-1-55652-633-6
  ISBN-10: 1-55652-633-4
  1. Cartoonists—United States—Biography. 2. Comic books, strips,
etc.—History and criticism. I. Title.
  NC1305.K37 2006
  741.092'2—dc22

                                    2006005410

Cover and interior design: Todd Petersen
Cover illustration: Ray Alma

First edition
Published by Chicago Review Press, Incorporated
814 North Franklin Street
Chicago, Illinois 60610
ISBN-13: 978-1-55562-633-6
ISBN-10: 1-55652-633-4
Printed in the United States of America
5 4 3 2 1

To my wife, Nadine Graham, my unofficial copy editor, for speaking her mind and telling me when anything in my manuscript was clichéd, trite, insipid, hacky, or just plain lame-ass. I love you too.

CONTENTS

ACKNOWLEDGMENTS

Throughout the course of writing this book, I was fortunate enough to have the help of many extraordinary people whose selflessness and loyalty were truly superheroic.

My three research assistants, Christina Harris, Anya Ciccone, and Max Bank, all deserve my deepest thanks for the seemingly endless hours they spent transcribing interviews and looking up obscure factoids.

Natalie Giboney of FreelancePermissions.com was indispensable in researching, requesting, and securing the permission to use much of the artwork found throughout this book.

I would also like to thank my wonderful editor Yuval Taylor for his guidance, and my incredible agent Rita Rosenkranz for helping to realize this project. Illustrator Ray Alma knocked it out of the park with his amazing cover art.

Lifelong friends Carl Kelsch and Rachel Gordon waded through my frighteningly overwritten first draft, helping me hack it down to a workable length.

Among those who made this book possible with their tireless efforts on my behalf are Joe Raiola, Charlie Kadau, John Ficarra, Nick Meglin, Sam Viviano, Greg Leitman, Jon Bresman, Dave Croatto, and Amy Vozeolas at *MAD* magazine; Paul Kupperberg and Thomas C. King at DC Comics; Gary Groth, Dirk Deppey, Kim Thompson, and Eric Reynolds at Fantagraphics Books; Denis Kitchen at the Kitchen & Hansen Agency; Elizabeth Clementson at W. W. Norton; Ed Orloff at the Wylie Agency; Michiko Clark at Random House; Aron Hirt-Manheimer and Joy Weinberg at *Reform Judaism* magazine; as well as John Romita, Anne Timmons, Sophia Quach, Al Jaffee, Peter Kuper, Patton Oswalt, Harris Miller, Lorraine Garland, Nicole Duncan-Smith, Lou Anders, Chris Roberson, Glenn Waldorf, Frank Santopadre, Jay Pinkerton, Chris Duffy, Dave Roman, Mike Lynch, Jim Salicrup, Bob Andelman, Mark Simonson, Barry Joseph, and Caroline

Bartels. Special thanks should also go to Bobby and Sara Kaplan (for not throwing away my comic book collection), and David Kaplan (for not *selling* my comic book collection).

And last but certainly not least, I'd like to thank the eleven masters of the comic book universe profiled within these pages, all of whom allowed me to interview them at such length. Your generosity is greatly appreciated.

INTRODUCTION

Neil Gaiman told me that when he first discovered American comics as a small child, it was like "reading postcards from Oz." I suspect it's like that for anyone who becomes enchanted with comic books at an early age; a comic book is a missive from another world. There's an energy in that combination of words and pictures, a sense that anything is possible.

So I found it odd when I started this project that no existing book chronicled the lives of the artists and writers who created the most seminal and memorable of these "postcards."

Oh sure, there are books of interviews with comics professionals. *The New Comics*, edited by Gary Groth and Robert Fiore, and Will Eisner's *Shop Talk* come to mind as particularly insightful. But these books are chock-full of shop talk and factoids. What they lack is a bigger picture of their subjects' lives. Who are the men and women who had the greatest impact on the comics industry over the past seven-plus decades? Who are they as *people*? Not as artisans, not as "behind the scene" technicians.

This book is a sort of oral history of the comics industry. The chapters are in chronological order: Will Eisner started out in 1936, so he goes first; Marjane Satrapi first published her work in 1999, so she gets the final chapter. This way you'll get a sense of how the industry has changed over the decades—from the teenage workhorses and street kids of the 1930s to the intellectual graphic novelists and superstar virtuosos of today.

Comics have become much more diverse over the years. I felt this fact was missing from many of the books on comics currently out there, and I wanted to shed light on it. Comics is the ultimate democratic medium. All you need—literally—is a pencil and paper to tell your story. Unlike film, with which comics storytelling is often compared, you don't need foreign investors, $100 million, and a major star attached. Because of this, many in today's comic book world have chosen to use the medium as a forum on the struggle of the oppressed. You see this in Kyle Baker's depiction of the Nat Turner revolt; in Art Spiegelman's war-torn Holocaust memoirs; in Marjane Satrapi's stories of the Islamic Revolution in Iran; in Will Eisner's chronicles of old-time Jewish New York; in Ho Che Anderson's Wellesian docudrama about the life and death of Martin Luther King; in Neil Gaiman's frank, honest depiction of human sexuality; in Gilbert Hernandez's tales of Palomar, the mythical Central American small town. You see it in Stan Lee's vision of a 1960s-era multicultural superhero community, and in Dwayne McDuffie's nineties-era version of same. You see it in Jerry Robinson's angry political cartoons and in Trina Robbins's equally trenchant feminist funnies. And while diversity in comics still has a way to go, I believe the cartoonists profiled herein are a damn good start.

So many of the people I interviewed for this book got into comics purely by accident. As you'll see in the ensuing chapters, almost everyone tells the same story: artist (or writer) falls in love with comics during childhood, then, convinced that comics have no potential to get their message across, abandons them to try and make it in more respected media, only to return to the form when they realize that it gives them the creative autonomy they've craved all along! But how they get from point to point, taking different twists and turns, makes each story gripping.

During the 1930s and '40s, comics were often thought of as the lowest point on the cultural totem pole, as both Stan Lee and Will Eisner kept reminding me when I interviewed them. Even today, there's an implicit message that almost any other medium is more worthy of artistic legitimacy than comics. As Kyle Baker told me, when he was starting out in "the biz" about twenty years ago, many comic book writers strove to break into ad copywriting. That sent a shiver down my spine. Hopefully, future generations will see comics for what they are: a medium comparable to art and literature, and equally capable of greatness.

Because of comics' status as lowbrow art, it required quite a bit of research to unearth the true stories behind the stories. I interviewed many of my subjects two, three, sometimes four times just to discover the more obscure anecdotes that even the most blasé comics fan *didn't* know about Eisner, Gaiman, Lee, Hernandez, et al. Along the way I found out little scraps of information about my subjects that had no place in the manuscript but were nevertheless revealing. When Kyle Baker was directing animated short subjects for Warner Brothers, the venerable film studio wouldn't let him turn Yosemite Sam into the more topical (but potentially troublesome) "Afghanistan Sam." Before I got to ask Marjane Satrapi word one of my carefully prepared questions, she went on an hour-long tirade about her problems with the Bush administration and the situation in Iraq (not that I didn't agree with her). Neil Gaiman, famous for crafting disturbing tales of existential horror, was surprisingly nostalgic in his praise for the light-hearted and zany Bob Rozakis and Stephen DeStefano DC title *'Mazing Man*. When Stan Lee and I got to talking about *Buffy the Vampire Slayer*, it dawned on Stan that the Slayer bore a certain resemblance to his webbed wall-crawler, whereupon he excitedly told me, "She could be Peter Parker's sister!"

In fact, *Buffy* also came up in discussions with Dwayne McDuffie and Trina Robbins, rabid fans of that show, who saw corollaries between the Slayer and their respective female superhero characters, Rocket and GoGirl. Another person whose name came up in virtually every interview was the legendary King of Comics, Jack Kirby. I found it fascinating that even Gilbert Hernandez, whose *Love & Rockets* provides an edgier alternative to the colorful, wide-eyed superheroes that dominate comicdom, considers Kirby a formative influence. In a way, the continuous mention of the King provided a connective tissue that bound many of the chapters, implicitly saying, "We may be creating different types of stories, but in the end, it's all comics."

Finally, while I truly believe that the people profiled in this book represent some of the most influential and important comic book creators in the history of the medium, it was terribly difficult narrowing down the list to just eleven. But, you know, space restrictions.

Oh well, there's always the sequel.

WILL EISNER

SELF-PORTRAIT.

"In the dark valleys of the underworld, where men laugh at the law and only the nimble survive, one man stands as a constant threat to the security of those whose cunning enables them to outwit the police! There are many to testify that not even death can halt The Spirit!"

—*The Spirit*, March 24, 1946

In every field there's someone who did things first and, more importantly, did them best. In comics there was Will Eisner, creator of the long-running comic strip *The Spirit* (1940–1952); author of the foremost book on the art of comics storytelling (1985's *Comics and Sequential Art*); and father of the modern graphic novel (1978's *A Contract with God*).

In the twenty-five years before his death in January of 2005, Eisner was elevated from beloved comics pioneer to nigh-omnipotent godfather of modern comics. He was famously consulted by author Michael Chabon while the latter was researching his Pulitzer Prize–winning novel, *The Amazing Adventures of Kavalier and Clay*, about two cartoonists during comics' Golden Age. He even had an award named after him: the Eisners, which Eisner himself presented every year from 1988 through 2004 at the San Diego Comic-Con, one of the nation's most lavish annual comic book fan conventions. What Ibsen was to modern drama, what Chaplin was to film, what Rodgers and Hart were to musical theater, Eisner was to comicdom.

WOW, WHAT A FUTURE!

Born on March 6, 1917, in Brooklyn, New York, William Erwin Eisner grew up in the crowded tenements that would become the backdrop for many of his graphic novels. As a teenager, he attended DeWitt Clinton High School in the Bronx, whose alumni also include fellow comics pioneers Bob Kane, Bill Finger, and Stan Lee; Eisner saw his first cartoons published in the school paper. He had a passion for the comics section of the newspapers he was selling on street corners to help his family make ends meet. But he didn't want to simply read comics; he wanted to *draw* them.

In 1936, Eisner began his comics career writing and drawing now-for-gotten comics features like "The Flame" and "Harry Karry" for the short-lived title *Wow, What A Magazine!* The magazine lasted only four issues, after which Eisner and *Wow*'s editor, fellow comics pioneer S. M. "Jerry" Iger, cofounded the Eisner-Iger Studio, one of the first comics produc-tion shops. They specialized in providing comics features to comic book and newspaper publishers who lacked an in-house art staff. Among Eisner and Iger's creations was "Sheena, Queen of the Jungle," the first success-ful female action hero in comics, who appeared in 1938 in *Jumbo Comics* #1. Basically a female Tarzan, Sheena influenced the work of future comics creators such as Trina Robbins (*GoGirl!*) and Dave Stevens (*Rocketeer*).

While running Eisner-Iger, Will Eisner employed future comics leg-ends such as Lou Fine (*The Ray*) and Mort Meskin (*Vigilante*). But although he was a consummate draftsman with an eye for talent, he still made a few errant judgment calls, including turning down a colorful char-acter named Superman created by two hardworking teens named Jerry Siegel and Joe Shuster. "I told them they weren't ready for prime time," Eisner laughed, shaking his head at the memory.

Another of Eisner's employees was his former *Wow, What a Magazine!* cohort, Bob Kane. "[Bob] worked as a freelancer for us—he didn't work in the shop," Eisner clarified. "Bob Kane and I were high school buddies. And he showed up one day when we just started Eisner and Iger, and we put him on a feature called "Peter Pupp." It was a Disney imitation. Shortly after that, he called me up, he came over and said, 'I'm leaving.' I said, 'Why are you leaving?' He said, 'You're only paying me five dollars a page.' I think [DC Comics] offered him seven or eight dollars a page to go do adventure features. I said 'Well, Bob you can't do adventure, you don't know how to draw that well!' [He said], 'No, I can do it!' And he started a thing called *Batman*. Actually the creation of superheroes starts when the character is very raw. I mean, Siegel and Shuster's early *Superman* was poorly done, based on the standards we have today. And they were primitive for the most part. So was *Batman*! But Batman was a good idea, and so was Superman. Anyway, superheroes of the day never remained what they were in the beginning. Matter of fact, the superheroes you have today have been done by a whole number of people over the years—none of them are being done by the original creator. So what you're seeing today are characters that were originally created because they're a novel idea, but they've been embel-lished and improved on, and so forth."

Another future comics legend who worked for Eisner in those days was the legendary "King of Comics" Jack Kirby, who would go on to cocreate the X-Men, the Hulk, the New Gods, and Captain America, among many other characters. According to Eisner, Kirby worked for him "around 1937 or 1938. He worked in the shop for about six months, that's about it. He was doing a classic comic for us. We were starting classic comics some time before the actual great classic comics." Eisner is referring to the Gilberton Company's "Classic Comics," which specialized in comics adaptations of literary classics. "It was a story called *The Count of Monte Cristo*. He did an adaptation of that for us, and so forth. A nice, hard-working guy."

Eisner and Kirby shared a belief that the artistic potential of comics rivaled that of film, theater, or prose fiction. Eisner knew that many of the other artists working under him didn't share this philosophy. "Most of the guys working at the Eisner-Iger Studio, all of them in fact, were there hoping to make enough money to move on uptown," Eisner said. "For them, becoming an illustrator one day [was their goal]. I was the only one in the shop that believed that he was going to spend the rest of his life in this medium. I was convinced it had a future."

How did Eisner maintain his dream of a life in comics, when so many others wouldn't even entertain the idea? "It occurred to me very early on that this medium had greater potential," Eisner explained. "That it was more of a literary medium than anybody else thought. I knew I could do it well. You know, you stay with it. I believed in the medium. . . . I guess psychologically, I wasn't as dependent on standard approvals as the other guys were. In other words, it didn't matter to me that nobody saw it my way." Did it ever upset him that comics were thought of only as cheap, disposable kiddy fare, and not as art with a capital *A*? "Yes, I was angry that nobody thought much of the medium, but I thought that I could prevail."

THE SPIRIT OF THE TIMES

Picture it: Captain Batt, a demented, nautical ne'er-do-well with rheumy, sightless eyes and a vulture's beak, pilots a rusty scupper known as the *Sea Rot II* northward through the arctic. The good Captain's looking for "a million in whale oil, bone, and meat." When one of his lackeys realizes that the blind Batt is a pirate, and that they'll be sailing under a Jolly Roger flag, he wants no part of it, and his neck is wrung like a dishtowel. The next morning when the lackey's corpse is discovered, The Spirit, a strapping galoot of a lawman with a domino mask and a lantern jaw, is dispatched to find the culprit and bring him to justice. Thus begins a typical installment of Eisner's landmark newspaper strip *The Spirit*.

In 1939, Eisner left his partnership with Iger after being wooed by newspaper syndicates, and in 1940 he debuted "The Spirit Section," a sixteen-page newspaper supplement (or "insert") composed of various comic strip features. The Spirit Section was designed to compete with the then-burgeoning comic book market, and its lead feature was of course *The Spirit* itself.

Eisner recalled that while the Golden Age of comic books (roughly 1938–1950) is fondly regarded today, those who lived through it have a more realistic take. "For those of us who were in the Golden Age, [we] didn't know it was the Golden Age! It was the Leaden Age as far as we were concerned," he laughed. "Aside from earning little money, the work you were doing was not regarded by the social, cultural arbiters as being worth anything! So we hardly thought of it as an era of great cultural prominence." For example, in the early 1940s, Eisner created an entire menagerie of costumed characters for Quality Comics, including Black Condor, Uncle Sam, and Doll Man—but his creative freedom, his ability to tell and sustain a good story, was severely hampered by an industry (and a readership) that just didn't care about such things.

It was partly because of comic books' bottom-rung reputation that Eisner started *The Spirit* (also created for the Quality Comics Group), as a newspaper insert. At that time, newspaper comics afforded greater artistic freedom (and financial compensation), and were regarded with more critical discernment than the lowly comic book, which was usually produced hastily and with only the bottom line in mind. Indeed, literary critic Gilbert Seldes and poet e.e. cummings both lavished praise on George Herriman's newspaper strip *Krazy Kat* (which Eisner called a "strong influence" on *The Spirit*), and one couldn't imagine a comic book in 1939 that enjoyed a similar position in the artistic limelight. Eisner explained that he felt compelled to undertake *The Spirit* "because I felt that [newspaper strips are] literature, I wanted to do literature. I didn't want to stay in what I regarded as the 'comic book ghetto.' The Register Tribune Syndicate came by and asked me if I would produce a comic book insert for magazines and Sunday newspapers. They weren't called comic books in those days, they were called 'comic magazines.' And I remember it was a very difficult decision at the moment because I was a partner in Eisner and Iger, and the company was doing extremely well, we were making a lot of money, and I had to make a decision. I had to leave Eisner and Iger. I couldn't do both, in other words. So I had to give up one.

"But the decision was made easier by the fact that this would be an opportunity at long last to work for a vehicle that would enable me to reach adults, so I could write adult stories. Remember, I grew up on pulps." Eisner recalled formative 1930s pulp magazines like *The Shadow* (by Walter Gibson) and *Doc Savage* (by Lester Dent), which clearly informed the action-adventure style of *The Spirit*. "I grew up on short stories. I was an avid reader. And I wanted, I needed, I guess, to write this kind of material. And [doing *The Spirit*] gave me the opportunity to do it." Indeed, the Spirit's mysterious demeanor is reminiscent of the Shadow, and his strapping, rough-and-tumble build and all-American boyish charm remind one of Doc Savage. Clearly, *The Spirit* was Eisner's chance to finally inject some literary merit into the superhero genre.

Eisner cited other influences on the Spirit as well, including the easygoing charm of actor Cary Grant and fellow cartoonists Milton Caniff (*Terry and the Pirates*) and Elzie Segar (*Thimble Theater*). But in the end, *The Spirit*'s entire twelve-year run can be read as one protracted Damon Runyonesque comic novel. The cartooning influences run deep, and one can see the Segar influence in the character of Commissioner Dolan, with his horseshoe jaw, abrasive manner, and corncob pipe all reminiscent of *Thimble Theater*'s most famous player, Popeye. One can almost imagine a young Eisner, hawking newspapers on the streets of New York, taking a lunch break to pore over the exploits of the spinach-scarfing sailor man, and letting Segar's magic weave its spell on his young, impressionable mind.

Many critics now say that *The Spirit*, a unique mix of bravura, derring-do, and tongue-in-cheek slapstick that ran until 1952, was one of the first attempts at the "action-comedy" genre in comics form, inspiring later efforts such as Stan Lee and Jack Kirby's *Fantastic Four* and Lowell Cunningham's *Men in Black*. Eisner used the strip to spoof conventions of the superhero and film noir genres, and *The Spirit* soon became famous for its uniquely cinematic layout and panel arrangements, including the "splash page," an opening page consisting of a single, dynamic, movie-poster-sized panel. Today, nearly every comic book opens with a splash page, a measure of Eisner's influence on the medium. Similarly, Eisner's use of light, shadow, and eye-popping camera angles recalls film classics such as *Citizen Kane* and *Metropolis;* and more recent cartoonists such as Dave Stevens, Gilbert and Jaime Hernandez (*Love & Rockets*), Seth (*Palookaville*), Frank Miller (*Sin City*), and Mike Mignola (*Hellboy*) are just as indebted to Eisner as they are to film history, employing a similarly moody, nuanced, "noir-drenched" tone in their comics.

In the pages of *The Spirit*, no story was too big or too bizarre to handle. Archaeologists in the far-flung future reading about how the Spirit battled the oldest man alive, unaware that the crusty old immortal is standing right behind them, ready to murder them both? Why not? Hitler wandering around New York trying to explain himself? No problem! But as much of a playground of ideas as *The Spirit* was, Eisner was itching for a bigger canvas. It might have been more literary than *Batman* or *Superman*, more cleverly written and cinematically rendered than *Captain America* or *Wonder Woman*, but it was still a superhero comic, still genre fiction. (Of course, the Spirit was a "superhero" only in the loosest definition of the term; he didn't have any innate superpowers, but then again neither did Batman, Green Lantern, or the original Sandman. Here the term superhero is used to mean "masked crime fighter," which the Spirit definitely was.) Eisner had even drawn a mask on the Spirit, his one concession to his boss at Quality, Everett "Busy" Arnold, who insisted that he bow to this superhero genre convention. After all, Arnold had said, "A superhero has to have a costume!" But Eisner drew the line at the Spirit's mask, refusing to put his hero in a cape and tights like Superman or Batman.

Two of the characters in *The Spirit*'s repertory company were broad ethnic caricatures: Blubber, who was a proper-speaking Eskimo boy and who filled in as the Spirit's sometime sidekick; and the Spirit's regular sidekick, the African American Ebony White. Ebony, with his *Amos & Andy*-style dialect and clownish appearance, is certainly offensive to modern sensibilities, as is Blubber, with his monkeyish demeanor. But it's also worth noting that during the strip's run, Eisner introduced the character of Detective Grey, one of the first black private eyes seen in a mainstream newspaper strip, who was as dignified and well-spoken as any of the other characters. In 1946, perhaps due to changing attitudes toward minorities in the postwar era, Eisner realized that Ebony's dialect humor was insulting, and the Spirit's sidekick was quickly sent to the all-black Carter School for Boys to rid himself of his "minstrel accent." The storyline: Ebony is embarrassed after his girlfriend makes fun of said accent. And it doesn't help that Ebony has a rival for his ladylove's affections, the African American army captain Fraternization H. Shack, who speaks with a very proper British inflection. Ebony never abandoned his accent, but the very fact that he was self-conscious about it meant that Eisner was as well. The Carter School for Boys was a chance for Eisner to introduce black headmasters, teachers, and other positive African American role models into the strip, all of whom spoke perfect English, and all of whom were depicted with dignity. Clearly, Eisner was beginning to develop more of a social consciousness in his work, and this would emerge further as the decades progressed.

It was also at this time that Eisner took on a young assistant named Jules Feiffer, the future *Village Voice* cartoonist, author of Broadway play *Little Murders*, and screenwriter of *Carnal Knowledge* and *Popeye*, among

A WHIMSICAL DRAWING OF THE SPIRIT DRAWING WILL EISNER. IN THE PAGES OF THE SPIRIT, EISNER SOMETIMES LIKED TO BREAK THE FOURTH WALL.

other accomplishments. But in 1946, Jules Feiffer was merely a bookish kid with an encyclopedic knowledge of the works of Will Eisner. So he called up his idol and arranged an appointment.

As Eisner remembered, "Feiffer came into the shop to work as a kind of general shop assistant. He did coloring and backgrounds, and things of that sort. One day, I was up against the schedule, and I said, 'Jules, would you do these balloons? Finish the story for me.' Because I would write the story, generally, through the very ending. And I looked at the balloon he did, and I said, 'This guy's incredible!'" Eisner was so impressed that Feiffer gradually progressed to writing whole *Spirit* scripts. Eisner is also quick to point out that Feiffer "could draw well enough to do a rough of the story, because the way we'd do a story in our shop was to start with big pencil roughs, sometimes we would do stick figures, and doing what you might call a storyboard, laying out the story with stick figures and dialogue. After a while, he did a number of stories. Matter of fact, the big joke between us now, when we get together, is he'll say, 'You wrote this story!' And I'll say, 'No *you* wrote that story!' We don't remember which stories we wrote."

Feiffer would work on *The Spirit* until 1952, eventually even drawing his own strip, a *Peanuts*-style feature called *Clifford*, as part of The Spirit Section. During their time together on *The Spirit*, Feiffer and Eisner used the series to experiment with the medium of comics, sometimes breaking the fourth wall to an absurd degree. Perhaps the most irreverent example of this "experimental" phase of *The Spirit* is seen in the December 31, 1950, installment, when Jules Feiffer is seen creeping into Eisner's studio, murdering Eisner, and taking over the series, whereupon Feiffer dresses Clifford up as the Spirit in order to fool the audience into thinking they're still reading *The Spirit*. "That gives you an idea of the kind of jokes that were running around the shop at that time," Eisner laughed. "We had a very good working relationship. We're still good friends to this day. And I admire what he's grown to be, and I admired him enough in the days he was in the shop. We had a good philosophical compatibility."

In *The Spirit*'s final months (July–October 1952), Eisner—aided by Feiffer, as well as *MAD* magazine cartoonist Wally Wood—embarked on a series of "Outer Space Spirit" tales, taking the masked galoot into the realm of science fiction. This final story arc involved the Spirit embarking on a government-sponsored experimental mission to the moon. Many of the breathtaking cosmic vistas and alien landscapes in these stories were courtesy of Wood, and were reminiscent of his work on EC Comics' *Weird Science* (which he was also producing at this time). This was further evidence of Eisner's desire to stretch *The Spirit* into as many realms as possible.

GOING UNDERGROUND

In 1948, while working on *The Spirit*, Will Eisner formed a commercial art company called The American Visuals Corporation, which created comic strips, cartoons, and humorous illustrations for corporate and educational use. His clients included RCA Records, the Baltimore Colts, and New York Telephone. He missed working in comics, but this work was more profitable, and in the 1950s, superhero comics seemed on their way out. "I had no intention of continuing *The Spirit*," Eisner explained. "I was no longer interested in it. Not that I disliked the character, I just said what I had to say!" But although he had left comics behind, comics fans were about to rediscover *him*.

By the 1970s, the American comic book was no longer the province of mom and pop candy stores and newspaper stands. It was now sold in direct market stores, commonly known as comic book shops, following a distribution plan engineered by entrepreneur Phil Seuling, who also pioneered the comic book fan convention. And one of the curiosities at these early conventions was back-issues of *The Spirit* from the 1940s and '50s, collected as reprints in comic book form. "One of the most surprising things in my career was the survival of *The Spirit*," Eisner recalled, still stunned. "I was

really astounded, in 1971 I guess it was, at a convention I went to, I found people walking around carrying copies of *The Spirit*. I had no idea that it was even known; I thought *The Spirit* was dead. The artwork was just lying in a vault; as far as I was concerned, it was finished." Eisner attributed the longevity of *The Spirit* to the fact that "I had been doing stories aimed at adults. The story material had a greater endurance. Superhero stories never really had the kind of endurance that good short

© Will Eisner Estate

COVER OF ONE OF KITCHEN SINK PRESS'S 1980s-ERA SPIRIT REPRINTS.

stories do." What a concept: good short stories in comics form. And younger cartoonists were latching onto the same concept, going "underground" for creative satisfaction.

Now that comics fans who came of age during the Golden Age were older and more discriminating, there was room for more adult-oriented product. Underground "comix" were the sometimes autobiographical, sometimes surreal, often raunchy alternative to mainstream superhero comics in the 1960s and '70s, usually inspired by the cartoonist's intimate personal experiences. Cartoonists like Robert Crumb (undisputed king of the undergrounds, creator of *Fritz the Cat*, and one of the founding artists of the comix anthology *Zap*), and Art Spiegelman (future creator of the graphic novel *Maus*) were at the forefront of this new generation.

No one was more surprised than Will Eisner at the leaps the comics industry was taking in those days. "Oh, I was very impressed! Matter of fact, I came upon [underground comix] at a convention in New York run by Phil Seuling," Eisner said, recalling that he was surprised to find himself regarded as a mentor to younger cartoonists like Spiegelman and Crumb. "First time I met the underground people, I realized that something revolutionary was happening. It was very much like the revolution that occurred when we started, way, way back, where we were taking daily strips and making complete stories out of them. They were dealing with social problems. Yes, they were raunchy, and they were crude and gritty, but they were using comics as a literary form!" In 1971, fueled by the resurgence of interest in *The Spirit* among the underground comix community, underground publisher/cartoonist Denis Kitchen reprinted a couple of Eisner's old *Spirit* stories under the banner of his Kitchen Sink Press, repackaging them as *Kitchen Sink Underground Spirit*. Starting in 1976, Kitchen Sink resumed publishing reprints of Eisner's *Spirit* strips, until the company stopped publishing comic books in 1999.

The underground comix movement inspired Eisner to return to the comics medium. This time, he forsook the genre conventions of his youth in order to tell stories with a more serious, novel-like scope. "As a matter of fact, I admit that those [underground comix] encouraged me to go back into the graphic novel," he said. Eisner had been thinking about creating a novel in comics form since the late 1930s, inspired by the woodcut novels of artist Lynd Ward, and he had even occasionally experimented throughout the years with the idea of bringing such a project to fruition. But back then, no one would take a novel-length comic book seriously. Now, it seemed, the time was right. The success of the undergrounds meant that his long-ago theories about comics as true art had finally been validated. "I was very energized by seeing the undergrounds. I thought, 'Gee, its time has come,'" he remembered. "The artwork was crude, very primitive art! But whether they intended it or not, they were using comics the way literature is normally used, to dramatically deal with a social problem. Up to that time, it's important to say, comics were used as an entertainment form. They were writing, they were telling stories. They were providing entertainment." Underground comix, however, was genuine social commentary, and the time was ripe for something more ambitious in this vein. So Eisner began work on what he had begun to call a "graphic novel."

THE GREAT AMERICAN GRAPHIC NOVEL

In 1978, Kitchen Sink Press released *A Contract with God*, a series of four related stories by Eisner about Bronx tenement life. The stories were nostalgic, taking place in the early years of the twentieth century, but any bucolic look at the "good old days" is overshadowed by their tone of despair and urban squalor. In the title story, "A Contract with God," protagonist Frimme Hersh, a pious Jewish man, has carved on a stone tablet a "contract with God" to which he attributes his lifelong lucky streak. Now elderly and embittered, Hersh is furious at God for allowing his young daughter Rachele to die of a sudden illness. He belts out at the heavens, "You violated our contract! If God requires that men honor their agreements, then is not God, also, so obligated?" With that, Hersh nullifies the contract, becoming increasingly miserly, corrupt, and lonely.

This story is a variant on the eternal philosophical question, "Why do bad things happen to good people?" Eisner was tackling straight drama, leaving behind the cape-and-costume genre trappings of his earlier days. "I was looking for stories that were purely adult, that were not 'cowboy and Indian,'" he explained. "From our childhood, I realized that we have been told that if we're good, God will reward us. We have a contract with God. And regardless of what religion you're in, the same contract exists. If you're a Christian you're told that if you don't sin, you'll ultimately go to heaven. And the Muslims believe the same kind of thing, Jews believe the same kind of thing." He could now talk about spirituality, racism, anti-Semitism, politics, and anything else under the sun in comic book form. And because of the ambitious scope of *A Contract with God*, he dubbed it a "graphic novel," a label that has become part of the modern pop culture lexicon.

Contrary to popular belief, Will Eisner didn't invent the graphic novel or even coin the term. The phrase "graphic novel" was believed to have been coined by Richard Kyle in 1964 in the pages of the Comic Amateur Press Alliance's newsletter, *Capa-Alpha* #2. The first time a comic book described *itself* as a "graphic novel" was on the title page of underground cartoonist George Metzger's *Beyond Time and Again* (1976), published by Richard Kyle. And various works from previous decades—such as Belgian artist Frans Masereel's 1919 series of woodcuts in book form, called *Passionate Journey*, and Gil Kane and Archie Goodwin's 1971 illustrated novel, *Blackmark*—can be con-

© Will Eisner Estate

EISNER POPULARIZED THE AMERICAN GRAPHIC NOVEL WITH HIS PIONEERING WORK A CONTRACT WITH GOD IN 1978.

sidered early graphic novel prototypes. With *A Contract with God*, however, Eisner popularized the term and perfected what had been an embryonic format. Eisner led by example, encouraging other cartoonists to think of comics as a forum for serious, ambitious storylines.

However, quite a few of his works aren't "novels" in the truest sense of the term, but rather short story collections. *New York: The Big City*, *The Building*, and *City People Notebook* are indicative of Eisner's "anthology" approach. His true "novels in comics form" are his larger, more epic works like *The Dreamer* (a fictionalized account of Eisner's own early escapades in the comic book business), *A Life Force* (a near-future sci-fi tale, but rendered with real dramatic heft), and the autobiographical *To the Heart of the Storm*. A multigenerational saga on par with Francis Ford Coppola's *Godfather* trilogy or Alex Haley's *Roots*, *To the Heart of the Storm* is "frankly autobiographical," Eisner claimed. The book is explicitly based on his family's experiences from the 1880s until his own entry into World War II. "I started [*To the Heart of the Storm*] intending it to be a discussion of anti-Semitism. And as I was doing it, I found myself depending on personal

A PAGE FROM WILL EISNER'S GRAPHIC NOVEL NEW YORK: THE BIG CITY. DEPICTING ONE OF THE MANY CROWD SCENES EISNER WAS FAMOUS FOR THROUGHOUT HIS CAREER, THIS PAGE ALSO DEMONSTRATES HIS MASTERY OF COMPOSITION.

experiences. And so a third of the way through, I thought to myself, 'My God, this is going to be an *autobiographical* graphic novel!' I said, 'I might as well go there. I have a strong visual recall.'"

Apparently, *quite* a strong visual recall. Turn-of-the-century New York is rendered with such accuracy and attention to detail that one has to wonder exactly how much research went into this mammoth work. Not much, it turns out. "A lot of it I pulled out of my memory," Eisner confided.

Ordinarily in creating such an intimate work of family history, one interviews the people involved, as Art Spiegelman did in creating *Maus*. However, *Heart of the Storm* was published in 1991, over one hundred years after some of the events in the book took place. Even the most *recent* events recounted happened fifty years prior. "I did *some* interviewing, but there wasn't much of a family around that I could interview," Eisner shrugged. "It was essentially an exercise in recall, like a therapy session, but when it was all finished I was quite exhausted. As a matter of fact, I went through a lot of difficult moments." Telling the story of your family members, warts and all, can be a tricky tightrope to maneuver. "First of all, there's the business of how to treat [characters based on] your mother and father," he pointed out. "You go through segments of guilt, particularly that your portrayal maybe wasn't fair to them. And you find yourself trying to avoid getting involved in what you feel might be an invalid memory."

One of the lessons Eisner learned from creating *To the Heart of the Storm* is that as we get older, we remember events from our life almost as though they were happening in comic strip form. "You learn in fact that we remember things in segments, almost in panels," he explained. "You remember the time you took cookies out of the cookie jar, but you don't remember before that, or you don't remember after that. Life goes on as a seamless flow, but the things you remember are not seamless at all. They're [dialogue] bubbles or they're panels. Panelization of memory, I guess you might call it that. Impressions last with you. You remember the smell in your grandmother's bedroom when you came in. You remember the smell of an uncle who always smoked cigars. These things stay with you. But they stay with you more viscerally than they do intellectually."

As a result *Heart of the Storm* was illustrated in a more sketchy style than the cleaner line work used on *The Spirit*. "I'm a great believer in the fact that the artwork in [*To the Heart of the Storm*] should be done impressionistically, because people remember that way. I try to avoid getting too accurately detailed in doing backgrounds. I did that in *The Spirit*, where it was important, but in this medium, readers are older, it's their memory that you're really dealing with." Eisner felt that this applied to his other graphic novels as well, such as *New York: The Big City*. "Matter of fact, the best compliment I've ever had for my work, I think, was about *New York: The Big City*," he recalled. "I was in Denmark or Sweden a couple of years ago, and this guy said to me, 'Hey I just got back from New York. I was there for the first time, and it looks just like your book!'"

Many of the characters in Eisner's graphic novels are Jewish New Yorkers, a reflection of Eisner's own background. "Well, that's not surprising, it's largely because I like to write about the things I know," he laughed. "I am not a promoter of Jewish culture . . . I guess you might say that I'm a Jewish Frank McCourt!" It's a valid comparison, especially in a work like *To the Heart of the Storm*, which depicts American Jews barely eking out miserable lives of squalor and desperation. Eisner creates a hermetically sealed world almost entirely populated by impoverished immigrant Jews, including a young Eisner himself, here called "Willy." "All my life, I've dealt with Jews," he said. "And in *Heart of the Storm*, I find that when I do have a gentile character, I treat him not quite as familiarly. But I understand Jews. I like to write about what I understand, and what I know."

Many of Eisner's graphic novels deal with Jewish themes, including the final major work published during his lifetime, *Fagin the Jew* (2003), Eisner's take on the life of the character from Charles Dickens's *Oliver Twist*. As in John Gardner's *Grendel* (*Beowulf* from the point of view of Grendel) or Gregory Maguire's *Wicked* (*The Wizard of Oz* from the point of view of the Wicked Witch), we get to see what makes an iconic literary villain tick and what drove him to such desperate ends. "He was referred to by Charles Dickens in *Oliver Twist* as 'the Jew' throughout the whole book. I take objection to that, I feel that it contributed to the stereotyping of Jews," Eisner explained. In the introduction to the book, he even compares himself to Dickens, using his treatment of Ebony in *The Spirit* as an example of how an author can fall into the trap of using harmful ethnic stereotypes. He also reveals some of the harsh Jewish stereotypes that pervaded the eighteenth and nineteenth centuries. "I did some research and found out that [in] the illustrations of the time (of 1740 and 1800), Jews were drawn very much like the Nazis drew the Jews," Eisner explained. "The big nose, the kinky hair. I drew what my research revealed was their true characteristic."

Fagin's father is murdered by anti-Semitic thugs, hardening the lower-class youth and sending him down his dark path. He's victimized without letup because of his ethnicity, denied a fighting chance at a proper education, and propelled into a life of crime. At one point it's revealed that the person to whom Fagin has been telling his story all along is Charles Dickens. "Fagin addresses Dickens, and says, 'Look, this is what I am, you who hate me.' The book is really more of an argument than it is a narrative story." Eisner argues that it was prejudice and a rigid class system that kept Moses Fagin from a more honorable life. This neither excuses nor glamorizes Fagin's actions; however, it does allow us to understand him.

ONE FINAL RETURN TO WILDWOOD

On January 3, 2005, Will Eisner died following complications from heart surgery. He was survived by his wife, Ann, to whom he'd been married since 1950. His last work was a six-page story in the sixth issue of the Dark Horse Comics title *Michael Chabon Presents: The Amazing Adventures of the Escapist.* Eisner teamed up The Spirit and The Escapist (a Captain

EISNER IN HIS NATURAL HABITAT (I.E., AT THE DRAWING BOARD), DURING HIS LATER YEARS.

America–style superhero Chabon created for his novel *The Amazing Adventures of Kavalier and Clay*) in a case involving a first edition of Joe Kavalier and Sammy Clay's first book. It was a final *Spirit* story, a fascinating example of metafiction, and an appropriate swan song for Eisner. But even though this was the last comics work he created, it wasn't his last work to see print. That honor belonged to 2005's *The Plot: The Secret Story of the Protocols of the Elders of Zion*.

Here Eisner takes his readers on a guided tour through a grisly chapter in Jewish history. We see the fabrication of *The Protocols of the Elders of Zion*, a notorious piece of anti-Semitic propaganda. Eisner explains how this famous document was disseminated in the late 1800s by Russia's secret police, who claimed it was a blueprint for conspiracy written by Jewish leaders planning to take over the globe. The book also shows real-life historical figures from Tsar Nicholas II to Henry Ford and Adolf Hitler, tracing the history of this disturbing document from nineteenth century Russia to the present-day Ku Klux Klan. And although the *Times of London* revealed in 1921 that the document is a fake, millions of people the world over continue to buy into its lies. Eisner shows documents and archival art, including many propaganda posters, that show how the *Protocols* have been used to foster anti-Semitism worldwide, and with a disturbingly high success rate. (He even shows how in 1992, a Mexican edition was listed in some Catholic schools as "required reading"!)

But as fascinating as *The Plot* is on a historical level, it leaves something to be desired on a story level and is far from Eisner's best work. This is possibly because he had just finished it when he died and didn't have the time to revise his manuscript. Or perhaps it was due to advanced age or illness. Whatever the cause, his later works such as *Fagin the Jew* are weighed down by mawkish sentimentality and broad characterization. Where his earlier books like *Contract with God* were edgy and even disturbing, his later graphic novels sometimes seemed like the work of someone going through the motions. Particularly in *The Plot*, huge blocks of exposition are glossed over with pictureless narration (unusual, in that comics follow the "show, don't tell" dictum of motion pictures), and the characters are unnecessarily broad and hateful. There's no central character to follow, and it's unclear who the protagonist is. Ironically for a work called *The Plot*, it's very light on plot and heavy on sermonizing.

However, this is not to dismiss Will Eisner's incredible lifelong body of work. Toward the end of his life, Eisner received the acclaim that was due him. He was routinely acknowledged as the grandmaster of comics, appearing as the quintessential comic book authority in film and television documentaries like *Comic Book Confidential* (1988) and *Comic Book Superheroes Unmasked* (2003). The comic book industry named its most prestigious award, The Eisner, after him. In 2002, he received the Lifetime Achievement Award from the National Federation for Jewish Culture. The award was presented to him by Art Spiegelman.

In 2005 Dark Horse Comics published *Eisner/Miller: One on One*. A dialogue between Eisner and *Sin City* creator Frank Miller, *Eisner/Miller* is poised to become the comics equivalent of the book *Hitchcock/Truffaut*. Also in 2005, the Museum of Comics and Cartoon Art (MOCCA) in New York held a career-spanning art exhibit, "The Will Eisner Retrospective." DC Comics has published Christopher Couch and Steven Weiner's *The Will Eisner Companion* and Eisner's *The Spirit Archives*, reprinting the adventures of the masked, blue-suited hero for a new generation. W. W. Norton is reprinting several of his graphic novels. *A Contract with God*, *Dropsie Avenue*, and *A Life Force* are collectively packaged as *The Contract with God Trilogy* as they all take place in the Bronx of Eisner's youth. *The Trilogy*, which includes new artwork and commentary by Eisner, crystallizes Eisner's nostalgic fondness for his childhood stomping grounds in the same manner as Woody Allen's *Radio Days* and Barry Levinson's *Diner*.

Throughout his unprecedented sixty-nine–year career as a professional comic book writer, artist, and editor, Eisner continually reinvented himself. Even his early, more frivolous *Spirit* stories were crafted with a draftsmanship lacking from many other Golden Age–era comics. His audience was privileged to see the maturation of his work from the action-comedy derring-do of *The Spirit* to the more personal stories recounted in *To the Heart of the Storm* and his other graphic novels. In creating graphic novels that focused on his role as the voice of a disenfranchised minority, Eisner inspired the works of later graphic novelists like Lance Tooks (*Narcissa*), James Sturm (*The Golem's Mighty Swing*), Howard Cruse (*Stuck Rubber Baby*), and Art Spiegelman (*Maus*). His work as advocate on behalf of comics as a venue for serious, adult storytelling elevated the art form immeasurably. Like the most lurid pulp superhero, Will Eisner used his power and influence for good, mentoring younger artists like Spiegelman and using his comics to document the New York Jewish community from whence he came.

Truly, his Spirit endures.

JERRY ROBINSON

"When crime lashes out at Gotham City with jeering evil laughter, there's only one answer . . . the Joker—malevolent mountebank of the underworld—is back with more brazen tricks up his capacious sleeve!"

—From *Detective Comics* #76 (June 1943)

Most of the artists and writers during comics' Golden Age plugged away at their craft until they were able to get better jobs in animation, commercial illustration, or newspaper cartooning. Some of these Golden Agers—most notably Will Eisner and Joe Kubert—started to tell more mature stories as they themselves aged. And then there's Jerry Robinson, arguably the most politically minded of the Golden Age illustrators. After a stint as a ghost artist for Batman creator Bob Kane, Robinson left behind the world of superheroes to become one of America's preeminent editorial cartoonists. Today, the artist formerly known as the creator of the Joker is regarded as one of the great activists, humanitarians, and political cartoonists working in the comics industry. He's won more awards than practically any other working cartoonist. He has fought hard to win recognition on behalf of friends such as Superman creators Jerry Seigel and Joe Shuster and uncredited Batman cocreator Bill Finger. He has smuggled money to persecuted Soviet cartoonists. And through his Cartoonists and Writers Syndicate, he's provided a forum for political cartoonists all over the world. Not bad for a skinny, malnourished wannabe journalist whose first job in comic books came almost by accident.

THE NINETY-EIGHT POUND FLEDGLING

Jerry Robinson was born on January 1, 1922, in Trenton, New Jersey, to Benjamin and Mae Robinson. Family legend states that he was born just at the stroke of midnight, as the bells of the New Year were ringing. The youngest of four siblings, Jerry liked to draw from an early age, but it was just something he did as a hobby. "I was the cartoonist for the high school paper, but that was my extent of drawing," he explains. "I just did it for fun." Robinson had never seriously considered a career in the arts. "I had intended just to be a journalist, a writer. And I'd graduated high school, and applied to three of the schools that the school counselor told me were the best for journalism. For no better reason than the fact that Syracuse sounded like it was more of a college town, I accepted Syracuse."

That summer, Robinson had a summer job selling ice cream via bicycle. The physical toll involved caused a bit of conflict with Robinson's mother who, like any mom, was prone to worrying about her son's health. "I was only ninety-eight pounds and on the track team as well, so I was thin as a rail," he reveals. "By the end of the summer, you couldn't see me if I turned sideways! And my mother persuaded me to take twenty-five dollars of my hard-earned money and go away to the [Catskills] mountains to fatten up, because she thought I'd never survive my first semester in college!"

Robinson was also a serious tennis player, and this inadvertently led to a chance meeting that would change his life. "The first day [in the Catskills] I went out to the tennis court," he explains. "And I wore a painters' jacket, which was a fad at that time among college kids. They were white painters' jackets with a lot of pockets. We would draw on them or you'd just decorate them yourself. I drew cartoons all over mine. Anyway, I'm out at the court wearing this jacket and somebody taps me on the shoulder and says, 'Who did those drawings?' And without turning around I said, 'Well, I did.' I thought I was going to be arrested or something, if I had anything scandalous on the back. And I said, 'Why, am I going to be in trouble?' And he said 'No.' It was Bob Kane. By sheer chance he was there that day."

Cartoonist Bob Kane was the creator of Batman, who had recently made his premiere in *Detective Comics* #27, cover-dated May 1939. Not that Robinson had heard of the caped crusader. "The first appearance [of Batman] had just come out, it was on the stands," he explains. "[But] I didn't know about it, and I'd never heard of comic books! So he took me down to a little store to show me. That was my introduction. I wasn't terribly impressed. I mean, I was used to seeing comics in the Sunday papers. You know, [*Terry and the Pirates* cartoonist] Milt Caniff, [*Prince Valiant* cartoonist] Hal Foster. And I liked the humor ones too, [George] McManus's *Bringing Up Father*. So [Bob Kane's] work didn't impress me. But what *did* impress me was when we got talking."

Kane quickly made friends with the young tennis buff. "So he got to know me," Robinson reminisces. "And he said, 'What are your plans?' And I said that I had been accepted to Syracuse. And he said, 'Going to

Syracuse, well that's too bad.' He said, 'I need an assistant to help me on *Batman* here in New York.' So I quickly called Columbia, to see if my application was still good, which it was, and then I called Syracuse and said, 'I'm not coming.' I called my folks at home, and said I got a job in New York. I went right from the mountains directly to New York. And I started drawing for *Batman* within a couple of weeks here in New York. And I thought of it then as just a way to earn my way through college. Meanwhile, I studied to be a journalist."

BAT GHOSTS

When Jerry Robinson started assisting Bob Kane on his Batman feature for *Detective Comics* in the fall of 1939, he was completely oblivious to the ins and outs of comic book illustration. "I absolutely knew nothing about drawing," he shrugs. "So I started out doing lettering and inking, but I came to it with a good eye. I mean I could copy anything I could see. It was tough in the beginning. I started burning the candle at both ends. That's how I started out for about two years, going to classes, until I became interested in the potential of comics. Then I started getting really interested in the art form and the characters. And the story and drawing. The combination. Words and pictures."

© DC Comics

Jerry Robinson's entry into the comic book world was also in many ways his entry into the adult world. And his guide through this brave new realm was *Batman*'s uncredited writer, Bill Finger, with whom Robinson worked under Kane's scrutiny for several years during the late 1930s and '40s. "Bill personally became my cultural

ONE OF JERRY ROBINSON'S MOST FAMOUS COMIC BOOK COVERS, FEATURING HIS MOST ENDURING CONTRIBUTION TO THE BATMAN MYTHOS, THE JOKER.

mentor," Robinson recalls. "New York was very exciting. I holed up in this room in the Bronx. I only knew Bob, myself, and an aunt. And once I met Bill, he kind of took me under his wing, as a friend. He took me down to the Museum of Modern Art, took me to the Met, took me to foreign films. I soaked everything up like a sponge, it was fantastic."

Another thing that Jerry Robinson hadn't thought about when he started working on *Batman* was that he'd be working as a "ghost artist" for Kane, inking, lettering, and often penciling the strip without ever getting credit. This was a frequent practice in those days. As Kane's second ghost artist (the first being Sheldon Moldoff, who some say worked on *Batman* as early as the Caped Crusader's second appearance, in *Detective* #28), Robinson understood that from his lowly rung on the artistic ladder, he wouldn't be able to share in the glory of an actual credit. However, he soon came to sympathize with the artistic plight of Bill Finger, who wrote the *Batman* stories from the beginning (and for a lengthy run during the 1940s), yet never received a writing credit for his chronicling of the Dark Knight's exploits.

"Bill was undoubtedly the best writer in comics at that period, in my estimation," Robinson claims. "He added a whole dimension of storytelling in the comics. He was an avid reader of the pulps, and of all fiction, and I'm sure a lot of these influences fleshed out his ability. When he plotted a sequence where 'Batman is springing down from here on the cranes,' or whatever, he did them like a movie script—otherwise, it wouldn't work! He knew what could be drawn, what couldn't be drawn, and what the artist needed. I remember getting the scripts and there would be things attached to it—a photo of a lie detector machine, you know, if the story was about it, he'd have a picture of it."

Bill Finger can legitimately be considered Batman's cocreator, since he either devised or coconceived Batman's backstory, the character's personality, his crimefighting arena of Gotham City, and Batman's supporting cast. Finger even suggested various visual cues, such as his cape with its unique scalloped edges (Kane wanted to go with wings). He wrote the first few years' worth of Batman stories, including the character's first appearance. And yet, you'll never see Bill Finger's name mentioned on a Batman comic book from this era, except in some of DC's recent reprint volumes. This was because Bob Kane—and only Bob Kane—signed the deal with DC to write and draw *Batman*. For the first year that they worked on *Batman*, both Jerry Robinson and Bill Finger worked directly for Kane. DC just assumed that Bob Kane was doing all the writing, and Kane paid his employees directly, ensuring that their involvement in the strip was kept on a very clandestine level. "Bill didn't know DC comics any more than I did," Robinson explains. "Bob hired me. I never met the [editors] at DC! Never knew them. They probably never knew that I existed, or Bill existed, until word got around that 'these two guys' were writing and drawing *Batman*!"

Of course, once word did get around, in 1941, Robinson and Finger were approached by DC to work for them directly. They agreed, but Bob Kane's unique contract with DC specified that *he* was the sole writer/artist of *Batman*. Robinson was hired to work on DC's growing roster of *Batman* titles as a ghost artist, still signing Bob Kane's name (before leaving in 1947), and Finger was not given credit as a writer, either.

"When Bob first went down and signed the agreement with DC for *Batman*," Robinson recalls, "he presented it as, 'By Bob Kane.' That was one thing I wouldn't excuse Bob for, that for all the things that he contributed, and for all the qualities that he had, *that* I wouldn't forgive him for! His treatment of Bill! Bill died broke, with a family and a child. Bill should've been equal in that arrangement. I saw what he created, he created all the other characters [in *Batman*]. The only one that really he didn't create was the only one that I contributed. That was the Joker."

THE MOST FAMOUS VILLAIN IN COMICS

That Robinson rather than Kane created the Joker is a long-dormant secret of comics lore that has only recently been revealed. The most famous comic book villain of all time (edging out Superman's arch foe Lex Luthor by a wide margin of recognizability), the Joker, a.k.a. the Clown Prince of Crime, is also one of the most visually striking antagonists in pop culture. With his shock of sea green hair, bone white skin, mouth continually set in a rictus grin framed by cherry red lips, and forever clad in a purple suit, the Joker looks like a serial killer's idea of a children's birthday party clown. Jerry Robinson tapped into a primal fear in creating the Joker. And that's what's made this evil harlequin so endlessly resonant for generations of comic book readers, since his initial appearance in spring 1940 in *Batman* #1 (*Detective Comics*'s sister title).

How did Robinson stumble onto the idea to create the Joker? "One day Bob and I were up discussing a story idea," Robinson recalls, "and we got a call that they were going to put out an issue of all Batman, which turned out to be *Batman* #1. But they were going to do one issue to see how it went. They needed it by a certain date that wasn't that long off. Bill immediately just said that'd be tough. I said, 'Well, maybe I could do one!' So all of a sudden, I began to be a writer for *Batman*. That night, I couldn't sleep. I was conceiving what I wanted to do for this first story. My first thought was, all the heroes and figures, in the bible, mythology, fiction, Sherlock Holmes and Moriarity, they all had an antagonist. So it dawned on me that we didn't have one. In all the comics up to that time, in *Superman*, et cetera, the villains were mostly small-time crooks, embezzlers, hijackers, things of that nature. I decided to come up with a villain first, and then it was a supervillain, something that was larger than life that would test Batman." Batman had previously faced gangsters, thugs, and mad scientists like Professor Hugo Strange. Even DC's flagship character Superman was facing off against run-of-the-mill thieves and wife beaters, but the concept of a truly distinctive, truly super "supervillain" hadn't really been invented.

Who would his supervillain character be? Luckily, Robinson, then studying writing at Columbia, recalled the old writer's maxim to "write what you know." "The [Joker] character came from two things in my background," he reveals. "One was [the idea of] a villain with a sense of humor. The other things I wrote [at Columbia] were humor and satire pieces. I love writing humor. And secondly, playing cards were part of my background. My mother and one of my brothers were contract bridge players. So there were cards around the house all the time. The next line of thought was the name. Names are so important for characters. So I

© Jerry Robinson

Original conceptual drawing of the Joker by Jerry Robinson, labeled "First sketch of the Joker—and his calling card."

thought, 'villain' and 'sense of humor,' and I thought of the Joker, the image of the Joker playing card I knew so well. I brought along a deck of playing cards and I found the Joker. Luckily it turned out to be the classic image of the Joker, which is what you see in that story [in *Batman* #1]. That's what I based it on, that sketch. Then it all began to come together. The playing card was his calling card you leave at the scene of the crime! I couldn't wait to get to the office the next morning to meet Bill and Bob to get together to show it to them, because this was my story. Well, they went crazy about it."

The one thing Jerry Robinson had to work hard to sell Bob Kane and Bill Finger on was the Joker's peculiar look. Nothing like the Joker had ever been seen in comic books before: despite his bizarre appearance, he wasn't an alien, a mutant, or a robot, and he wasn't simply wearing makeup. "[Bob and Bill] said, 'What about his hair? It's green! Why is he white?'" Robinson recalls. "And I said, 'That's his bizarreness! Don't explain it!' And we didn't. They did explain it years later, I understand [in the story "The Man Behind the Red Hood," from *Detective Comics* #168, February 1951], but we didn't do that. I think I was slightly influenced in a way by *Dick Tracy*, who at the time had these bizarre villains. Bob and Bill were really excited about the Joker story. Bob said, 'Jerry, Bill should really write it.' And he asked, 'Do you mind?' And I said, 'Yes.' But I had to agree that they had a deadline, and who knew how long it would take me to write this thing. Literally, when I gave it over to them, it was like giving away my baby. So Bill, from that point, wrote the first Joker story.'"

ROBINSON THE BOY WONDER

Another character that Jerry Robinson had a hand in creating (albeit to a lesser extent) was Batman's sidekick, Robin the Boy Wonder. Batman had operated solo as dark avenger of the night for a year. Bob Kane, knowing that the audience for comic books was mostly young boys, wanted someone this demographic could more easily identify with. "When we came in to kick it around," Robinson recalls, "I suggested [the name] Robin. And then designed his costume, based on Robin Hood. That's where my inspiration for Robin came from, contrary to a lot of other stories. You know, it supposedly came from Robin the bird, and one article even said it came from my name. So, once we got the idea of Robin, Bill added 'the boy wonder' as a tagline. So they called him Robin the boy wonder. So then, they began to kid me that I was 'Robinson the boy wonder!' Well, that sounds great now, but back then I hated it!"

Batman himself is a sort of Robin Hood–style vigilante, but where did Jerry Robinson get the idea to dress his sidekick in the trappings of Robin Hood? "It was based on my recollection of the paintings of N. C. Wyeth," he reveals, "who was a great illustrator of Robin Hood. The reason I knew that so well, is because for a confirmation present, I was given a beautiful, handsome book of full-color illustrations of N. C. Wyeth. I remembered his concept of Robin Hood. So, when we first thought of [Robin], I sketched out how I remembered [the book]." Bob Kane also added details to Robin's visual conception. "We both really drew it together," Robinson adds, "but it started from my concept. And I remember, my last touch was, I added that *R* design, the logo on Robin's breast."

THE BULLPENNERS

In 1941, DC lured Jerry Robinson away from Bob Kane; Robinson was still working on the *Batman* titles, but not for Kane directly. DC's higher-ups were afraid that Robinson and Finger would be lured away by the competition if they weren't officially hired to work there. They also didn't want to lose two of the people who had set the tone of the *Batman* stories.

This was Robinson's first time working in the so-called "bullpen," a row of desks in which artists would sit side-by-side cranking out comic book pages. Here he worked alongside future giants of the comic book industry, like rowers in a Roman slave galley. One of those giants was Jack Kirby, later known as the "King of Comics," creator (or cocreator) of the Hulk, the Fantastic Four, the X-Men, the New Gods, and scores of other classic characters. Kirby and Joe Simon had just created Captain America for Timely Comics, after which the two jumped ship for DC.

Even then, Kirby had an industrywide reputation as a cartoonist's cartoonist. While Robinson noodled away on *Batman*, Kirby and Simon were drumming up many of their "kid gang" features like *Boy Commandos* and *The Newsboy Legion*. "I always loved Jack," Robinson recalls. "He was a wonderful, kind person in all my interactions with him. I was still quite young [when I was] working at DC doing Batman. And for a while, we worked at adjoining desks. Jack was an extraordinary artist, a pioneer. He dramatically expanded the parameters of the visuals. His drawing style literally exploded! We all worked in two or three dimensions. I think Jack worked in *four* dimensions. I mean, his composition went forward, backward, sideways. Things that we all *tried* to do. But he was able to incorporate his own style, his own persona. And he was very fluid, and very fast. He could rough out a page very quickly. I thought I was really quick myself, but it was nothing compared to Jack!"

Not that Jack Kirby was the end-all, be-all of the DC bullpen in those days. "We all learned from each other because we worked so close," Robinson explains. "It was an exciting time. We were all experimenting, and attempting new things with our art and storytelling. It was a time of establishing the idiom itself. The medium had no past. There was just the present and the future. We had a great bullpen. Joe Shuster was there working on one side, and Jack was on the other. There was Mort Meskin, who was a very close friend. I brought him up to DC, and that's how he started there."

Meskin, who worked on DC characters like the cowboy hero Vigilante and super-speedster Johnny Quick, was known as a superior draftsman. Bernie Klein, another strikingly proficient cartoonist and a great friend of Robinson's during this period, was a former boxer whom Robinson describes as resembling "a young John Garfield," and worked on titles such as *All-Star Comics* for DC, delineating superheroes like Dr. Fate. "Mort, Bernie Klein, and I had an apartment together," Robinson remembers. "Then Bernie was drafted into the army, and Mort and I took it over. Bernie was a combat photographer and was killed in Italy. It was a great tragedy for me; he was like my brother. He came from my hometown." After the tragic loss of Bernie Klein, Jerry Robinson and Mort Meskin forged on, eventually working together on a variety of comics titles such as *The Vigilante*.

DAREDEVILED EGGS

Robinson was also moonlighting at other companies to make extra income. During the early 1940s, he did quite a bit of work for Lev Gleason Publications, as did Klein. In late 1940, the two contributed features to the second issue of a new comics magazine called *Daredevil*, named for Charlie Biro's red-and-black-suited superhero, who headlined in the lead feature (not to be confused with the blind Marvel superhero created during the 1960s). "The idea was that [*Daredevil*] would help the war effort," Robinson explains. "It was hard to get an allotment for paper. You had to apply to the war production board. Lev Gleason had an allotment of paper, and if he didn't use it up by a certain time, he'd lose the allotment. So, Charlie Biro called me excitedly one day and said, 'If we get a magazine out by Monday, to the printer, we can get the magazine published!' And the only thing we had was the lead character, Daredevil, which was Charlie's. We got [cartoonist] Bob Wood, [his brother] Dick, myself, [fellow *Batman* ghost artist] George Roussos, and Bernie Klein, and we rented a bare apartment, on Fifty-third Street I think."

However, now that Robinson was on board for *Daredevil* #2 (cover-dated 1941), he and the other artists had a unique dilemma; how were they going to write and draw an entire comic book over the course of a weekend? "We had two big drawing boards, very wide," Robinson explains. "And we holed up for Friday, Saturday, and Sunday to turn out the whole book. Conceive the characters, write the scripts, and draw them. So two artists could work at the drawing board at the same time, while the script writer was on the floor. And when we had to take a nap, one would get off the drawing board, lie on the floor and take a nap. And we met the deadline."

But working in close quarters during wartime, when basic necessities were scarce, made for some unforgettable incidents. "An extraordinary thing happened that weekend, which was referred to in a couple of books like Michael Chabon's *The Amazing Adventures of Kavalier and Clay*," Robinson recalls. "We were snowed in. The whole city came to a standstill. We didn't have the mobile snow equipment you have today. But I remember, we were just off of Fifth Avenue, between Fifth and Sixth, and there was no traffic. We had no food there. We were starving. So we drew straws, and one of us had to go out to forage for food. And I think it was Bernie who lost, and he disappeared. He went out in the morning, and he disappears for hours We thought he had frozen in the snow. Turned out that everything was closed on Sixth Avenue, and he had to walk all the way down through the snowstorm to Fourteenth Street—we were in the Fifties—before he had found some saloon. And he was able to bring back a half a dozen raw eggs. That's all he could find. But there was nothing to cook them on, no kitchen. And in our inventive way, we tore tiles off the bathroom wall and made a hot plate on the floor. We heated the tiles and then fried the eggs. We could have eaten our shoes, à la Charlie Chaplin, we were so hungry."

Jerry Robinson's contribution to *Daredevil* #2 was his Axis-pummeling costumed vigilante, London, a hero who emerged "from the debris and chaos of war-torn England," as Robinson's narration put it. This was the first time Jerry Robinson signed his own name to a feature rather than ghosting for someone like Bob Kane. Finally, here was a character that was Jerry Robinson's baby all the way. That was the idea behind the various features appearing in *Daredevil*. "Each one of us was to create a character of their own," he explains. "Bernie did a boxer [named] Whirlwind, because he had been a boxer. Instinctively, we all thought of what we were comfortable doing, because we had to do it right away! I vaguely had an idea to be a political cartoonist. And it was at the height of the German blitz over London. It was the turning point of the war, meant to bring about the defeat of England. That was before we entered the war of course, December 1940. And if London hadn't held out, [the Germans] could have won the war. So this was in the news, so that's how it came about that I thought of doing a strip about London under the blitz. So my hero became the character of London. The masked character was kind of a dapper Englishman, almost a precursor of James Bond. A red cape, over a full dress suit. He was a superhero, but with a British sensibility." London only lasted about a year, at which point *Daredevil* folded with issue 11, the victim of a fickle market and slumping sales.

SCIENTIFACT

In 1947, Jerry Robinson stopped working directly in the DC bullpen, ending his run ghosting *Batman*. The anonymity was getting to him. "I was tired of not being able to sign my work," Robinson says. "I probably signed Bob Kane's name more than *he* did!" Robinson started collaborating with Mort Meskin on DC features like *Johnny Quick* and *Vigilante* from a studio the two shared. All their work together was signed "Robinson/Meskin." Like Simon and Kirby, the two worked on all phases of the art together, from pencil roughs to finished pencils to inking and lettering. During this time, they also collaborated on non-DC superhero features, like *Black Terror* and *Fighting Yank* for Standard Publications. And from the late 1940s into the early '60s, Jerry Robinson also illustrated the adventures of various licensed characters adapted from other media, like *Lassie, Rocky and Bullwinkle*, and *Bat Masterson* (all for Dell Publishing). During this prolific period, he also illustrated some war, sci-fi, and mystery titles for Timely Comics, then under the editorship of an energetic spitfire named Stan Lee. "There was a good rapport between us," Robinson recalls. "I thought he was a very good editor. I was an already established professional, I knew what [Timely] was doing, and I guess he just liked my work and trusted me."

But the project that Robinson worked on during this period that was the most indicative of things to come was *Jet Scott*, because it gave him a taste of the world of newspaper comic strips. "I got a call from a Herald Tribune editor who knew my work and asked if I'd be interested in doing a new strip," Robinson recalls. "I'd be the cocreator of it and they already had the writer, who was [screenwriter] Sheldon Stark." *Jet Scott*, which lasted from 1953 to 1955, was a new type of comic strip. It was a science-fiction series, but not a wildly whimsical or futuristic one, like *Flash Gordon* or *Buck Rogers*. Unlike its sci-fi forebears, *Jet Scott* would try to predict what sort of technological accomplishments could plausibly be made. There would be no giant robots, no jetpacks.

"We carved out a particular niche," Robinson recalls, "which was science fiction, but just what's in the immediate future. That was an area that hadn't been explored before. So we didn't have people flying around in spacesuits. Jet, the hero of the strip, was the head of the office of Scientifact, a government agency." However, the daily grind of doing an adventure strip lost its appeal after awhile. "An adventure strip always requires research to do things semirealistically," Robinson explains, "I didn't have a day off for those two years, I was doing all the research myself. We were doing all right, we had maybe seventy-five papers. I remember really debating whether to renew the contract. I decided not to."

His next newspaper strip was a humor strip, and therefore perfect for him. Not only was it less labor-intensive than something like *Jet Scott*, it also involved one of his long-time passions: politics. This comic strip was the one that would really establish Robinson in the world of newspaper comics. It was called *Still Life*.

A POLITICAL ANIMAL

By 1961, Robinson was phasing out his comic book work in favor of a new passion—editorial cartoons. "I love politics," Robinson explains. "During all the time I was doing comic books, I followed the news regularly and was one of the few comic book artists who searched out editorial cartoons every day. That became my ambition—to be a political cartoonist. At that time, the papers didn't have op-ed pages as we know them today. If there was a columnist, he or she appeared on the editorial page. And the editorial cartoon was on the top, and the editorial of the day was on the left, and maybe some letters to the editor went on the bottom. I knew I had to do something that was an editorial cartoon but didn't look like it, so it would not be in competition with the editorial cartoon of the paper.

"That's when I dreamed up *Still Life*, which were inanimate objects that commented on the news. And it was in a panel shape—usually an editorial cartoon was more horizontal. So that was my idea." A prime example of the trenchant wit of Robinson's *Still Life* gags is the timeless cartoon in which the Presidential seal is saying, "The President is in conference with his most trusted advisor," and then adds, "he's alone."

Robinson acknowledges that when coming up with the rather unique idea for his strip, he relied on outside help. "My wife Gro came up with the name *Still Life*," he admits, "And the idea to use inanimate objects to talk about the news of the day. Usually they would be different objects all the time, but a recurring set of characters were the wastebasket on the street corner—because the wastebasket got the day's paper thrown in, and he'd know the news—and the fire hydrant. I developed a presentation of about thirty. I took the cartoons down to the *New York Post*, as I recall. They said yes they could use an editorial cartoonist—maybe not doing *Still Life*, but I'd have to work on staff and be available to do other drawings." Robinson relished the freelance lifestyle, and found staff jobs confining. What was he to do?

Suddenly, fate intervened. "New York went into a big newspaper strike," he reveals, "which affected all the papers for at least a month. And what sprung up were a lot of what they called 'interim papers.' They were like six or eight pages edited by the editors from the major papers. So these independent publishers sprung up, staffed by editors and writers and reporters from the major dailies. They were all professionally produced. I thought this maybe is a way to get *Still Life* published. Because these other papers were looking for material, I assumed, and they couldn't use any syndicate material, so they didn't have much graphics. So I picked out what I thought was the best interim paper, and I went in to see the editor. He took one look at it and said, 'I can run this one tomorrow.' I said, 'No, I'm sorry. I designed those for national syndication. But I'll do a new one for you every day.' He said 'OK, can you start tomorrow for tomorrow's paper?' It was as simple and fast as that. I was so elated! So I figured this gave me ammunition to sell a syndicate eventually."

So flush with success was Jerry Robinson that he immediately went and got *Still Life* on television. "They had an expanded TV news program on NBC, again to make up the gap for the lack of newspapers of the day," he explains. "So they expanded the news show to fit in a lot of news. I was so excited about the success that morning, I went straight up to the NBC offices. And lo and behold, I get in and see [the producer]. And I show him the things and he says, 'They're great!' All of a sudden, I was appearing in a daily New York paper *and* NBC News! I kept this up during the whole strike period, for the paper and for NBC."

Work with a big newspaper syndicate still eluded Robinson, but he now had a growing body of work as an editorial cartoonist. "I called my friend Warren King, who was then the political cartoonist for the *New York News* And I said, 'Could you possibly get me an appointment with the editor of the *News*?' This was Richard Clarke, one of the best editors I've met. Well, long story short, before I left [Clarke's] office, his secretary came in and dictated the contract on one page, and I walked out, and I was signed with Chicago Tribune–New York News Syndicate! I did one [cartoon] a day for some thirty-two years until I finally had to give it up. But it was a wonderful time, that's the longest stint I ever did of any one thing."

During that thirty-two-year period, *Still Life* underwent considerable changes. In 1977, it became known as *Life with Robinson* and morphed into a more conventional horizontal panel cartoon, now featuring people rather than inanimate objects. But the strip still retained Robinson's sharp wit,

© *Cartoonist & Writers Syndicate*

IN 1977, ROBINSON'S GAG PANEL <u>STILL LIFE</u> BECAME KNOWN AS <u>LIFE WITH ROBINSON</u> AND MORPHED INTO A MORE CONVENTIONAL HORIZONTAL PANEL CARTOON, NOW FEATURING PEOPLE RATHER THAN INANIMATE OBJECTS.

as when a political prisoner is about to be executed, and the commanding officer orders his firing squad to "Shoot him! He refuses to participate in our free and democratic elections!"

(SUPER)MAN OF THE PEOPLE

During the 1970s, Jerry Robinson's political leanings had alerted him to various injustices that were affecting cartoonists the world over, especially in countries that lacked a free press. In the late seventies, he spent three years working to free the Uruguayan cartoonist Francisco Laurenzo Pons from jail, where he was being tortured. Since 1973, a military junta had taken over the government. Pons tried to flee with his family, but was eventually tracked down, branded a communist, and imprisoned. Amnesty International got in touch with noted political cartoonist/playwright Jules Feiffer, who relayed word about Pons's plight to his colleague Jerry Robinson. Robinson, then president of the Association of American Editorial Cartoonists, devised a scheme by which to spur the release of Pons.

"I invented a new cartooning award, The Distinguished Foreign Cartoonists Award," he explains. "The idea was that we would award it to Pons and request that he come to America to receive it, pretending that we didn't know he was in prison. To further the ruse, we made it a joint award, the other winner being the Polish cartoonist Eric Lipinski. We explained to the Uruguayan ambassador what a big honor it would be for Uruguay to have Laurenzo Pons win this award! Several months passed, and the Uruguayan government sent us word that they'd let Pons's wife and son come to accept the award, but not Pons himself. This was amazing, because normally even the family of a political prisoner wasn't allowed out of the country. So Mrs. Pons came to accept the award, and when she went back to Uruguay and visited her husband in jail, he was amazed that American cartoonists were working on his behalf. This gave him hope!"

Another thing that gave Pons hope was the publicity generated by Robinson's efforts on the persecuted cartoonist's behalf. Because of this, the Uruguayan embassy even took Pons to the hospital at one point for fear that otherwise he'd die in jail, making the government look cruel and inhuman. One day, Robinson received a call from Pons's wife, saying that her husband was being released after serving only six years of his eight year sentence. "They didn't even have to release him at all," Robinson points out. "They could have just kept him in there forever to rot!" But they didn't, largely because of the bad publicity generated by Jerry Robinson.

Some American cartoonists were also being mistreated. Two such comics pros were Robinson's old friends Jerry Siegel and Joe Shuster, the creators of Superman. After selling their initial concept and first Superman story to DC for a flat fee of $130 (admittedly a large sum in 1938, but a flat fee nonetheless), they'd received no royalties. After taking DC to court in the mid-1940s over financial compensation for the Superman character—during which time they'd won a limited settlement—DC had their "created by" credit taken off the various *Superman* titles. In the decades since, they'd attempted to sue DC several times, always unsuccessfully.

Jerry Robinson's friendship with Siegel and Shuster stretched back to his early days in the industry. "One time Joe worked at the next table from me at DC Comics," Robinson recalls, "and Jerry would come in from time to time and work there. And I liked them both very much from the beginning as individuals and as creators. Jerry was gonna be married shortly. But Joe was a perpetual bachelor, and we would go on several dates together. I had the assignment of getting Joe the date, because he was very shy, very reserved, very unassuming. You'd never know he was the creator of Superman." But Siegel and Shuster were no longer the carefree kids Robinson knew in his youth; now they were impoverished, obscure, and understandably bitter. "Over the years I knew they were both in bad shape. There was something in the papers that Jerry and Joe had made a settlement with DC, and that they had income for the rest of their lives. Actually it wasn't true. Joe had moved out to California, to be near Jerry, so I lost contact with them both."

Then, in 1975, while working in his studio late one night, Jerry Robinson saw something on television that filled him with righteous indignation. "My assistant Bob Forgione and I were working on a deadline and *The Tomorrow Show* came on," he recalls. "Jerry was in the audience, telling of his plight, that they lost everything, the whole sad story. That was the first time in years that I had heard from them, and I was really terribly upset that I was wrong, that they hadn't settled anything. Jerry had been working as a postal clerk, and Joe was broke and destitute. It was terrible. Joe was certifiably blind at that time."

By this time, a *Superman* movie was about to go into production. This was a big-budget affair, helmed by A-list director Richard Donner. And if Robinson hadn't intervened, Siegel and Shuster wouldn't have seen a dime from the film, and their creator credit would still be left off Superman to this day. "I immediately called Jerry in California," Robinson recalls, "and I told him how terribly I felt about the situation, and [asked], 'What could I do to help?'"

Unbeknownst to Robinson, another *Batman* cartoonist—superstar illustrator Neal Adams—had been recently attempting to help out Siegel and Shuster with their cause. "I called Neal and said maybe we should work *together* wherever we can and rally the profession, which we set out to do," Robinson explains. "There was a comic book organization, ACBA, and Neal went to them to get all the comic book people." Meanwhile, Jerry Robinson contacted the National Cartoonist Society, whose membership roster includes over five hundred of the world's major cartoonists, representing newspaper strip cartoonists, comic book artists, editorial cartoonists, animators, greeting card illustrators, advertising illustrators, and magazine and book illustrators. Robinson was a past president of both the NCS and the Association of American Editorial Cartoonists, and did what he could to encourage various public figures to support the cause, including author Pete Hamill, novelist Kurt Vonnegut, television newsman Mike Wallace (an old tennis buddy), and fellow cartoonists Will Eisner and Jules Feiffer.

Jerry Robinson and Neal Adams had their work cut out for them in their fight on Siegel and Shuster's behalf. There were many issues to consider—health care, pension, profit participation—all of which the aging comic book creators should have been entitled to. Every day, either Adams or Robinson would call Jerry and Joe to report on their progress. "A lot of the negotiating was done by phone between Neal, myself, and Jay Emmett, VP of Time Warner," Robinson recalls. "It was a different generation, several decades after the original [Siegel and Shuster] contract was signed, so they didn't have the baggage that the original [regime] did. Now DC was owned by a big firm, and was more susceptible to pressure. Meanwhile, Jerry had already had a heart attack, and the main concern was to get some settlement for his daughter and wife before something happened to him. Jerry said to me, 'I can't go on with this anymore! Settle it tomorrow, get the best deal you can get. It's better than nothing.'"

The sticking point was of course still the issue of the creator credits. And knowing of Jerry Siegel's fragile health, Jerry Robinson decided to zero in on this aspect of the agreement. "I said to Jay Emmett, 'Restore their names, that won't cost you anything. These are human beings. They are proud of their creation.' And I played every card that I needed for that. And finally he says, 'Jerry, let me call you back in an hour.' I knew what he was going to do, he was going to call his lawyers. He wasn't in a position to OK it himself; he had to talk to them every hour. He said, 'We can't restore their names to everything, but we can do it on *some* publications.' I said, 'No, Jay, you have to go all the way! Restore their names in all print

HOLY COBRA, BATMAN! I THINK THE JOKER AND PENGUIN ARE UP TO SOME NEFARIOUS TRICK!

THIS 1984 SUPERMAN PIN-UP BY JERRY ROBINSON SHOWCASES HIS
GIFT FOR CARICATURE, AS MANY 1980s-ERA CELEBS ARE IDENTIFIED.
AMONG THEM ARE FORMER NEW YORK CITY MAYOR ED KOCH,
FRANK SINATRA, CHER, WOODY ALLEN, MICHAEL JACKSON, AND
ROBINSON'S FRIENDS JERRY SIEGEL AND JOE SHUSTER (BETWEEN THE
TANGLE OF MICROPHONES AND A RANDOM WELL-WISHER'S ELBOW).

matter, and the movie.' He said, 'No, I can't do that.' I said, 'Of course you can.' He calls back and says, 'OK, I'll restore all print matter.' And with the movie he said, 'I can't do the movie, the credits are already all final in the film.' I said, 'Jay, I've worked on movies before. It's not like reshooting a scene!' He said, 'All print matter, and we'll get the credits on the film. But I can't do the licensed products [like toys]. I thought that was the best possible deal and that's what we did. The big thing was that we got the names restored."

The signing of Siegel and Shuster's *Superman* agreement took place right before Christmas, on December 23, 1975, a joyous ending to a year fraught with anxiety and tension. They all decided to get together at Robinson's Manhattan apartment that night to celebrate. "I was coming out of the Time Warner office to get to the party and it was pouring rain," Robinson recalls. "We're all gathered around the TV set, watching the *CBS Evening News*," Robinson remembers. "Walter Cronkite had the story, we had phoned him. It's finally at the end of the program, and Cronkite used it as the sign-off story for the end of the show. He said, 'And this proves that truth, justice, and the American way won out!' He had an animated graphic of Superman in the background. With Jerry and Joe standing there at the party, there wasn't a dry eye, it was such a moving experience."

Toward the end of their lives, Joe Shuster and Jerry Siegel (who passed away in 1992 and 1996, respectively) were on good terms with DC, and Warner executive Steve Ross and multimedia mogul Ted Turner went to bat on their behalf to make sure that DC upped their pensions. Jerry Robinson is also quick to point out that the mistreatment of Siegel and Shuster is largely the fault of DC's founding regime circa the 1930s, and "if [DC's current publisher] Paul Levitz and [Levitz's predecessor] Jenette Kahn had been in charge back then, this wouldn't have happened."

CARTOONISTS OF THE WORLD, UNITE!

Today, Jerry Robinson runs the Cartoonists & Writers Syndicate (CWS), a forum for political cartoonists from all over the world. CWS's artists are seen through the *Views of the World* feature in many newspapers worldwide, as well as online at cartoonweb.com. "My basic motivation for doing it," he explains, "was that I thought a syndicate should be founded by a cartoonist who knew the problems of cartooning. This would correct what we thought the other [syndicates] could do fairer. The cartoonists own the original work, all the [assurances] that cartoonists would want."

Robinson started the CWS in 1978 after publishing a book called *The 70s: Best Cartoonists of the Decade*. While compiling cartoons for the book, it dawned on him that books of this type were usually relegated to American cartoonists, and he didn't think that was fair. "I traveled often at that time, and I went all around the world," he explains. "I saw these great cartoonists in every country. So I took the idea to McGraw-Hill. I said I'd like to do a book, but I said that I won't do it unless at least half the cartoonists are foreign and half are American. So they fought me on that. They said, 'The American public doesn't know these other countries, why would they be interested in their work?' So I said, 'They don't know because they haven't seen them. And also, anybody who is interested in cartooning, they want to see the best, and America is not [always] the best. And you're doing something unique that you've never done before.' So we agreed on that, the book was published, and it got great reviews. Critics all said, 'Too bad we don't see these foreign cartoonists more often, except in anthologies like this!'"

Robinson envisioned a new syndicate, an *international* syndicate. "To syndicate the best from the world," he explains. "That's when I came up with the idea of *Views of the World*. I tried to present it in a form of a large-panel, one-third of the page, that had five or six cartoons in it, that represented leading opinions from around the world on the issues of that week. I showed a diversity of opinions. I hoped to convince the editors that by showing a round of them, we weren't endorsing any one view. We wanted to show our readers what the world opinion was on these issues. This was the time where we were becoming more one world, that the issues affecting France and Germany and Russia and Italy and Brazil and South Africa were affecting our readers, too. America's papers were very isolationist except for the *New York Times* and a few others. I formed the syndicate right after the book, but it took me two years to put that package together.

"I think the first *Views of the World* was maybe around '81. We started off with a group of maybe seventeen or twenty artists from maybe fifteen countries. Today we have artists from seventy-five countries. And we have five of the top American political cartoonists: Jeff Danziger, formerly worked with the *Christian Science Monitor*, multiple Pulitzer nominee; Kevin Kallagher, the *Baltimore Sun* and the *Economist* in London; Jim Morin, of the *Miami Herald*; Joel Pett, of the *Lexington Herald-Leader*, Pulitzer Prize winner; and recently, we signed Anne Telnaes, the top American female political cartoonist, also a Pulitzer Prize winner. So we have a great American contingent now."

Sometimes Robinson would come up against foreign governments who would keep the royalties he'd send his artists. So he had to resort to covert tactics. "At first I was sending it to the Arts Commission, because that's who gave them permission to sign with CWS," he explains. "But after I met the artists from Moscow, they said they got such a small percentage that sometimes they didn't even know I sent any royalties. The Arts Council would just keep it! So finally I took the chance to smuggle it in. They never searched me. I wore a money belt most of the time. I made about four to five trips for various reasons to Moscow. Every time I was there, I would meet the artist and take the occasion to bring in royalties. I remember one time, this was back in the eighties or early nineties, one of them who got $1,000 fell on the floor, literally. He said, 'Jerry, you don't know what this means for us! I can live for two or three years from this!' I realized how much these royalties meant to people."

Truly, Jerry Robinson has come a long way—from not even being able to sign his own name to his work on the *Batman* comics of the late thirties and forties, to becoming one of the world's most prominent political cartoonists, to helping fellow cartoonists earn credit and royalties for their work and creating a global cartooning community. Like very few other cartoonists, Jerry Robinson has used his industry clout to affect real social change. As a result, he has opened up the minds of other artists to the possibility that comics can literally change the world.

STAN LEE

PORTRAIT OF STAN LEE BY LEGENDARY SPIDER-MAN ARTIST JOHN ROMITA.

"And so, we take our leave of Peter Parker for now, as he and the girl he loves go their separate ways—both tragically kept apart by the mysterious, ever-present figure whom the world knows only as—Spider-Man!"

—*Amazing Spider-Man* #30, 1965

A n archetype found time and again in American popular culture is the hero who's least likely to succeed, and yet does so in the face of insurmountable odds. Stan Lee fits solidly in this tradition. He'd been working in the comic book industry for over twenty years as a comparatively undistinguished writer and editor before he really started to make a name for himself with *Fantastic Four* #1 in 1961, a comic book that changed the industry forever. *Fantastic Four* simultaneously inaugurated what's come to be known since as the Marvel Age of Comics and turned a minor comic book company into an industry leader.

Since then, Lee has gone on to cocreate some of the industry's most famous and psychologically complex superheroes, including the neurotic Spider-Man, the schizophrenic Hulk, and the societal outcasts known as the X-Men, all of whom changed the way that mainstream superhero comics were written by showing that heroes can have feet of clay. In the years since his triumphant run (roughly 1961–1972) writing and editing most of Marvel's major titles alongside artists like Jack Kirby and Steve Ditko, Stan Lee has served as Marvel Comics's spokesperson and public face, going on lecture tours and making television talk show appearances. He acts as a creative consultant and executive producer on the various film and television adaptations of Marvel's properties, developing his own multimedia properties (many of them in the realm of television animation). Occasionally he finds time to write the odd comic book series, such as 2000's *Just Imagine Stan Lee Creating* . . . series for Marvel's chief competitor DC, where he reimagined various DC stalwarts such as Superman and the Flash, showing how different each of these iconic heroes would be if Stan Lee had written them.

Stan Lee is probably the most famous American comic book writer in history, but his journey from working stiff to creative visionary is as unexpected as Peter Parker's journey from clumsy nerd to suave arachnid superhero. . . .

SECRET ORIGINS

Stan Lee was born Stanley Martin Lieber on December 28, 1922, on the Upper West Side of Manhattan. Early on, his Jewish-Romanian immigrant parents Jack (a dress cutter) and Celia (a homemaker) moved the family to a cramped apartment in an even more cramped neighborhood in the Bronx. Young Stanley Lieber, forced to sleep in the living room, found it hard to adapt, but life wasn't without its joys. "My mother used to have me read to her," Lee remembers. "And she gave me a hell of a superiority complex! I was always a ham. I think I always wanted to be an actor. And if I learned a poem in school or something, I'd come home and I'd read it to my mother, and she'd say, 'Oh you read so beautifully, oh I love it!'" During his teen years, Lee even flirted with the idea of a life in the theater, appearing in plays sponsored by Franklin D. Roosevelt's Works Progress Administration. "The WPA had something called the Federal Theater, and I belonged to one of the branches, and was in a few shows," he clarifies. "But it didn't pay anything, so I couldn't stay with it very long. I was able to make more money writing." In fact, Lee would soon come to regard himself as a writer above all else.

A TIMELY CAREER

In those less-than-halcyon days of early childhood, Stanley and his kid brother Larry would spend Sunday mornings poring over newspaper comic strips such as George Herriman's *Krazy Kat*. After attending DeWitt Clinton High School in the Bronx (where fellow literary-minded schoolmates included future television scribe/playwright Paddy Chayevsky and novelist James Baldwin), Lee indulged his love for newspaper comic strips by working for their fledgling sister industry, comic books. The comic book industry was relatively easy to break into in 1940, and Lee's cousin was married to Martin Goodman, publisher of Timely Comics.

After getting a start as a copy boy at Timely working for editor Joe Simon and art director Jack Kirby (the duo had recently hit creative pay dirt by creating Captain America), Lee was assigned gigs writing "filler" copy for various comic books. The name "Stan Lee" first saw print in *Captain America* #3, cover-dated May 1941, in the story "Captain America

Foils the Traitor's Revenge." This was a rather pulpy, hastily churned out short prose piece designed to fill up space between the various comics features in the magazine. But Lee treated the story with an unusual degree of passion, describing the fight scenes with a natural storyteller's flair. Two issues later, in the pages of *Captain America* #5 (August 1941), Lee wrote the story "Headline Hunter, Foreign Correspondent," about a reporter behind enemy lines, which was the first actual comic book script (as opposed to filler story) to be credited to Stan Lee.

Stanley Lieber used the pen name Stan Lee because at the time he had more serious literary ambitions, and comic books were perceived as a temporary pit-stop on the road to greater glory. "Comics in those days, everybody looked down their noses at them," Lee says today. "They were at the bottom of the cultural totem pole, so to speak. And I figured, 'Someday I'm going to be a great writer. I don't want to use the name Stanley Martin Lieber for these lousy comics,' little dreaming I'd stay in comics forever." However, even though he might have simply been marking time until he wrote the Great American Novel, he took to comics writing with relish, signing his pen name to every script he wrote at a time when comic book writers were often anonymous.

Lee's early comic book work was hardly groundbreaking. His 1940s-era superhero comics were written just as well as anyone else's, but there was little room for innovation or complex characterization under the watchful eye of Martin Goodman. As writer and (by late 1941, after Simon and Kirby's departure) editor of Timely, Lee was writing many of Timely's comics under various pseudonyms aside from Stan Lee, the better to make the small company appear to be a larger operation. (His other noms-de-comics included Neel Nats, S. T. Anley, and Stan Martin.) But even though he was practically running Timely a year after joining the company as a copy boy, he was still writing comics the way Goodman wanted him to. And Goodman wanted his comics to be like everyone else's, so that they would be guaranteed to sell. As the ultimate company man, Stan was more than happy to oblige Goodman's craving for product, churning out such lurid costumed characters as Father Time, who cleaned criminals' clocks with a scythe, and the Whizzer, a super-speedster who gained his powers after a transfusion of mongoose blood.

This last description typifies the sort of fare Timely—as well as most of its competitors—commonly produced at that point. Comics stories of this period were as a rule poorly constructed escapist melodramas, often created by artists and writers who would go on to transcend these early efforts. Working with talents like the young Al Jaffee (later of *MAD*) surely made the days fly by faster, but Stan Lee was getting restless. After a four-year stint in the army, he returned to Timely during the fall of 1945, only to discover that testosterone-driven superheroes had to make room for a relatively new genre: *Archie*-style "teen" comics such as *Patsy Walker* and *Millie the Model*. Lee now had to edit these by the truckload.

By 1953, the trend turned to science-fiction titles, and Lee dutifully obliged Goodman by creating a barrage of sci-fi anthology titles such as *Journey into Mystery* and *Strange Tales*. In 1950, Timely had been rechristened Atlas, and by 1957, Jack Kirby was back in the fold freelancing there, having split amicably with Joe Simon, who had left for a career in advertising. From 1958 to 1961, Lee and Kirby collaborated on various "monster" stories (usually inspired by either *Godzilla* movies or the UFO paranoia then gripping the nation) about slobbering, slimy, and often prehistoric creatures. Lee commonly dubbed these creatures BEMs, which stood for "Bug-Eyed Monsters," that being a pretty apt description of the scaly abominations. The BEMs laid claim to names like "Xom, the Creature Who Swallowed the Earth," "Torr," "Grottu the Giant Ant-Eater," "Krogarr," and "Fin Fang Foom." Lee and Kirby didn't know it at the time, but in forming a creative partnership with these crude monster tales, they were laying the foundation for a collaboration that would change both their lives.

A FANTASTIC FORCE

In May of 1960, Martin Goodman was playing golf with DC publisher Jack Liebowitz, who was bragging about the success of DC's new superhero team book *Justice League of America*. So in early 1961, Goodman ordered Stan Lee to come up with a group book to counter *Justice League*. This imperative came at just the right time: Lee was feeling used up and worn out, his best days in the comics industry behind him and no idea how he was going to make a name for himself as a "real writer," as he'd always dreamed. He'd worked in comics since he was seventeen, and felt that it was time to switch professions. And then his wife Joan intervened.

"I was all ready to quit," Lee laughs. "Because I was sick of writing these one-dimensional stories that the company wanted, that my publisher wanted. And my wife said to me, 'Look, if you're going to quit anyway, why don't you just do one book the way you'd like to do it, and the worst that'll happen is you'll get fired, and so what? You *want* to quit!'" With this in mind, Stan Lee created a superhero team book that was the antithesis of the sunny, congenial *Justice League of America*. That book, cocreated with Jack Kirby, was the *Fantastic Four*. *Fantastic Four* #1, with its dramatic and

COVER OF FANTASTIC FOUR #1, THE COMIC BOOK CREDITED WITH SINGLE-HANDEDLY BIRTHING THE MARVEL UNIVERSE.

unusual take on the superhero genre, appeared on newsstands in November of 1961. Very quickly it proceeded to turn around the fortunes of Martin Goodman's small but prolific publishing company, which by 1963 started officially calling itself Marvel Comics (a name that had been used on and off in various capacities for years).

The *Fantastic Four* is the story of scientist Reed Richards, his fiancée Sue Storm, her hot-headed kid brother Johnny Storm, and Reed's tough-but-lovable friend Ben Grimm. When they find themselves assaulted by a storm of cosmic rays that give them superpowers—Reed's body is suddenly as pliable as Silly Putty, Sue can turn invisible, Johnny can burst into flame, and Ben has been permanently transformed into a walking pile of orange rocks—they decide to use their powers in the fight against evil as (respectively) Mr. Fantastic, Invisible Girl, the Human Torch, and the Thing.

From this brief description, one might think that this was standard superhero fare: the heroes are imbued with powers and use them to promote the ideals of truth and justice. But in the *Fantastic Four*, Stan Lee's innovations are in the details. These characters are constantly bickering. Ben Grimm has to be convinced that beating "the commies" in the space race is the right thing to do, whereas in a DC book, that would go without saying. And when they first get their powers, the first thing they do is fight with one another. Elsewhere in the book, when Johnny flies overhead, his powers short out and he almost plummets to his death, when he's saved by the superelastic Reed. This is the equivalent of John Wayne falling off his horse in a Western—it just wasn't done!

Another thing that Lee did that "just wasn't done" was make these books *character driven* superhero comics. In other words, Reed was always cerebral and preoccupied with his scientific inventions, and Ben and Johnny were always bickering, almost at each other's throats. This led to scenarios like the one in *Fantastic Four* #4. Johnny Storm leaves the group after a fight with the others, and the bum that he meets while holed up in a flophouse turns out to be none other than Carl Burgos's legendary 1940s Timely character the Sub-Mariner. The Sub-Mariner, a.k.a. the aquatic Prince Namor of the lost city of Atlantis, distrusts surface-dwellers, but he immediately falls in love with Sue Storm. And Sue is torn between Reed, who is eternally preoccupied with science, and Namor, the exciting bad boy rebel.

This was pretty heady, psychologically complex stuff for a superhero comic in the early 1960s. These are modern heroes, with faults and foibles, who aren't always in control of every situation like DC's Superman or Wonder Woman. And they are dealing with relationships on a more or less adult level, as opposed to Superman, who never had a serious fight with Lois Lane that didn't involve one or both of them being brainwashed by an alien mind control ray. "I did the *Fantastic Four* the way I felt I would like to write, the way a story ought to be written," Lee enthuses. "To me, the only interesting stories are stories where you care about the characters, and you know their personalities and their individual quirks and hang-ups." Indeed, everything Stan Lee wrote from then on followed the character-driven, angst-laden template of the *Fantastic Four*. He had finally found his voice in the world of comics, a voice that would set him apart as the great writer he always wanted to be.

BUILDING A MARVELOUS UNIVERSE

Stan Lee and Jack Kirby's 1960s run on *Fantastic Four* lasted an impressive 102 issues, during which time they established it as the most busily bubbling cauldron of creative ideas in the Marvel Universe. And it constantly broke precedent with what you were "supposed to do" in a superhero comic. Never mind that these are superheroes who walk around without the benefit of secret identities or masks. Sure, they have flashy nicknames, but everyone knows who they are and what they look like, and they don't feel the need to don a bat-suit or a pair of glasses to disguise themselves. In fact, they only wore their costumes starting in issue 3 (in response to readers who wanted to see the FF in costume). Even then their costumes felt less like superhero suits and more like uniforms, akin to the kind a fireman, policeman, or rescue worker would wear.

Lee and Kirby were clearly experimenting with ideas such as: What would it be like if superheroes walked among us, not in a fictional "Metropolis," but in real live New York City? What relationship problems would they have? How would they earn a living? Would the government feel threatened by their presence? In a very real way, Lee and Kirby were taking the first furtive steps toward sculpting the postmodern superhero, a concept that would be more fully realized during the 1980s by such graphic novels as Alan Moore and Dave Gibbons's *Watchmen* and Frank Miller's *The Dark Knight Returns* and *Batman: Year One*.

Another novel-like innovation in the early *Fantastic Four* stories was the rich, dense mythology that Lee and Kirby wove around the four title characters. Their creators would often take the FF to hidden realms such as the technologically advanced African nation of Wakanda and alternate dimensions such as the Negative Zone. As in other forms of genre fiction, readers would grow accustomed to returning to these settings, and to revisiting the strange and varied characters that populated them.

It all became part of Lee's grand editorial plan for a shared Marvel Universe, a concept that would achieve greater fruition with the subsequent Marvel titles. In the course of the *FF*'s first 102 issues, Lee and Kirby introduced an enormous roster of supporting characters, many of whom later spawned their own successful spin-off titles. This "extended family" includes such future Marvel stalwarts as the Silver Surfer, Galactus, the Watcher, the Black Panther, Wyatt Wingfoot, the Inhumans, the Skrulls, and the Kree. "These characters came easy to me," shrugs Lee, who admits

© *Marvel Characters, Inc.*

STAN LEE AND JACK KIRBY USED THE FANTASTIC FOUR AS A PLAYGROUND OF IDEAS THAT WERE BOTH WHIMSICALLY IMAGINATIVE AND GROUNDED IN REAL HUMAN DRAMA.

that "our big problem was finding a way to squeeze them all into [the *Fantastic Four*]. We had dozens of characters we wanted to do. And we only had twenty-page stories!"

In fact, when considering just how integral so many of these characters continue to be to the current Marvel Universe, one gets the idea that Lee was thinking ahead in a way never before done in comic books. He was creating a storehouse of characters so that the Marvel books would never run out of material, in effect using the *Fantastic Four* as a "series bible" for future Marvel titles. Lee was also establishing a set continuity, a shared universe in which these characters could all coexist without having to rewrite the rules of the Marvel Universe every few years, as often had to be done in other companies. In other words, he was rewarding long-time readers while making the books user-friendly to new readers who didn't want to play catch-up.

MULTICULTURAL MARVEL

Another way Stan Lee the editor was courting more readers was by introducing characters into *Fantastic Four* who reflected the diversity of the readership.
This included integrating minority characters into the Marvel Universe. Up
until this point, minority comic book characters, especially black ones, were
usually depicted as domestics, or they were played for cheap laughs. In 1966,
Stan Lee and Jack Kirby shattered this negative stereotype by presenting the
first major black superhero, The Black Panther, in *Fantastic Four* #52.

The Black Panther was in reality T'Challa, monarch of the fictional
African nation of Wakanda, a technologically advanced civilization hidden
by sophisticated camouflage from the prying eyes of the rest of the world
(including the white world). "Here I wanted to get a black hero, and I wanted
to go totally against type," Stan Lee explains. "[T'Challa] looks like an ordinary black man, and his village in Africa looked like an ordinary village. But
underneath was one of the most scientific, high-tech establishments you can
imagine anywhere. And this guy who seemed like an ordinary black war-
rior chief of a tribe in Africa was really a great scientist, and the city was
more modern than most of the places in the rest of the earth. And they had
just had the village on top, for camouflage, so no one would suspect that this
great civilization was beneath." Lee made a genuine effort "to make the
Black Panther a fellow who was better educated, more gifted, and more of
a genius than most of the people around, and I hope that that came across."

The Black Panther was Stan Lee's acknowledgment of the struggles
of black American culture, and the evils of racism. "Intolerance is an
important issue to me," Lee elaborates. "People who hate other people
because of their color, because of their race, the color of their hair, their
religion, whatever stupid reason. And you know, any little thing I was able
to do in the [Black Panther] stories, I tried to do." The Black Panther
would later become a member of the superhero group the Avengers, and
eventually get his own title for a time, but he was far from the only minority character Stan Lee would introduce in the 1960s.

In August 1967, in the pages of *Amazing Spider-Man* #51, Stan Lee
and artist John Romita, Sr., introduced the character Joe "Robbie"
Robertson, African American city editor of the *Daily Bugle* and friend
to Spider-Man's alter ego, nebbishy newspaper photographer Peter
Parker. Robbie Robertson was created in direct contrast to the *Daily
Bugle*'s editor in chief, the cantankerous J. Jonah Jameson. "The balance
that I had in the stories," Lee states, "was that Jonah Jameson, the rich
white guy, is intolerant and a braggart and a bigot, and Robbie, the black

city editor, is sort of the voice of reason. He's really the clear-thinking, intelligent one of the two. And without him, who knows what trouble the newspaper would be in?"

Marvel soon became known as the most progressive mainstream comic book company out there in terms of introducing minority characters, and many of these characters were cocreated by Stan Lee. In *Fantastic Four* #50, May 1966, Stan Lee and Jack Kirby introduced Johnny Storm's Native American roommate Wyatt Wingfoot, who would become a recurring supporting cast member, often helping out the FF on their missions, and eventually—long after Lee's run on the series ended—becoming romantically entangled with She-Hulk (who was herself a "person of color," if you count the color green). In June 1969, Lee and artist Gene Colan introduced the white-and-red–clad African American superhero the Falcon in the pages of *Captain America* #117. The Falcon and Captain America became the first interracial superhero team, foreshadowing later pairings like Cloak and Dagger.

SPINNING A WEB OF STORIES

As with the *Fantastic Four*, one of the strengths of Stan Lee's other superhero efforts was his mastery of characterization. Every character sounded different. Whereas an upset Reed Richards might say, "See here! I demand an apology," Ben Grimm would say, "Pal, you just earned yourself a knuckle sandwich!"

Lee's gift for complex character development hit its apex in the character that he and Steve Ditko introduced in August 1963's *Amazing Fantasy* #15—Spider-Man, who emerged (as the Fantastic

© *Marvel Characters, Inc.*

Steve Ditko's idiosyncratic style of artwork complemented Stan Lee's storytelling prowess, though the two didn't always see eye-to-eye.

Four had done) a fully developed personality with a very specific set of quirks. He would often make fun of the villains he fought, as when he repeatedly referred to the Green Goblin as "Gobby" during a fight. He would frequently sit on rooftops and soliloquize, Hamlet-style, about his various romantic and personal problems. Even the other characters in the series had their own quirks and catchphrases, as when girlfriend Mary Jane Watson nicknamed him "Tiger."

In fact, Stan Lee gave Peter Parker a succession of love interests including *Daily Bugle* secretary Betty Brant and the ill-fated Gwen Stacy, all of whom had their own attitudes and world views. Betty Brant initially brushes Peter off as a loser. But she comes to appreciate and even love him—until her longing for a life of stability makes Peter choose between his career as a superhero and her.

Another important element of the Spider-Man character is that instead of the muscle-bound heroes of old, e.g., Superman or Captain America, Spider-Man is slight of build, a wiry figure who has more in common with the agile Bruce Lee than the chiseled Bruce Wayne (or the Hulking Bruce Banner). Spider-Man's physicality reveals something of his character as well, because before he was bitten by the radioactive spider that gave him his powers, he was nebbishy Peter Parker, a lonely, bespectacled high school student who lived with his Uncle Ben and Aunt May in Forest Hills, Queens. When his Uncle Ben is murdered, Peter realizes that he could have stopped it and decides to wage a never-ending war on crime as Spider-Man.

Before Spider-Man, teen characters in comic books were usually either of the kid sidekick variety, like Robin of *Batman* fame, or they were lovable Andy Hardy–style kids like Archie and Jughead who had nary a care, their world an idyllic teenage dreamland filled with sock hops and dates at the malt shop. But Spider-Man broke from those stereotypes in a couple of key ways: a) he was nobody's sidekick, and b) he was a hunched-over, neurotic mess, often unable to pay the rent or get a date. This was Stan Lee's innovation in writing the Spider-Man character; he strove to inject realism into the series. "My feeling is, if you can get the reader to suspend disbelief for one fantastic element [of the story], you then have to make everything else as realistic as possible," Lee declares. "So, all right, I was going to ask the reader to accept the fact that a guy could be bitten by a radioactive spider and gain the power of a spider. And I wanted him to be a real guy that you can empathize with! So he had money problems, and he wasn't the handsomest, most popular kid with the girls, and he had family problems, and he was shy, and he was neurotic, but he was also very bright.

So again, even though if you think about it it's a silly premise, getting bitten by a spider and suddenly you can do everything that a spider can do, if you accept him as a human being, then perhaps you're willing to go along with the premise. And that's the way I tried to treat all of these characters."

OUTCASTS AND OUTLAWS

One recurring theme in all of Stan Lee's Marvel comics is that all the characters are outsiders of one kind or another. Ben Grimm hates himself and feels like a freak who doesn't belong anywhere, least of all in his own rock-hard skin. Peter Parker fears that he'll never find a woman who will understand him because of his dangerous double-life. Bruce Banner lives in a constant state of panic, always wary that the monster inside him will erupt, and therefore he can't form meaningful bonds with anyone. But this "outcast" theme really emerged in full force in the pages of September 1963's *X-Men* #1. Stan Lee attributes the creation of the X-Men to "laziness," explaining, "I realized I wanted to do a lot more heroes and I thought, 'Well, if I just say that people are mutants, you know, mutations exist in nature, and they exist in fruit and animals and people, so I'll just say a lot of people were born that way. And then I don't have to dream up gamma rays, or radioactive spiders, and it made it very easy for me.' So it was just laziness." Stan Lee's modesty aside, there's a serious side to his and Jack Kirby's creation of the X-Men.

The X-Men were heroes, but society branded them a menace, because unlike the Hulk, Spider-Man, or the FF, the X-Men weren't doused with radiation. The X-Men were mutants, meaning that they were born with their superpowers. They were born *different*. And as the X-Men were all adolescents, their powers could be read as a metaphor for puberty—indeed, the X-Men didn't realize they were mutants until their powers first manifested during adolescence.

But as society hated and feared them for being innately different than everyone else, the X-Men are often seen as a metaphor for the ethnic "other," specifically African Americans, Jews, and homosexuals. Later *X-Men* writers like Len Wein and Chris Claremont would bring this metaphor even further into the forefront of the series, bringing black, Jewish, Asian, Latino, and Native American characters into the group (and of course, the two *X-Men* feature films directed by Bryan Singer used the "mutant as minority" angle quite effectively). In much the same way as films of the period such as *Invasion of the Body-Snatchers* and *Night of the Living Dead* were shrewd commentaries on the Red Scare and racism, Lee and Kirby were here using the X-Men to examine society's paranoia and hatred against those we see as different or threatening. And during the 1960s, a time when the civil rights movement, the gay rights movement, and the feminist movement were all gaining momentum, Stan Lee was using science fiction in time-honored fashion, like H. G. Wells, Rod Serling, and many others had done before him, as a potent means of holding a mirror up to society.

"I was just trying to make [the X-Men] contemporary," Lee explains. "Trying to make them as hip as I could. And whatever people were thinking about or arguing about at the time, whenever I could, without being heavy-handed about it, I tried to insert some of that in the stories." By making stories like the *X-Men* edgy and current, Stan Lee was courting an older audience. This audience appreciated that Lee, Kirby, Ditko, and company were respecting their intelligence, and Marvel Comics became the first mainstream superhero comic books to be read widely on college campuses.

Another innovation in Stan Lee's *X-Men* stories was its ethical graying. In creating a series about superhero outcasts, there were few clear-cut, black or white villains, only shades of gray. So it is with the X-Men's arch foe Magneto, the master of magnetism, who like his nemeses is also a mutant. In the Lee and Kirby *X-Men* stories, Magneto would occasionally ask why the X-Men's leader, Professor X, was fighting him, rather than working with him, since they were both self-appointed defenders of mutantkind (and thus in Magneto's eyes, potentially on the same side). And in *X-Men* #4, we learn that the Scarlet Witch, one of Magneto's allies, owes Magneto her life. When she was about to be burned as a witch in her small European village, Magneto interceded and saved her. So there is some good in even the darkest of hearts.

Stan Lee's use of ethical graying is also apparent in his other Marvel titles of this period, such as *Fantastic Four*, where the character of Medusa—who can wrap you up with her long crimson tresses—at first seemed to be a villain, and was later revealed to be a misguided member of an ancient race of beings known as the Inhumans. Once they win the FF's trust, the Inhumans prove themselves to be powerful allies.

THE POWER COSMIC

After the smash success of *Fantastic Four* and *Spider-Man*, Marvel was riding high, and Lee realized that he now had won the creative freedom to explore ever-more innovative and ambitious themes in his comic books. And while the *X-Men* and the *Hulk* explored the inner lives of monsters and mutants, those monsters and mutants were still (technically) mortal. Meanwhile, some of Stan Lee's other titles of this period explored other-worldly realms, worlds beyond this mortal ken.

In August 1962, the same year that they were unleashing the Hulk on audiences, Stan Lee and Jack Kirby created Thor, God of Thunder (with Lee's brother Larry Lieber coscripting the first installment) in the pages of *Journey into Mystery* #83. What was unique about Thor is that unlike other superheroes, he wasn't an alien, nor a genetically altered mutant or radioactive human. He was a god. Thor was the story of crippled doctor Don Blake who, when he discovers an ancient staff and taps it on the ground, is transformed into Thor, the ancient Norse god of thunder. Thor could be powerful without being sacrilegious, because let's face it, his followers are long gone. He could therefore be the ultimate superhero!

Because Thor is an immortal, and thus ignorant of modern street slang or even present-day English, Lee wrote the character's dialogue in a flowery barrage of "thou shalt nots" and "so be its," clearly having fun every step of the way. And Lee was also able to wring an occasional bit of fish-out-of-water comedy out of Thor's stylized delivery, as when in 1967's *The Mighty Thor* #143, the strapping blond god chugs a milkshake and then asks the soda shop owner, "Alas, I find I have no Earthly coin of the realm upon my person—but if thou wilt permit me to *charge* yon frothy drink?"

Around the same time, Stan Lee joined with Steve Ditko to fashion another magically inclined hero. In July 1963, in the pages of *Strange Tales* #110, Lee and Ditko introduced a sorcerer named Stephen Strange to unwitting audiences, and the unique character quickly gained an immense cult following. Doctor Stephen Strange was an arrogant surgeon who, after a car accident, found that the nerves in his hands had been damaged and his medical career was over. Journeying to India, Dr. Strange seeks out a legendary mystic known only as "The Ancient One." After putting Dr. Strange through a trial to test his mettle, The Ancient One takes on the humbled former surgeon as an apprentice and teaches him the ways of the mystic arts.

Dr. Strange laid claim to a unique use of the English language. Lee had him utter intensely bizarre and descriptive incantations, such as, "In the name of the All-Seeing Agamotto!" Lee was fully aware of how bizarre these magical phrases sounded, and he was also aware that this was part of Dr. Strange's appeal. "In trying to do a magician, I tried to do dialogue that's right for the character," Lee says. "So when Dr. Strange was going to create some sort of magical effect, I couldn't have him say 'Abracadabra!' I figured I would have him say, 'By the hoary hosts of Hoggoth!' I tried to make up expressions that would sound right, and would sound as though there's some sort of reason or there's some sort of legend behind them."

Of course, Lee's very specific-sounding incantations often struck readers as being a little *too* specific. "It's funny," Lee recalls, "because I used to lecture a lot at colleges, and inevitably in the question and answer period, somebody would get up and say, 'Stan we've been researching these Dr. Strange stories and I noticed that you took a lot of the material from the ancient druid writings or from the inscriptions at Stonehenge!' And they were always so disappointed when I would say, 'No, I just made them up!'"

Lee had a good reason for always making up the magic words in the Dr. Strange stories: as Marvel's editor in chief, production manager, head writer, and de facto art director during most of the 1960s, his dance card was full. "I never had time to do research!" he exclaims. "The stories that I wrote, I would come into the office, and whoever was taken charge of the scheduling in the production would say, 'Stan, we need a Dr. Strange story tomorrow morning!' Or, 'We need *Thor* by the afternoon!' I only had a few hours to do those things." But Lee doesn't wish that he'd had more time to do research. "I hate research. It's more fun to make stuff up."

© *Marvel Characters, Inc.*

The third and final of Stan Lee's 1960s-era "cosmic" characters was someone that he couldn't do any research on, because unlike a mystic sorcerer or a Norse god, this character was from an alien world. The Silver Surfer, a chrome-plated being who rides through the air on a shiny plank, was introduced by Lee and Jack Kirby in 1966's *Fantastic Four* #48. The herald of the planet-devouring alien giant Galactus, the Silver Surfer's job is

STAN LEE USED THE CHROME-PLATED SILVER SURFER TO COMMUNICATE PHILOSOPHICAL POINTS ABOUT THE NATURE OF LIFE ON EARTH.

to scout planets for his master, who then consumes the energies of the chosen worlds, leaving them barren and lifeless. However, when the Silver Surfer scouts the Earth for Galactus, he falls in love with its flawed, yet endearing, citizenry, and tries—with the aid of the Fantastic Four—to prevent Galactus from consuming the Earth. This heads off a three-part saga that was among the most memorable of the many sprawling multi-issue story arcs Lee and Kirby spun. At the end, the Silver Surfer strikes a bargain with Galactus: his beloved Earth will be spared, but as punishment for delaying his master's lunchtime the Surfer is cursed to remain in the Earth's orbit, never again to freely roam the galaxy's spaceways. He is trapped on this tainted blue orb.

The Silver Surfer became one of the most popular recurring characters in the *Fantastic Four*, eventually starring in his own series. Stan Lee used the chrome-plated alien to communicate philosophical points about the nature of life on Earth. "[With] the Silver Surfer, I tried to get across a lot of my own feelings about things, without getting into a religious area," Lee muses. "I never wanted to seem to be pushing any religious ideas of mine on the minds of the readers. That wouldn't be right. But there are a lot of things that were philosophically [resonant]. For example, the main thing I tried to have the Silver Surfer say [was] the fact that the human race must be crazy! I mean, we're living on a planet that's the closest thing to the Garden of Eden, it has fresh air and sunlight, the change of seasons, all the food we could ever want, fresh water all over, it's a perfect world for human beings [to] live on. And instead of appreciating it, we hate anybody who's different than us, we have wars, crimes, there are people going hungry, and it seems to me that if you came from another world, like the Silver Surfer, and saw what goes on on Earth, you'd think we were a race of madmen!"

People have often read the story of the Silver Surfer as a metaphor for yet another larger-than-life story. "A lot of people felt he was my version of the Second Coming of Christ," he laughs. "But I didn't think of that. I just thought, 'What if somebody from another planet who was a good guy came down here and saw the terrible things we're doing to our planet and to each other?' When I lectured at colleges, inevitably during the question-and-answer period, somebody would get up and say, 'Hey Stan, did you intend the Silver Surfer to be like Jesus Christ?' And they'd read all this religious stuff into it." Lee facetiously muses, "If I had time I might have tried to start a new religion, but I was just too busy." And he's very proud of how the Silver Surfer continues in his tradition of characters whom you could recognize just by reading their dialogue balloons. "I tried to write his dialogue so that it was a form of prose-poetry," he reveals. "If you read it aloud, it almost scanned."

THE MERRY MARVEL MARCHING SOCIETY

In early 1965, Stan Lee started an innovative publicity gimmick called the Merry Marvel Marching Society, Marvel's official fan club. The MMMS was launched after Lee had planted hints—often little cryptic blurbs on the corner of the covers of Marvel titles proclaiming that "The MMMS Wants You!" Before the club was officially started, fans wrote in en masse trying to guess what the acronym stood for. Once the MMMS was made public, fans who sent a dollar to Marvel Comics certainly got their money's worth: an official membership kit that included a membership card (with a Marvel pledge of allegiance on the back), a membership button, a letter welcoming you to the organization, a collection of stickers, and most impressively, a 33⅓-RPM record with the voices of Stan Lee, Jack Kirby, and others (the notoriously press-shy Steve Ditko declined to participate) cracking jokes and welcoming you into the Marvel inner circle.

This was only one of the tricks in Stan Lee's PR utility belt. Another was the "No Prize." If a fan wrote in pointing out a continuity error or other story mistake in one of the Marvel books, Lee or one of the other Marvel staffers would send that dedicated fan an empty envelope with Marvel's return address in the upper corner, and the declaration, "This envelope contains a genuine Marvel No Prize, which you have just won!" This was Lee's tongue-in-cheek (not to mention cost-efficient) way of mocking obsessive fans, while at the same time rewarding them with a rare keepsake, the envelope itself having quickly become a collector's item.

Stan Lee also spared room in each Marvel title for a page of promotional news dubbed the "Bullpen Bulletin," fostering the homey, old-fashioned image that a small cluster of artists, writers, editors, and production people were hunkered over a drawing board in a mythic "bullpen," churning out Marvel Comics, factory-style. At the bottom of each "Bulletin" was a yellow-coded area dubbed "Stan's Soapbox," Lee's personal note to the reader. He would usually sign off with the phrase, "Excelsior!", the New York State motto meaning "Ever Upward," a hopeful credo that also gave readers the right message: Marvel Comics was always looking toward the future, never mired in the past.

Another one of Stan Lee's personal publicity touches was that he was the first comics editor to—as a rule—credit everyone who worked on each comic book, from the writer to the penciler to the inker to the letterer (later in the decade, he also started crediting the colorist and editor). Other publishers, like Bill Gaines's EC Comics in the 1950s (*MAD* and *Tales from the Crypt*), had often promoted their artists like Wally Wood and Harvey Kurtzman, creating a "star system" of sorts. But here Marvel was promoting not only their illustrators but the whole creative team, so that fans would have two reasons to buy the books: 1) to see their favorite characters, and 2) to see the work of their favorite comic book *creators*! And even here, Lee says, "I wanted to make it fun. And I think the thing I enjoyed most was writing credits, like, 'Written with passion by Stan Lee, drawn with fervor by Jack Kirby, and lettered with a scratchy pen point by Artie Simek.' I loved having a little gag even in the credits! And the readers seemed to love it."

Chief among Lee's artists was Jack Kirby, who had a hand in the creation or development of almost every major Stan Lee Marvel superhero during the 1960s. If there was ever one person who could be seen as Stan Lee's coconspirator in charting the Marvel Universe, it's Jack Kirby. "His contribution was enormous," Lee says of Kirby. "He was able to combine drama with action with excitement. No matter what he drew, it never looked dull. And even if nothing was happening on the page, even if there was no fight scene or anything, he found a way to draw the characters' expressions, and to do the perspective, and whatever magic he worked. Every page looked interesting, and compelling, and you wanted to read it. And he had a way of making a hero look incredibly heroic and a villain look indescribably evil. And he was just great at emotion, and storytelling. I don't think the [*Fantastic Four*] would have been as successful had Jack not been the artist. He also contributed a lot of the story points as we went along. I can't praise him highly enough!"

Just as Lee demonstrated how a Marvel comic should be written, Kirby was instrumental in demonstrating how a Marvel comic should be drawn. His work was for years indicative of what became known as the Marvel "house style," something that went a long way in terms of establishing Marvel's brand identity. Today, over a decade after Kirby's death, Stan Lee still acknowledges the importance of the artist who was in many ways the DeNiro to his Scorsese, and younger artists like Kevin Eastman (cocreator of *Teenage Mutant Ninja Turtles*) and Mike Mignola (creator of *Hellboy*) are blatantly influenced by this artist whom in younger days Stan Lee nicknamed "The King."

EVER UPWARD

In 1972, Stan Lee became publisher of Marvel. With this new responsibility he had to drop some of his old tasks, such as scripting chores on the four monthly Marvel titles he was still writing by that point, the *Fantastic Four*, *Amazing Spider-Man*, *Thor*, and Joe Simon and Jack Kirby's *Captain America*. Ever since Lee became Marvel's publisher, a new Lee-scripted comic book has become a special event. In 1978 Stan Lee and Jack Kirby collaborated for what would be their final work together, the superhero sci-fi graphic novel *Silver Surfer*. Often considered one of Lee and Kirby's finest accomplishments, the one-hundred-page book finds the Surfer once again defending the Earth from Galactus, who sends a gold-plated female seductress, Ardina, to try to convince our hero of humanity's worthlessness. Stan Lee next returned to the Silver Surfer character in a 1988 one-shot entitled *Judgment Day*, illustrated by John Buscema, in which the Surfer fought against Mephisto (a villain clearly reminiscent of Satan).

Then came Lee's two-issue limited series, published in late 1988 and early 1989, called *Silver Surfer: Parable*, in which the Surfer faces off against both Galactus and a power-hungry preacher who proclaims Galactus a deity. The gullible populace of Earth only become disillusioned with Galactus when their newfound god callously lets an innocent woman die. This is one of Lee's most uncompromising stories, and the fact that he doesn't go for an easy, happy ending denotes a trend in his career. As with the 1971 "drug abuse" arc he'd written into *Amazing Spider-Man* #96–98 (in which Peter Parker's roommate Harry Osborn becomes addicted to pills), here we see Lee using his industry clout to tell important, mature stories about the human condition, rife with social commentary.

STAN THE MOGUL

By the time Lee stepped up to the plate as publisher of Marvel in the early seventies, he was also very much in demand as a celebrity, and the Marvel name carried with it a certain hipster cache. As early as the mid-1960s, the world of arts and letters took note of Marvel's success, and in 1965 legendary filmmaker Federico Fellini visited the Marvel offices. In that same year *The Village Voice*, a bastion of the hip alternative press, wrote an article on Marvel that paid specific attention to Lee. Author Ken Kesey (*One Flew Over the Cuckoo's Nest*) was an outspoken fan of Lee and Ditko's psychedelic Dr. Strange, and future *Bonfire of the Vanities* author Tom Wolfe was such a Marvel fan that he appeared alongside Stan Lee and read aloud from issues of Marvel comics at Lee's 1972 Carnegie Hall performance. French director Alain Resnais and Troma Films cofounder Lloyd Kaufman each served as screenwriting partners with Stan Lee during the 1970s.

Lee did sell a couple of screenplays and treatments to Hollywood, but the majority of his work during this decade was divided between his growing fame as a lecturer on the college speaking circuit and his attempts to help sell Marvel's properties such as Spider-Man and the X-Men to various film and television production companies. At the time, the showbiz world was reluctant to invest in big-budget movies and television shows based on two-dimensional superheroes.

For years, the only adaptations of Marvel properties that were successfully translated to the small screen were of the Saturday Morning variety, animated cartoons such as the 1967 cartoon serial *Fantastic Four* or the 1981–1986 series *Spider-Man and His Amazing Friends* (for which Lee provided voice-over narration in his crisp, grandfatherly tones). Live-action treatment of Stan Lee's Marvel characters was not as kind, and typically resulted in fiascos such as the 1978 *Spider-Man* television series starring Nicholas Hammond, or the grade Z, 1994 straight-to-video *Fantastic Four* movie, executive produced by low-budget mogul Roger Corman. When a Marvel character *did* receive dignified treatment on the big or small screen, such as in Kenneth Johnson's 1978–1982 television version of *The Hulk* starring Bill Bixby (on which Stan Lee served as consultant, and one episode of which featured Jack Kirby in a cameo as a police sketch artist), it was the exception, not the rule.

All that changed when a new generation of genre auteurs cropped up during the 1990s. These filmmakers were technologically savvy enough to use the new CGI (Computer Generated Imaging) technology to create quality filmic adaptations of the Marvel Comics images they'd grown up with. Soon, A-listers like James Cameron (*Terminator*, *Titanic*) were jockeying to direct feature-length big-budget adaptations of Spider-Man and other Stan Lee characters. Finally, in 1998, the film *Blade* (based on a Marv Wolfman and Gene Colan character from Marvel's *Tomb of Dracula*) was released. While not based on a Stan Lee creation, Lee's name was on the slickly produced blockbuster film as executive producer. He and his characters were both now viable Hollywood commodities. This also had a lot to do with the current CEO of Marvel Studios (Marvel's entertainment division), Avi Arad, a former toy designer who has made it his mission to bring Lee's characters to the big and small screens with dignity and top-name talent.

Then in 2000 another film Stan Lee executive produced, *X-Men*, became a mega-hit, becoming the first hit feature film based on a Stan Lee–scripted comic book. This film, which also made a major movie star out of Australian stage actor Hugh Jackman, proved that the success of *Blade* was no fluke. Whereas DC heroes such as Superman and Batman had been box office gold in the past, now there was an established precedent for Marvel heroes succeeding at the box office.

The critically acclaimed smash hit *Spider-Man* in 2002 continued Marvel's winning streak of film adaptations. *Spider-Man 2*, released in 2004, was cowritten by Pulitzer Prize–winning novelist Michael Chabon, long known as a fan of Stan Lee's work. Chabon's novel *The Amazing Adventures of Kavalier and Clay*, about two Depression-era comic book artists, was loosely inspired by the lives and careers of Lee and his contemporaries such as *Superman* creators Jerry Siegel and Joe Shuster, *Spirit* creator Will Eisner, and of course *Captain America* creators Jack Kirby and Joe Simon. Lee does admit that for someone who spent years trying unsuccessfully to sell Hollywood on his various Marvel concepts, this sudden rush of showbiz success is a bit surreal. "It really does feel wonderful," he shrugs. "I've gotten quite friendly with Michael Chabon, who's one of the nicest guys, a great fella. I think my only regret is that I never wrote one of those Marvel movies myself!"

Using his newfound Hollywood clout, in 2002 Lee founded POW! Entertainment, which has produced projects such as the 2003 SpikeTV effort *Stripperella*, an animated series that starred Pamela Anderson as the titular exotic dancer / superhero. Recently Lee announced plans to develop animated series starring such luminaries as *Playboy* founder Hugh Hefner and former Beatle Ringo Starr. Through POW!, Lee also has several projects in development with Bruce Willis and Arnold Rifkin's production company Cheyenne Entertainment, and he's recently stepped into the reality-television ring, producing a reality series called *Who Wants to be a Superhero?* "The idea is that anybody who thinks he can be a superhero, or has an idea for a great superhero, we're going to try them out." Stan Lee is certainly keeping busy. "With POW! Entertainment, we're working on everything. We're doing movies, television, animation, DVDs, and we're even doing features for cell phones! I like to do different things. And that's what I'm doing now, a lot of different things."

WITH GREAT POWER . . .

When we first meet Spider-Man, Stan Lee's narration informs us that "with great power there must also come—great responsibility!" With great power also comes great controversy, as Lee has learned. For just as he's been lauded for his contributions to comic books both as a business and an art form, Lee has also been at the heart of a handful of controversial debates in the industry, most of which relate to the various characters he's created for Marvel.

Or more to the point, *co*created. And therein lies the issue. In the early days of comics, everyone wrote comic book scripts using what is now known as "full script," meaning a very detailed script that dictates what happens on every page, panel by panel, laying out the dialogue and stage directions for every panel and sometimes even describing what a certain character or location might look like. This type of comic book script is similar in format to a screenplay. However, even in those days, some comic book writers wrote in a different format, known as "plot style," in which a writer talks over the basic plot and structure with the artist, then types up a one or two page synopsis (known as a "plot" or a "premise") laying out the general dramatic beats of the script, then hands that over to the artist, who works from this to break down the story (via rough pencil drawings) into its panel-by-panel specifics, often even making notes for the dialogue in the margins. This is then handed back to the writer, who can suggest changes to the plot and structure, but who mainly then writes the final dialogue balloons, narration, and captions.

Until Lee began writing the lion's share of the Goodman line of comics in the 1950s, even *he* wrote full scripts. But then the sheer workload necessitated that he use "plot style" on all his scripts. This style henceforth became known as the "Marvel method." Because Lee popularized the Marvel method, the artists who worked with him, such as Jack Kirby, Steve Ditko, Don Heck, Bill Everett, and John Buscema, could legitimately be called Stan Lee's writing partners. After all, they often took his loosely written plots and fleshed them out panel by panel, turning his short synopses into full-length stories on which Lee could then hang his dialogue and narrative captions. And turning a treatment into a fully structured story is one of the things that a writer does. Coupled with the fact that artists such as Ditko and Kirby created characters that were not in Lee's synopses (e.g., the Silver Surfer), and considering the fact that they often deviated quite seriously from the details of those synopses (Lee's synopsis had the FF landing on Mars after their accident, instead of back on Earth), it seems that the artists did some of the writing themselves.

Stan Lee is quite candid about the fact that he frequently handed both Jack Kirby and Steve Ditko minimal scraps of written material, from which they were to spin out a full, beat-by-beat story. "Don't forget," Lee says, "when we did the *Fantastic Four*, I think I gave one page to Jack Kirby, and that was the whole thing! And when I did *Spider-Man*, I don't even know if I wrote anything! I think I just *told* it to Steve Ditko! I can't remember! But if you have the right idea, it doesn't take a lot of describing. You can sum it up in a few words. I find it's only when the idea isn't too sharp and isn't too crystallized that it takes forever to describe it and make it sound good."

This doesn't downplay Lee's own literary contributions to the stories themselves. As both writer and editor, Lee would often further restructure any given story after he received the pages back from the artists, using the dialogue and captions to deepen the characters' relationship dynamics, sharpen their personalities, and provide narrative elements such as backstory (and using thought balloons, he could also get across a sense of their inner desires and aspirations that even the strongest illustrator couldn't communicate). And Stan Lee would often make strong, writerly decisions that his artists sometimes chafed at. Ditko was notoriously unhappy that when the Green Goblin was finally unmasked, Lee revealed the mysterious villain to be a character we'd come to know and like, Norman Osborn. Steve Ditko felt strongly that under the mask, Green Goblin should be a person we'd never seen before, and this difference of opinion over the identity of "Gobby" reportedly contributed to Ditko's 1966 resignation from Marvel. Ditko felt an almost paternal sense of ownership toward the characters he worked on, which came from having invested so much in the stories as well as the artwork.

For this reason, Steve Ditko demanded a "plot" credit on the *Spider-Man* and *Dr. Strange* titles he drew, meaning that he plotted the books; in essence this is tantamount to saying that he cowrote them. But Jack Kirby, company man that he was, never demanded such a credit, although he certainly could have. After all, he'd cocreated most of the major Marvel superhero line from 1961 to 1969. But what really upset Kirby was the fact that Stan Lee rarely spoke up to challenge the media's exclusion of Kirby or Ditko's role in the creation of a given Marvel character. Kirby's disgust with what he perceived as Lee's credit-hogging was one of the main factors leading to his ending his collaboration with Lee and defecting to DC in 1970.

In 1972, in the pages of DC's *Mister Miracle*, Kirby created the character of Funky Flashman, a sleazy huckster willing to sell out his grandmother if it yielded a profit. With his tinted sunglasses, toupee, beard (which Lee wore at the time), and manic chatterbox delivery, Funky Flashman is a more-than-obvious dig at Lee. In fact, Funky's sidekick, Houseroy, is a parody of Lee's protégé Roy Thomas. Kirby was none-too-subtly making the point that Thomas was like a houseboy to Stan Lee, almost an indentured servant. Kirby's frustration was understandable; throughout the 1970s and '80s, Marvel's press materials trumpeted Lee as the sole creative godfather of the Marvel Universe, and he was the only representative that Marvel sent out on lecture gigs or television appearances. He was management, and Kirby was a mere freelancer, no matter how enormous his contribution to Marveldom.

It didn't help that throughout the 1980s, Kirby was engaged in a battle with Marvel over his original artwork, which he'd hoped to have returned to him. This was not Lee's fault, nor was it his battle (here Jack Kirby was fighting Marvel Comics, *not* Stan Lee). However, again, Lee could have spoken up in Kirby's defense but chose to remain silent. For these reasons, in several published interviews during the 1980s with such luminaries as *Spirit* creator Will Eisner and *Comics Journal* editor Gary Groth, Kirby went on record not only disputing Lee's version of the creation of the Marvel Universe; he also downplayed Lee's importance in creating anything for the company, claiming that Lee was nothing more than a conduit to get to Martin Goodman's ear, and snorting, "Stan Lee and I never collaborated on anything!"

So, did Lee really write (or cowrite) the 1960s-era Marvel stories? The majority of evidence would scream a resounding "Yes." Kirby later regretted his harsh words regarding Lee's authorship, and took them back as untrue. But after a 1998 *Time* magazine article credited Lee as "Spider-Man's creator" (rather than cocreator), Steve Ditko similarly questioned Lee's authorship of the *Spider-Man* and *Dr. Strange* stories. The reclusive Ditko has never quite recanted his accusations that Lee never wrote any of the stories on which he's credited as writer. However, in this case, as in Kirby's case, the claims seem suspect, the vengeful words of a justifiably disgruntled employee.

Kirby's work after his partnership with Lee could be well-written (certain *New Gods* and *Mister Miracle* stories come to mind, as do some of his *Kamandi* tales), but Kirby's work with Lee maintained a discipline and a focus it never quite recaptured after they parted ways. Kirby's solo work often suffered from cardboard characterization, awkward dialogue, and erratic pacing. And Kirby's work with creative collaborator Joe Simon in the forties and fifties—while still good comics storytelling—never yielded the literary merit of a *Fantastic Four* or an *Incredible Hulk*. Furthermore, Ditko's post-Marvel work has often been wildly inventive and atmospheric (especially in series like *The Creeper*), but also increasingly didactic and corny. Left on his own—or collaborating with scribes other than Stan Lee—Ditko's writing becomes ponderous.

On examination, it's clear what Stan Lee brought to the table as coauthor of the Marvel Universe: a sense of characterization and dramatic structure that was lacking when artists like Kirby and Ditko were let loose as solo artists. Lee, Kirby, and Ditko brought out the best in one another. Finally, as one last gesture toward his friendship with Kirby, Lee was instrumental in setting up a pension for the artist's widow, Roz Kirby, during the final years of her life.

Authorship issues notwithstanding, most of Kirby's beefs were with Marvel itself, and not Stan Lee; indeed, Lee often had little or no control over Marvel's treatment of their former star artist. But if Kirby felt that his friend and colleague Lee had burned him at certain points during their relationship, Lee himself would experience a far greater betrayal at the hands of his longtime friend Peter Paul. In January 1999, Lee and Paul founded Stan Lee Media, an Internet startup with an eye toward developing Web-based content (an online animation studio), comic books to be sold both over the Web and via direct market distribution, and film and television franchises, not to mention Stan Lee–based theme park attractions. By buying out a holding company that was already publicly traded, Stan Lee Media sneaked onto the NASDAQ board and let the public at large put a price on what Stan Lee was worth. By selling Lee as a source of global entertainment licensing through the Internet, SLM soon had a market capitalization valued at $3.5 million, and Lee briefly even thought about buying Marvel.

From the time it went public in August 1999 until late 2000, Stan Lee Media embraced the dot-com boom, creating several "webisodes" of an online animated superhero series, *The 7th Portal*, about a group of software beta testers who battle villains on the Internet. In *The 7th Portal*, Lee himself provided the voice for the wizened sage Izayus. The licensed characters from *The 7th Portal* became part of an interactive touring 3-D movie attraction that played at several amusement parks nationwide. SLM also published a sold-out run of *The Backstreet Project*, a Backstreet Boys comic book cocreated by Lee and Backstreet Boy Nick Carter, in which the Orlando boy band acquired superpowers. In addition, Lee was in talks to develop a series of webisodes featuring a superhero version of rapper The RZA (of the Wu-Tang Clan). As Peter Paul told the *Los Angeles Business Journal* in August 2000, "We're really the Disney of the twenty-first century." It certainly looked that way . . . for a while.

And then the bottom fell out of Stan Lee Media. The new company burned through cash at a rate of $18.5 million in the first nine months of

2000 (versus revenue of $1.2 million). Also, Peter Paul was revealed to be someone other than the staunch ally Lee had thought he'd befriended. He had a checkered past: In 1979, he'd spent thirty months in prison after being convicted on twin charges of cocaine possession and attempting to swindle the Cuban government out of $8.75 million. As cofounder of SLM, he'd borrowed $250,000 from Lee, which he never repaid. But more importantly, according to federal indictments later filed, Paul and SLM vice-president Stephen Gordon borrowed large sums of money on margin from Merrill Lynch, using Stan Lee Media shares as collateral. They converted their stock to cash without selling it outright and lowering the stock price. Paul, Gordon, and others bought and sold large portions of Stan Lee Media shares to artificially maintain and inflate its price. They also paid Wall Street analyst Jeffrey Pittsburgh and stock promoter Charles Kusche to tout the stock with misleading research reports. In late 2000, Paul and Gordon stopped paying Pittsburgh and Kusche. Stan Lee Media's stock plunged; investors were stuck with worthless stock, and Merrill Lynch was owed $5 million in loans.

On December 15, 2000, Stan Lee Media ceased production, and almost all their 150 employees were laid off. Trading of its stock (which had shrunk to 13 cents a share) was halted. In June 2001, Peter Paul was indicted for his alleged part in a stock manipulation, fraud, and check kiting scheme at SLM. The indictment claims that Paul went to great lengths to exploit and cash in on both Stan Lee's legendary cache and on the Internet boom. In August, Paul was arrested in Brazil, and in 2003, he was extradited back to the United States to stand trial. Stephen Gordon was convicted (with his brother Jonathan) in December 2002 of fraud charges. To this day, Stan Lee is hesitant to talk about the whole affair, only saying that he wants to put it behind him. The Stan Lee Media fiasco revealed a friend as a traitor and threatened to ruin Lee's hard-won reputation. He refers to it as a nightmare he's still trying to forget.

And Jack Kirby—who settled his returned-art dispute with Marvel in 1987—wasn't the only member of the Lee-Kirby team to have a bone to pick with the "House of Ideas." In 2002, Stan Lee sued Marvel. He'd claimed entitlement, under a prior agreement with Marvel, to share profits generated by the 2002 *Spider-Man* movie, as well as other film and television productions utilizing Marvel characters that he'd cocreated. In April 2005, Marvel Enterprises announced that it settled all pending litigation with Lee. The settlement covered Lee's participation claim for both past and potential future payments. This was a watershed moment for the veteran comics creator, and he feels rightfully vindicated.

"It's very simple," Lee explains. "People misunderstand. They think that I [was] suing because I feel I created these characters, and I should be paid for it. But if that were the case, I'd probably be suing for all the artists that I worked with, for the writers and so forth, but it's not that at all! See, I've worked for this company for sixty years, and for the past few decades I had a contract, and years ago one of my contracts said that I was to receive ten percent of Marvel's profits, for any movies or television, et cetera, that they made. So at the time when the contract was written, they weren't really working on very many movies and so forth. But now that all these movies have been done, I said, 'OK, it's in my contract! Where's the money?' So that's what the discussion is all about. It's actually written in my contract, I should be getting ten percent of their profits from movies and other things! So, it's not that I suddenly came out of the woodwork and decided to sue them. I just wanted my contract to be lived up to!"

MEDIA MUTATIONS

Today, Stan Lee is no longer publisher of Marvel Comics; as Chairman Emeritus, he is no longer involved with the day-to-day workings of the company. However, he is still very important to Marvel as its public face. Occasionally he writes a regular Marvel title such as the 1980 *Incredible Hulk* spin-off series *She-Hulk* or the 1992 dystopian sci-fi series *Ravage 2099*, and he writes the *Spider-Man* newspaper strip with brother Larry Lieber. In 2001, at the behest of movie producer Michael Uslan (1989's *Batman*), Stan Lee worked on his first project for the Distinguished Competition (as he used to call DC), *Just Imagine Stan Lee Creating. . . .* In the pages of *Just Imagine*, Stan Lee refashioned iconic DC characters like Batman, Superman, Green Lantern, and the Flash, writing them as he would have scripted one of his own Marvel Comics from the 1960s. "I was asked to do it, and I have trouble turning down anything that sounds interesting," Lee shrugs.

Stan Lee's version of the Flash, far from being straight-arrow police scientist Barry Allen (DC's Flash from the 1950s to the 1980s) or devil-may-care ladies' man Wally West (DC's current Flash), is a frightened teenage girl who can't fully control her powers. The series pointed out the glaring difference between Marvel characters (neurotic, feet of clay, outsiders) and DC characters (heroic, colorful, optimistic), and it also brought Stan Lee's career full circle. The man who had built up a small but prolific company into an industry titan in order to realistically compete with unbeatable comic book powerhouse DC was now invited to write a special project for DC, giving their pantheon the special "Stan Lee" touch. If that isn't an ironic twist worthy of a Marvel Comic, nothing is.

So, as the Silver Surfer might say, *what hath Stan Lee wrought?* How do we gauge his influence on modern popular culture? One doesn't have to look very far to answer that question. Even looking outside of the official canon of Marvel film and television properties such as *Spider-Man* and *X-Men*, the world of entertainment is rife with characters influenced and inspired by the works of Lee. As actor Mark Hammill (who played Luke Skywalker in the first three *Star Wars* movies) has said, the visual concept of villainous Darth Vader—a metallic face-mask surrounded by a hooded cape—is quite reminiscent of FF villain Doctor Doom, who has an origin story somewhat like Vader's own (both Darth Vader and Doctor Doom were handsome, brilliant, troubled young men who donned masks and turned to evil when their faces were horribly scarred).

Then there's the Oscar-winning Disney/Pixar CGI-animated film *The Incredibles* (2004), written and directed by Brad Bird. This film, about a family of superheroes, one of whom can turn invisible, one of whom can stretch like plastic, and another of whom can light himself on fire, is clearly an homage to Lee and Kirby's *Fantastic Four*. This is especially obvious in the film's visuals, e.g., its retro-sixties décor and the Incredibles' costumes, which resemble the FF's monochrome unitards. The FF spoofery is also there in some of the film's supporting characters, such as the subterranean supervillain the Underminer, clearly a parody of the FF's first villain, the Mole Man.

Joss Whedon, whose 1997–2003 smash hit television series *Buffy the Vampire Slayer* has many similarities to *Spider-Man* (both are about neurotic, superpowered teens with chaotic love lives), wrote the first twelve issues of the new Marvel title *Astonishing X-Men*, continuing the storyline of some of Stan Lee and Jack Kirby's best-known characters. Other major film directors have written comic book series continuing the adventures of Stan Lee characters: Kevin Smith had an acclaimed run several years ago on *Daredevil*, and Reginald Hudlin (director of *Boomerang* and *House Party*) is currently penning the best-selling *Black Panther* comic book. So even as Stan Lee has influenced the content of movies and television shows, he's also influenced filmmakers to pull up their sleeves and get involved in the comic book industry itself.

Then there's the fact that for the past five years and counting, summer movie season equals Stan Lee movie season. Indeed, with the summer 2005 release of the *Fantastic Four* movie, and with both *Ghost Rider* (not a Stan Lee character, but Lee does have an executive producer credit), starring Nicholas Cage, and *Spider-Man 3* set for 2007, Stan Lee's characters seem to have tied up the "event movie" schedule much in the same way that in years past, a new George Lucas or Steven Spielberg movie was the blockbuster to look out for.

Stan Lee, the man who staged the most dramatic career second-act comeback in comics history and changed the way comic books were written, seems to have also had a profound influence on every other visual medium. His concepts, once considered too bizarre for Hollywood, are now the rule rather than the exception, with nearly every genre filmmaker out there paying either direct or indirect homage to his works. And he continues to write, to produce, to develop, and to create, well into his eighties.

As Stan Lee himself would say, Excelsior!

TRINA ROBBINS

SELF-PORTRAIT.

"Lindsay Goldman's mom was Go-Go Girl, a superheroine in the 1970s. Lindsay's inherited her mom's ability to fly and, wearing her mom's old costume, she becomes the teenage superheroine, GoGirl!"

—From *GoGirl!* #2, 2001

S adly, today's comic book industry is frustratingly male-dominated. This is especially obvious in the world of superhero comics, where the pulpy pages reek of adolescent testosterone. It's also obvious in many comic book specialty shops, where passersby are frequently confronted by a cardboard "standee" of a scantily clad female with breasts each just slightly smaller than her head. Thankfully, the world of underground comics isn't quite so awash in pubescent male fantasies. Female cartoonists have found the undergrounds—with their focus on the trials and triumphs of everyday life—to be an artistically rewarding forum for ideas. But this wasn't always the case: once upon a time, underground comics were as much of a boys' club as their superhero contemporaries.

In the late 1960s, Trina Robbins was a true pioneer, the first major female underground cartoonist. Since founding 1970's *It Ain't Me Babe*, the first comic book with an all-female staff, she's written and illustrated scads of influential comics titles. Many of them were designed with the express purpose of getting more girls to read comics, as you can tell from a rundown of the titles: *Wimmen's Comix, Trina's Women, California Girls.* She's penned the adventures of that amazing amazon *Wonder Woman* and the world's favorite glamour doll *Barbie*, and is the creator and writer of the retro teen superhero series *GoGirl!*, on which she collaborates with artist Anne Timmons. Add to this impressive list the fact that Robbins is also the premier feminist comics historian currently active, and you've got one woman with a mission: to help today's girls recapture the wonder she felt reading comics as a kid. Now that the comics industry has let the world at large know that comics aren't just for kids, she seems to be saying, let's spread the message that they're not just for *boys* either.

WHAT WERE WE DOING IN THAT NEIGHBORHOOD?

Trina Robbins was born in New York City (a lady never gives her age) to a schoolteacher mother and a journalist father, each of whom instilled in her a deeply ingrained sense of moral responsibility. She grew up in South Ozone Park, Queens. "It was the pits," she says, laughing ruefully. "It was an Irish, Italian, Catholic working-class neighborhood. Very politically reactionary, very bigoted, and in the middle of it is us Jews, with my Communist father. Well, [he was] a 'fellow traveler.' Meaning he wasn't a party member, but he was very politically radical. *At least* a [socialist]. And certainly, my liberal mother. And we were sore thumbs. What were *we* doing in that neighborhood? My parents thought moving to a nice suburb in Queens was a good way to bring your kids up, because they had been living in the Lower East Side!"

But in the midst of this place she considered "the pits," Robbins escaped through the world of books. "My mother taught me to read at the age of four," she remembers. "And I took to it. Boy, did I take to it! I read every book in the house and we had a lot of books." Another form of reading material that piqued her interest from an early age was comic books. "[In] those days, a lot of parents and teachers didn't approve of comics," she explains, "because they thought that if you read comics, you wouldn't read [regular] books. [But] my mother didn't mind. And of course, I was drawing. I mean, I was drawing since I could hold a crayon in my little fists. So ever since I started reading, I also started writing and making up stories. I actually wrote my first poem at the age of three, before I could read, because I have a very good ear for lyrics and rhyme. So it was just real obvious to put the things together. My mother, being a teacher, kept me supplied with 8½ x 11 white board-of-education paper and board-of-education pencils. And I would take a piece of paper and fold it in half, giving me four pages. And I would just start at the beginning, the way kids do—you don't plan it ahead. First you do one [comic strip] panel and draw the whole thing, then you do the second panel and draw the whole thing— you know how kids do it. And that's how I would make four-page comics."

Even in early childhood, Robbins started expressing a preference for certain comic books, specifically ones that had a decidedly matriarchal bent. "I would just go to the corner candy store whenever I got my allowance and buy a comic," she explains. "I was open to any comic that had a female lead. That was the only thing that was important. I couldn't have been less interested in superheroes. Guys were just boring. They wore gray suits and had short hair. Women wore technicolor! They had red lips and they wore bright colors. So I was only interested in women. Now that means I read *Wonder Woman*, I read *Mary Marvel*, I read *Sheena Queen of the Jungle*—she was definitely a favorite. She was the one, when I used to pretend—that was my favorite fantasy—that I lived in a treehouse with my pet chimpanzee, and swung from vines and rescued people from the evil white traders, that kind of thing. So it was all the female characters. The teen characters too. *Patsy Walker, Millie the Model, Katie Keene,* teenage girls."

As with many children of her generation, Robbins threw away her comic book collection when she entered adolescence. "When I hit high school, my mother told me that now I was a teenager, comics were kid stuff, I should give away my collection," she remembers. "Which I did. I believed her. I was a good daughter. She didn't have to throw away my collection, which some parents did. She gave my collection away to the neighborhood kids. Thousands of dollars' worth of comics. And I didn't read comics [again] until the sixties, when college students and hippies started reading Marvel. You know, the new Marvel. Spider-Man and the X-Men and Fantastic Four! And it was new and different. Somebody turned me on to them. Somebody said, 'Look what's coming out in comics now!' The hippies and the college students who read it—to us, it was very revolutionary! Jack Kirby's work was psychedelic. And Steve Ditko's Dr. Strange—I have to use the term psychedelic. It's the only term I can use. We used to read this stuff, us hippies, and go, 'Wow, those guys working at Marvel must all be on acid!' Which of course was totally wrong and totally incorrect, but that's what we thought."

BACK TO THE LOWER EAST SIDE

Her interest in comics reignited thanks to Stan Lee's Marvel Comics, Trina Robbins soon found herself more interested in representational art than the abstract movement then in vogue. This rubbed her professors at Manhattan's prestigious Cooper Union the wrong way, and she soon found herself at odds with the venerable arts institution. "I got kicked out of Cooper Union. [I was] studying art," she says. "But the thing is, I just wanted to draw little pictures on paper. And they weren't like huge canvases that you stretch yourself, and big abstract designs. [That] wasn't what I wanted to do, so I kind of lost interest and kind of cut a lot of classes and they kicked me out at the end of the [first] year."

Having already been kicked out of Queens College prior to this, Robbins moved to Los Angeles with her then-husband where she lived the "typical L.A. Sunset Strip / rock 'n' roll hippie" life, making clothes for rock stars like Joni Mitchell, David Crosby, Donovan, and Mama Cass. Then she and her husband split up and she landed back in New York. In fact, she moved back to the Lower East Side, the very part of Manhattan her parents had been so anxious to escape.

In 1966, Trina Robbins's first professionally published comic strip appeared in the underground newspaper *The East Village Other*, which soon also became a forum for other underground cartoonists like Willy Murphy and Bill Griffith. "So we have to start with [the fact that] I'm all turned on by Marvel, right?" she points out. "So I realize that all the while I've been doing these little drawings, and what they are is they're proto-comics. They're not quite comics yet, but they're what comes before comics. They're almost-comics. So I start trying to draw comics. But here I am, under the influence of Marvel, so what do I try to do? I try to do this psychedelic super-hero—based on Timothy Leary—this guy who invents a drug that enables him to fly. I am not a superhero artist, so I abandoned it, 'cause it just wasn't coming out right. I can't draw those kind of guys, I'm not Jack Kirby.

"But then, shortly after that—and this is also at the peak of the Bat-man pop art craze—I'm living in Los Angeles. Somebody shows me a copy of *The East Village Other*, out of New York, and says, 'Look what they're doing in New York!' And I look at the stuff, and there's comics in it. There's comics in it, but they're not superheroes. They're psychedelic, they're spacey, they're cosmic, and they don't necessarily make sense, but they're really intriguing. And I went, 'This is what I can do!' So I started just doing this kind of stuff. The first things I did were really just single panel draw-ings with a lot of speech balloons coming out of them. Very design-y, but they tended to look like Aubrey Beardsley. So shortly after that, I moved [back] to New York, and I had a friend from L.A. who was working on *The East Village Other*, Eve Babitz. She was, I think, the managing editor. I started doing comics for *The East Village Other*. Obviously I wasn't getting paid. In those days, you were just so thrilled to be in print!"

Since she wasn't getting paid to draw cartoons, Robbins ran a bou-tique on the Lower East Side, selling clothes that she herself designed. She decided to draw a comic strip for *The East Village Other* to advertise the store's merchandise. "I designed one-of-a-kind clothes and the store was called 'Broccoli,'" she remembers. "That was when everything had a cute name, like 'Iron Butterfly' and stuff. So the store's called 'Broccoli,' and I named the strip 'Broccoli Strip' or 'Broccoli's Trip,' and it was supposedly an ad for my store. Except it was so psychedelic that most people just thought it was a comic strip, just this weird comic strip, which was OK!"

There was a cute girl [in the strip]. Suzie Slum Goddess was her name, based on the song by The Fugs."

Robbins's work next appeared in *Gothic Blimp Works*, published from 1968 to 1969 by *The East Village Other*. It was an all-comics tabloid, billed as "the first Sunday underground comic paper." It boasted art not only by Vaughn Bode (who edited the first two issues), but also such comics legends as Kim Deitch, Berni Wrightson, Mike Kaluta, and Steve Stiles. To Robbins, appearing in *Gothic Blimp Works* represented a new step in her fledgling career. "I finally had a chance to do an entire full page comic, not just a little strip," she recalls. "And somewhere around then—before *Gothic Blimp Works*—I had discovered that New York wages were miserable. And that [in] my boutique, in the month of February, nobody had bought anything. Everyone was just indoors, grumbling to themselves. So the next February that I was living in the Lower East Side with my boutique, I just closed the store! Actually I sublet my apartment to a friend and let a friend of mine live in the store, too, and went to California for the whole month. I spent a lot of time in Los Angeles, where I had lived, but then I also visited people in San Francisco."

It was in San Francisco that Robbins's eyes were fully opened to what an underground comic book could be. Her new San Fran friends exposed her to *Zap*, the underground comic that the legendary Robert Crumb wrote and illustrated solo (after the first issue, he shared the space with fellow underground cartoonists Gilbert Shelton, Victor Moscoso, Robert Williams, S. Clay Wilson, Spain Rodriguez, and Rick Griffin). Robbins's mind was blown. "OK, so these people meet me at the airport, and without even speaking a word to me, they hand me a copy of *Zap* #1," she recalls. "And it was like, revelation: 'My God, you can do this in a comic book! It doesn't have to be in an underground newspaper, it doesn't have to be a little strip in an underground newspaper. It can be a *comic book*! Just like the Marvel books except different!' That was an amazing revelation."

Robbins's most notable contribution to *Gothic Blimp Works* was one of the more bizarre characters to emerge from the underground comics movement of the late 1960s, which is saying something considering that this is the same movement that gave us such off-the-wall titles as Gilbert Shelton's *Wonder Warthog* and Frank Stack's *The New Adventures of Jesus*. While Robbins's creation wasn't a superheroic swine, or a blasphemously comical take on Christendom's messiah, it *was* a human-animal hybrid that went by the unlikely name of Panthea. "It was really derived from my childhood *Sheena* fantasy," she says. "I was trying to think of what was the sexiest fantasy I could come up with. It was a woman who was part woman and part lion, and I [created] Panthea. As in Pantheism or Pantheon."

BOYS' CLUB

In December 1969, Robbins moved permanently to San Francisco, which has been her home ever since. Many other underground cartoonists were migrating to San Francisco in the late 1960s and early '70s, among them Robert Crumb. She also started to notice a disturbing trend in the underground comic book industry. "Around that time," she explains, "little naive me, who has always believed in peace and love, starts noticing that the men are kind of leaving me out, the guys in the comic scene. Kind of doing their thing. Not just the comics! Ed Sanders of The Fugs had an exhibit of underground cartoonists in some storefront, and he didn't invite me, he invited all the guys and left me out."

Robbins also noticed that her male contemporaries in the cartooning field laid bare some of their relationship issues on the page. She found this upsetting, to say the least. "I started noticing a recurring theme in the comics the guys were doing, which was extremely misogynistic," she explains. "Crumb kind of started it. He came to New York, and I loved his stuff! It was really charming in those days, very old-fashioned, reminiscent of the twenties and thirties, really cute, you know. Then he showed all of us this one strip he had just done. And it was incredibly misogynistic, and all the guys were laughing! And I suddenly thought, 'Whoa! This makes me very uncomfortable. I don't like this. This is very hurtful toward women.' And the guys are going, 'Ha ha! You have no sense of humor! Don't you see? It's funny!' And this kind of thing was building up! It's like Crumb's work was becoming more and more misogynistic, and the guys, they were like really defending him." Was there anyone at this time who spoke out against this sort of thing? "Only me, in comics," she points out. "A lot of feminists spoke out against it, but in comics, it was only me."

In 1970, the blatant chauvinism of underground comics prompted Robbins to cofound *It Ain't Me Babe*, the first underground comic book completely produced by women. The cover featured a group of licensed cartoon and comics characters from various media—Olive Oyl, Little Lulu, Wonder Woman, Mary Marvel, Sheena, and advertising mascot Elsie the Cow. Each of them is raising a militant fist and breaking out of the confines of the comic book cover, presumably to fight the good fight and to claim autonomy for themselves in a male-dominated world.

"*It Ain't Me Babe* was the very very first ever in the world all-womens' comic," Robbins explains. "At that point it was so hard to find women who were actually drawing comics. And I kind of had to actually seek them out, but I found that the most important one was Willie Mendez. There was a time when Willie and I were the only two women drawing comics in San Francisco, and Willie was also being left out. We were good friends, and in our misery, we clung to each other, and so we did books with each other. I put her into *It Ain't Me Babe*, she did the back cover, I did the cover, she did the first story. Then because we were involved by having done this, we put out our own books. We put out a book called *The Womenation*, which I contributed to. And together we did a book called *All Girl Thrill*. And I did my own book, I did *Girl Fight* #1, and then *Girl Fight* #2. *Girl Fight* was just all my characters."

It Ain't Me Babe lasted only one issue, but it united the growing sub-culture of female underground cartoonists, and it caused Robbins to more ardently use comics as a forum for feminist issues. "It was *It Ain't Me Babe* that started all this, because we had done this [one] book," she says.

Robbins was carving a niche for herself in the comics underground, breaking boundaries and making waves. Many of her comics focused on radical new depictions of women. "I did draw the first black woman in comic books," she says. "I drew a character called Fox, who was a political revolutionary who was wanted by the FBI, based on Angela Davis. I first did her [in 1971] for an underground newspaper called *The Good Times*, put out by the Good Times collective. It was a continued strip. She was reprinted in *Trina's Women* also." Robbins says that her positive portrayal of black characters—she also drew strips for *High Times* depicting her black heroine Lulubelle—caused some readers to wonder if she herself was black.

In 1972, *Wimmen's Comix*, also cofounded by Robbins, more directly picked up the slack where *It Ain't Me Babe* left off. And where *It Ain't Me Babe* lasted only one issue, the *Wimmen's Comix* anthology lasted almost twenty years (1972–1991) as the first ongoing comic book written and drawn exclusively by women. Aside from Robbins, *Wimmen's Comix* involved such respected female comics creators as Sharon Rudahl, Aline Kominsky, Lee Marrs, and Terry Richards. *Wimmen's Comix* functioned as a collective, meaning that there was no set editor. Instead, the book was run by a rotating editorship, with each issue edited by two different women working as a team.

As she did in her solo work, in working with the *Wimmen's Comix* collective, Trina Robbins was determined to shatter taboos and depict images of minorities usually marginalized (if not rendered downright invisible) in most comics. *Wimmen's Comix* frequently touched on issues ignored in undergrounds created by men, such as abortion, birth control, and homosexuality. "*Wimmen's Comix* published the first comic by a lesbian," she points out. "Not the first comic *about* a lesbian, because I did that one. That was called 'Sandy Comes Out' and it was in the first issue of *Wimmen's Comix*. But then [openly gay cartoonist and *Bitchy Bitch* creator] Roberta Gregory sent us this great thing—it was almost a parody of the romance comics—it was called, 'A Modern Romance.' That came out in '74, issue number 4."

Some of Trina Robbins's work from this period could be rather didactic; witness "The Woman Who Couldn't," from 1976's *Trina's Women* anthology, in which Robbins takes issue with a male party guest's assertion that "women just aren't creative!" She goes on to tell him the life story of Suzanne Valadon, a lover of both Renoir and Toulouse-Lautrec, who would've been a major painter herself if she hadn't been hampered by a patriarchal society's constraints. It's a fascinating story, but told in such a way that renders its pro-girl message subtle as a sledgehammer. Still, this and many of Robbins's other stories from the underground era were important attempts to reach out to women, a segment of the potential comics-reading audience that was, then as now, largely ignored.

During the 1940s and '50s, half of the comic books being produced—including Robbins's childhood favorites such as *Millie the Model*, *Sheena*, and *Katy Keene*—were geared toward girls, even though the majority of them were produced by men. Robbins's theory is that the death knell for the majority of girls' comics was Dr. Frederick Wertham's 1953 book *Seduction of the Innocent*, which postulated that comic books were the cause of America's rising strain of juvenile delinquency. After this, Robbins says, many comics about love and relationships were the first to get the axe, because of what Wertham and his followers saw as their sexual undertones. Even superhero comics were on the wane, until Lee, Kirby, and Ditko revolutionized the superhero genre with their 1960s Marvel Comics.

Then in the early 1970s, entrepreneur Phil Seuling changed the way that comics were distributed, setting up the first comic book specialty shops, so that the majority of comics were sold not through candy stores or newsstands, but through mostly male-owned comic book stores, which looked imposing and threatening to female passersby. It was then that the comics industry—obsessed with testosterone-drenched superheroes and selling their product in dungeon-like shops that didn't sell "girl comics"—forgot about half of their readership, the readers of *Katy Keene*, *Patsy*

Walker, and *Sheena*. Robbins's career has largely been dedicated to winning back that missing fifty percent. But comics like *It Ain't Me Babe*, *Wimmen's Comix*, and *Trina's Women* were just the beginning of her crusade.

MISTY MODELS, CALIFORNIA GIRLS, AND WONDERFUL WOMEN

Throughout the 1970s, Trina Robbins didn't just create comic books centered around serious issues such as female empowerment. She also had a more playful side. This was the decade during which she created comic strips and illustrations for the humor magazine *National Lampoon*, then at its peak. Working with legendary *Lampoon* art director Michael Gross, Robbins contributed strips like "Rosie the Riveter" (a postmodern riff on the World War II–era firebrand) and "Radio Rae" to the magazine's "Funny Pages" section, whose other contributors included fellow underground cartoonists Vaughn Bode and Shary Flenniken. Some of Robbins's *Lampoon* work also made it into critically acclaimed works like 1973's ambitious *The National Lampoon Encyclopedia of Humor*. "*National Lampoon* was wonderful because they paid so nicely," she says. "It was so enjoyable! Michael Gross was the art director. He's such a great guy, I love that man."

Robbins was happy at the *Lampoon*, a magazine that, like the underground comics movement, was also largely a boys' club. But this boys' club didn't rub her the wrong way. "The Lampoons were never hostile," she points out. "There was never this hurt, or this anger that there was [in the undergrounds]. They were simply funny."

Then, during the 1980s, a curious thing happened to Trina Robbins's career. "I started doing nicely in the eighties," she explains, "because people who were not in the underground liked my work and asked me to contribute. So that's when I did those [Lulubelle comics] for *High Times*." She also found a home at three non-underground comic book companies—DC, Marvel, and Eclipse.

By the mid-1980s, Marvel Comics had instituted its Star Comics sister line to reach out to younger readers. Star Comics produced the comic book adventures of licensed characters from film, television, and the Sunday funnies, like *Heathcliff* and *Thundercats*. It also implemented a few original titles, like Robbins's *Meet Misty* (1986), geared toward young girls. The whimsical adventures of a bubbly blonde supermodel and her friends, *Misty* was a seven-issue limited series, and it contained several of Robbins's trademarks. Every few pages there was a spread containing paper dolls of the characters, which readers could cut out and play with. The characters' outfits were largely based on suggestions from readers, who would be credited for their original designs in captions littered throughout the books. And finally, the letters page was not like most letters pages, where people would write in and ask about continuity errors ("Spider-Man isn't wearing his black and purple costume in this issue, even though the events in this issue take place after his adventures on planet Arcturus Rann in issue 459! I demand an explanation!"). Misty's letters tended to be more about the characters—which ones grabbed them, which ones didn't—and they were often addressed to Misty herself, rather than to Robbins. This was largely because Misty's readership consisted of young girls who didn't discriminate between fictional character and real-life creator, but Robbins encouraged this playful attitude.

But despite its sense of playfulness and Robbins's engaging drawing style, *Misty* wasn't the sales success she had hoped for, and the limited run didn't lead to a regular series. Robbins is understandably perplexed by the fact that *Misty* was considered a flop. "*Misty*, if sold today, if it sold that many comics, it would be a raving success," she explains. "But in those days, you had to sell ever so much more. I got so much fan mail from *Misty*— girls loved it. Moldering in a storeroom in my basement there are two cartons full of fan mail for *Misty*. 'Dear Misty, I love your story!' Oh it was so sweet, and sometimes they would have problems, and that used to break my heart. 'Dear Misty, what should I do? I used to have this girlfriend, and then this new girl came to school and now my old girlfriend only hangs out with her, and I feel so left out. What should I do?' And I was giving advice! I mean it wasn't just a letters column, it was an advice column, and I used to read these things and go, 'Oh, the poor kid!' And I would get things from really, really little girls, like five years old, drawing designs for me, and you could barely make out what the design was, but I would fix it, and use it in the book, and these kids would be so happy. It was a limited series, but I have always said that if [then–Editor in Chief] Jim Shooter had been the father of a seven-year-old girl, that book would be going right now— it'd continue. His daughter would have loved it so much, she would have said, 'Daddy, you can't stop *Misty*,' and she would have just started crying. I mean, that's how much these little girls loved it!"

Misty sold about twenty-five thousand copies a month. Today, many Marvel and DC titles are lucky to get those kinds of numbers, but in those days it wasn't good enough. But sales figures weren't *Misty*'s only enemy. Robbins also says that the comic book stores wouldn't carry a comic for girls. "I would go to stores and they wouldn't have it," she recalls. "And I'd say, 'Where's *Misty*?' And they'd say, 'Oh, we sold out.' In the beginning, I'd think, 'Wow, that's great,' but then I'd discover that they sold out because they only ordered two copies! And they never would reorder."

The same fate befell Robbins's 1987 Eclipse series *California Girls*, about Max and Mo, a pair of unflappable twin teens. From 1981 to 1993, Eclipse was one of the larger "independent" comic book companies, meaning that it occupied a middle ground between underground (Last Gasp, Rip Off Press) and mainstream (DC, Marvel). Eclipse Editor in Chief Catherine Yronwode had collaborated with Robbins on the writing of the book *Women and the Comics* in 1983. Yronwode was happy to welcome Robbins's new teen comic onto Eclipse's roster. Many *Meet Misty* readers migrated to this new title,

which also featured Robbins's signature paper dolls, readers' suggestions for the characters' clothing, and letters written directly to the California Girls themselves as though they were real people.

But even with her ardent *Misty* fan following behind her, Robbins's *California Girls* was short-lived. Again, comic book stores refused to stack very many copies of the book. "This teenage boy sent me a design that I used in *California Girls*," she recalls. "And then he wrote to me, and said, 'I can't get a copy! My local comic store doesn't carry it.' So I actually phoned his comic book store, I sent the comic book personally, and they were very impressed that I was

UNFORTUNATELY, CALIFORNIA GIRLS WAS A VICTIM OF WHAT ROBBINS CALLS THE "DREAD COMIC BOOK STORES," WHICH ACCORDING TO HER OFTEN NEGLECTED TO STOCK FEMALE-ORIENTED TITLES.

phoning them, but they still wouldn't order it. Of course I sent the poor kid a copy, but [the store] simply would not carry my comic."

Robbins says that this trend continues; it's very hard to get comic book stores to stock "girl comics." Why are comic book stores and publishers so shy about promoting female-oriented comics? "I can only reach one conclusion and that is that they don't want women in the field," she shrugs. "They don't want girl cooties. It's a boys' club and they don't want girls in the boys' club, just like the guys in the underground didn't want me in their boys' club."

In between shepherding *California Girls* and *Meet Misty*, both original creations, Robbins chose to render her version of a classic superhero in the four-issue 1986 DC miniseries *The Legend of Wonder Woman*, billed as a "last loving look" at the "Golden Age" Wonder Woman of the 1940s.

Wonder Woman was originally created in 1941 by writer William Moulton Marston, and the character had been retooled many times over the years. During the mid-eighties, the Powers That Be at DC decided to com-

pletely overhaul their major characters and hired Robbins to draw and coplot (with writer Kurt Busiek) a miniseries ushering the Golden Age Wonder Woman into the great beyond. DC wanted to signal a changing of the guard, from old Wonder Woman to new. It was an especially fitting tribute, seeing as Robbins's art style was clearly influenced by original Wonder Woman artist H. G. Peters's work.

The story concerns Wonder Woman's battles with Atomia, queen of the Atomic galaxy. It also concerns Wonder Woman's friendship with a bratty little girl, Suzie, who, as the series goes on, comes to admire the amazing Amazon as a

THE COVER OF DC'S LEGEND OF WONDER WOMAN #1, TRINA ROBBINS'S TAKE ON THE AMAZING AMAZON.

big-sister figure. Robbins has admitted that she modeled Suzie's appearance (if not her personality) on herself as a young girl. And the series's gentle, colorful art style and whimsical stories—at once mythic, kid friendly, and full of wonder—set it head and shoulders above many more recent versions of *Wonder Woman*, where the character is drawn like an S&M pin-up and the writing feels like excerpts from a WWF steel-cage brawl. "Oh, I hate that! I hate that," Robbins says emphatically. "I've said this, and I've done entire slide shows on Wonder Woman! If you've read *The Great Women Superheroes*, you know that the first chapter is an homage to Wonder Woman. She unfortunately is a slave to whoever draws and writes her."

COMICS HERSTORIAN

By the 1990s, Trina Robbins was still writing and drawing various comics stories; she contributed the true-life teen pregnancy story "A Town Without Pity" to a 1990 comics anthology she also edited, *CHOICES: A Pro-Choice Benefit Anthology*; she drew a set of "Valerie Solanas Paper dolls" (satirizing Andy Warhol's would-be assassin) for *Real Girl Comics* in 1995; and she wrote the 1998 one-shot *Wonder Woman: The Once and Future Story*, illustrated by Colleen Doran. However, during this decade Robbins found her time increasingly taken up by the writing of books about other female cartoonists. After the 1983 publication of her *Women and the Comics*, her status as an author soared. When she and Catherine Yronwode had written that book, many of their male colleagues in the industry doubted that there even were enough women cartoonists to fill a book. Robbins proved them wrong, and throughout the nineties she would offer several more volumes of proof.

In 1993, Robbins wrote *A Century of Women Cartoonists*, profiling women cartoonists for the past one hundred years. The book starts with Louise Quarles's illustrated puns from 1901, then goes on to explore such pioneers as *New York Evening Journal* cartoonist Nell Brinkley, *Brenda Starr* creator Dale Messick, and more recent doodlers like *For Better or For Worse* creator Lynn Johnston.

In 1996, Robbins's *The Great Women Superheroes* corrected, like her earlier books, many misnomers about the comics industry. Contrary to popular belief, Wonder Woman wasn't the first female superhero (that honor belongs to The Woman in Red, introduced in 1940). Like *A Century of Women Cartoonists*, *The Great Women Superheroes* is incredibly comprehensive, dealing with older characters like Wonder Woman, Missy Fury, the

Blonde Phantom, Sue Storm of the *Fantastic Four*, and Supergirl, as well as newer characters like Elektra and Ghost. It discusses how images and portrayals of females in mainstream comics have changed over the years, citing incidents like an old *Batman* story where Batgirl couldn't join Batman and Robin in clobbering the bad guys until she fixed a run in her tights. As she does so, the villains stop what they're doing to ogle her thigh. Trina Robbins's *From Girls to Grrlz: A History of Women's Comics from Teens to Zines* was published in 1999, and in 2001 she wrote *The Great Women Cartoonists*.

These latter two books expand the subject matter of Robbins's earlier works to also include the rapidly growing world of alternative cartooning, which has become much less of a boys' club. Today, as Robbins notes in her books, one finds important female cartoonists working in the alternative press, such as Mary Fleener (*Slutburger*), Barbara Brandon (*Where I'm Coming From*), Allison Bechdel (*Dykes to Watch Out For*), and Jessica Abel (*Artbabe*). "There are more women than ever," she smiles. "More women than ever in the entire twentieth century doing comics. And they're all doing indies and self-published comics. You go to one of those alternative comic conventions, there are more women on both sides of the table— selling their comics and buying comics—than ever before. Alternative comics is no longer a boys' club."

YOU GoGIRL!

Robbins's adventures as a nonfiction author haven't quieted her passion for creating her own comic books. *GoGirl!*, which Robbins created and writes, collaborating with artist Anne Timmons, was published by Image Comics starting in 2000. The series is about perky blonde teenager Lindsay Goldman, who also happens to have inherited the superpowers of her mother Janet, who in the 1970s was known as the superhero Go-Go Girl. Janet got married, however, and her husband felt threatened by having a wife who could fly, so Go-Go Girl hung up her white boots and minidress. Now, Janet's passed her costume down to Lindsay, who fights crime and navigates the rocky waters of high school life as the costumed heroine GoGirl!

As with *Meet Misty* and *California Girls*, each issue of *GoGirl!* contains Robbins's trademark paper dolls; and as a feature particular to *GoGirl!*, readers are also treated to pin-up miniposters of GoGirl! by various comics luminaries, like *MAD* cartoonist Sergio Aragones, *Barbie Comics* artist Barb Rausch, and veteran Marvel and DC artist Steve Leialoha (*Howard the Duck, Action Comics*).

Trina Robbins first met cartoonist Anne Timmons at the 1996 San Diego Comic-Con. "Anne and I had met at the convention," Robbins recalls. "And we became e-mail pen pals. And one day, Anne e-mailed me and said,

GoGirl! and her mother, the 1970s-era superheroine Go-Go Girl!

'Why don't we do a comic together? You write it and I draw it.' And I went, 'Ha! That wouldn't have a chance in a million. Nobody wants girls' comics.'"

Still, the idea of doing another comic for girls intrigued Robbins. "[I figured], 'What the hell! I have a filing cabinet in my brain, of various schemes I've always wanted to do," she recalls. "I tried to rifle through the filing cabinet. And I said, 'How about a teenage superheroine?' And she said, 'Great!' So I came up with the whole concept, and wrote the first story, and Anne drew it. And we showed it to [then-publisher of Image Comics] Larry Marder. And I thought, 'No way is Image gonna want this! 'Cause, you know what [sort of comics] Image was doing." At the time, Image was known for lurid, violent, boy-friendly titles like Todd McFarlane's *Spawn*. What chance did a more benign comic like *GoGirl!* have?

But Robbins was underestimating Larry Marder, who had previously created the acclaimed independent comic book *Tales of the Beanworld*. He understood what Robbins and Timmons were trying to do with *GoGirl!* "Larry, what a sweet guy," Robbins remembers. "He wanted to do something different, and he liked it. And then when he left, [Marder's successor] Jim Valentino was also really nice. Except, because [*GoGirl!*] was a comic book and not a graphic novel, the only place where you could sell was the cursed comic book store." Robbins has a habit of referring to comic book specialty shops as the "cursed comic book stores" because of their tendency not to stock female-oriented comics. "This is why *GoGirl!* couldn't get [color printing]," she explains. "They just couldn't get enough advance orders. We thought [the deal] was gonna fall through completely. But then Jim Valentino said we could do this in black and white. The people who did believe in us, God bless 'em, they're all going to heaven."

Trina Robbins, a big fan of television's *Buffy the Vampire Slayer*, wrote *GoGirl!* #3 as a *Buffy* homage with its demonic teacher character, Ms. Steele. Where does Robbins see *GoGirl!* in the pantheon of other female superheroes like Buffy and Wonder Woman? "I didn't design *GoGirl!* to fit in any pantheon," Robbins admits, "but I suppose you could say that she's Buffy for kids—for young girls."

Speaking of young girls, *GoGirl!* generates an unsurprisingly large amount of fan mail from that demographic. What *is* surprising is that the series continues to generate fan mail from men as well. "A lot of grown men like it," Robbins smiles. "Girls and mothers especially love it, and young women, but it's really quite amazing how many grown men like it. I get a lot of fan mail from them. A lot of them like it because it's 'retro.' That's one word they use a lot about *GoGirl!* *GoGirl!* came from my love of sixties comics, which got me back into comics. [But] the funny thing is, people call [the series] retro—I never thought of it as retro. But I'm still not quite sure what is retro about it except that she's very influenced by [Fawcett's] *Mary Marvel*. Mary Marvel was like that—she was just a nice, sweet teenage girl who happened to be a superheroine."

The universality of the *GoGirl!* characters accounts for their appeal, as does their multiculturalism. This is one of the few superhero comics that features a truly diverse cast. Aside from Lindsay herself, who's Jewish, there's her African American best friend Haseena, and cheerleader Heather Wu, who's Asian and who befriends Lindsay during the course of the 2005 *GoGirl!* graphic novel *The Time Team*.

Trina Robbins points out that creating a multicultural cast of characters for this series was something she was very conscious of. "One of the things I can't stand about comics," she explains, "is that when they do have black kids, they're always these ghetto kids, and they're always going, 'Yo, yo, wassup.' There were so many black educated kids where I grew up. I wanted to show a normal black person. And also, the opposite too, that in [*The Time Team*] with the Asian Heather, I wanted to show that the Heathers—the spoiled kids—don't always have to be white either. [In real life] there are lots of Asian cheerleaders!" Lindsay Goldman herself is a nonstereotypical depiction of a Jewish female. Robbins was determined to have a matter-of-fact presentation of the characters' ethnicity. "Why can't she just be Jewish?" Robbins asks. "It doesn't have to be a big deal about her being Jewish, she doesn't have to be oppressed. She doesn't have to have the Klan burning a cross in her yard. She's an American girl who just happens to be Jewish, just like me!"

GoGirl!'s initial run garnered much critical acclaim, with Carol Cooper of *The Village Voice* a particularly staunch advocate of the series. However, this didn't ensure stellar sales, especially in an increasingly competitive and crowded market with so many media jockeying for the attention (and allowance money) of young girls. In 2001, after *GoGirl!* #5 was published, Image stopped publishing the series.

This looked like the end of the road for Lindsay Goldman, but the following year, Dark Horse Comics stepped in and published a trade paperback compilation of the first five Image issues. Dark Horse, easily the third-largest comic book company in America (just behind Marvel and DC, and ahead of Image) is an independent publisher founded by Mike Richardson in 1986. Dark Horse's hipster cache and business savvy gave *GoGirl!* a much-needed injection of lifeblood.

"Dark Horse was our knight in shining armor," Robbins smiles. "Anne Timmons had gone to school with [Dark Horse editor] Chris Warner. And she ran into him at some convention, and said, 'There's this comic we've been doing, and Image isn't publishing it anymore. Would you be interested?' And we sent him all the [back] issues, and he said, 'Let's do this, let's collect this as a trade paperback and see what can happen.' And it sold! It sold so well that we got royalties! We got royalties twice! And in fact, the first printing is sold out and they're doing a second printing. So that was enough for him to realize that the answer was to do it in graphic novel form, get it into bookstores, get it into school libraries, so we can bypass the dread comic book store. So it's coming out twice a year."

. . . AND THE NEW WOMAN

Today, in addition to new *GoGirl!* graphic novels, Trina Robbins is one of the founders of the group Friends of Lulu (named for Marge Henderson's

classic comics character), an organization devoted to getting more women into comics, both as creators and readers. Robbins is also expanding her role as a feminist author and historian to include subjects outside of the comics realm. Aside from her books *The Great Women Cartoonists* and *Nell Brinkley and the New Woman in the Early 20th Century* (about the Art Nouveau cartoonist and creator of the "Brinkley Girl"), 2001 saw the publication of the non-comics-related *Eternally Bad: Goddesses With Attitude*, which focuses on some

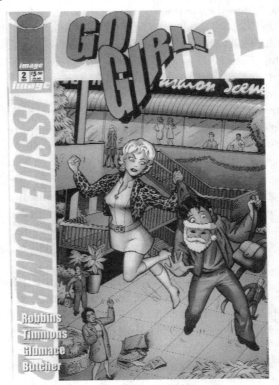

GoGirl! © Trina Robbins; art © Anne Timmons

Cover of GoGirl! #2.

of the less "dainty" female deities one encounters in world mythology. Robbins is also the author of 2003's *Tender Murderers: Women Who Kill*, a study of history's more notorious female criminals, including Bonnie Parker (of Bonnie and Clyde), Valerie Solanas, Amy Fisher, and Lizzie Borden. She continues to write still more books, often on the subject of women throughout history, at the rate of at least one a year.

Robbins is also working on other comic book projects, but she prefers to stick to writing and not illustrating these days. Among the comics she's penning are a series of educational comics on female historical figures like Elizabeth Blackwell, the first woman doctor in America; early movie star Hedy Lamarr, focusing on the famed actress's escape from her pro-Nazi husband and her work developing a code during World War II; and pioneering nineteenth century Paiute Indian rights advocate Sarah Winnemucca. In addition, she's working on a fictional story set in Nazi Europe, "about a sister and brother who escaped from the Nazis, and I'm on my own on that one. I'm allowed to make up my story, and is that ever going to be fun!"

And as she's aware that American girls today are a rapidly growing audience for *manga* (Japanese comics), Robbins has been writing English dialogue for various Japanese comics titles typically classified as *shojo manga* (*shojo* being Japanese for "young girl") for the independent publisher Viz. "And it's really fun," she says. "I really enjoy it. Look, I'm a girl, I love these comics! I really enjoy what I'm writing."

Trina Robbins continues to fight the good fight, and it's clear that she won't rest until the missing fifty percent of comics' potential audience—the distaff half—is reading, drawing, or writing comics themselves.

ART SPIEGELMAN

ART SPIEGELMAN CLOWNING AROUND WITH SOME OF HIS FRIENDS.

"In May 1968 my mother killed herself. (She left no note.) Lately I've been feeling depressed."
　　　—From *Maus, Volume II: And Here My Troubles Began*, 1991

Ever since the first six issues of his Holocaust memoir *Maus* were compiled into a 1986 graphic novel, Art Spiegelman has been lauded as the dean of contemporary nonmainstream cartooning, one of the only comics personalities who's a household name even to people who'd never pick up a comic book. And in American culture, where the comic book industry is considered an obscure, arcane subculture, that's saying something.

But of course even before *Maus* Spiegelman had been breaking new ground in the comics industry, as he has continued to do since he won the Pulitzer Prize for *Maus* in 1992—from his work at Topps starting in the mid-sixties developing novelty cards like *Wacky Packages*; to the comics anthology *Arcade* magazine, which he coedited with Bill Griffith during the mid-1970s; to his brilliantly avant-garde comics magazine *RAW* (which originally serialized *Maus* starting in 1980); to his controversial work for *The New Yorker* from 1992 to 2002; to his *Little Lit* series of comics anthologies for kids, which has attracted contributors including Lemony Snicket, Neil Gaiman, and Jules Feiffer; and to his disturbingly apropos collection of 9/11 strips entitled *In the Shadow of No Towers*.

But in the 1960s, *Maus* was a long way off, and Art Spiegelman was just a young cartoonist trying desperately to find his voice, and ignoring his parents' pleas for him to become a dentist. . . .

HELL PLANETS AND FUNNY AMINALS

Art Spiegelman was born on February 15, 1948, in Stockholm, Sweden. His parents, Vladek and Anja, were both Auschwitz survivors who'd endured the Nazi atrocities. During early childhood, Spiegelman emigrated with his family to the United States, and he grew up in the Rego Park section of Queens, New York. As a child, Spiegelman was obsessed by *MAD*, especially the early comic book issues of *MAD*, which were edited, written, and occasionally illustrated by Harvey Kurtzman, before it became the more well-known *MAD* magazine. Kurtzman's anarchic style of cartooning and his passion for political and social satire would deeply inspire Spiegelman's own comic book work.

Another favorite of young Art Spiegelman was Will Eisner's comic strip *The Spirit*; not surprising since Eisner, like Kurtzman, was a virtuoso storyteller and the comics equivalent of a filmic auteur who was in full control of everything on the page. His head full of dreams of being the next Kurtzman or Eisner, the teenaged Spiegelman and his friend, fellow future underground cartoonist Jay Lynch, contributed comic strips to Joe Pilati's self-published fanzine *Smudge*.

In his teens, Spiegelman attended the High School of Music and Art in Manhattan. In 1966, after graduating, Spiegelman started working at the Topps Company creating novelty cards and stickers. That same year, against his parents' wishes that he pursue a career in dentistry, he majored in art and philosophy at Harpur College (now the State University of New York at Binghamton). As creative consultant for Topps, a post he kept for just over twenty years, Spiegelman drew up rough sketches and wrote gags and jokes for many of the gum cards. He developed or cocreated such famed trading card series as *Wacky Packages* and *Funny Little Joke Books*.

A pivotal year for Art Spiegelman was 1968; that year, the budding cartoonist suffered a nervous breakdown at Harpur (possibly due to frequent ingestion of LSD) and was taken to a mental ward, where he recovered after a month's stay. Shortly after his release, Spiegelman's deeply troubled mother, Anja, committed suicide. He would later dramatize this tragedy in the autobiographical comics story "Prisoner on the Hell Planet" in 1973's *Short Order Comix* #1. The story laid bare Spiegelman's complex relationship with his clearly depressed mother, and the mixture of guilt, anger, and helplessness that her death provoked.

After this confluence of tragic events, Spiegelman officially chose underground comics as his preferred form of "art therapy," creating psychologically revealing (and sometimes broadly sexual) comics throughout the late sixtiess and early seventies for titles like *Bijou Funnies*, *Gothic Blimp Works*, and *Conspiracy Capers*. However, his cartoons from this period, with few exceptions, were all over the map. By his own admission, Spiegelman had yet to find his voice. "Oh God, a bunch of it was misguided," he laughs.

He also points out that some of the cartoons from this early period are very indebted to influences like Kurtzman and Eisner. "A lot of the stuff that I did in comics prior to 1972, I was just messing around. I did a strip called 'The Viper' [in 1971's *Real Pulp* #1], and it was intentionally mean spirited, and following the trail that'd been blazed by people like [*Checkered Demon* and *Zap* cartoonist] S. Clay Wilson, just get everything as unpleasant from your id as possible, and staple it to a sheet of paper." Indeed, the pulp fiction parody series "The Viper" (and the specific "Viper" installment Spiegelman is citing, called "Pop Goes the Poppa") is a classic example of the young artist's penchant for shock value, which one saw over and over again in the early undergrounds. In the story, the titular hero is hired to solve the murder of Solly Putz, who leaves behind his beautiful wife and young towheaded son Eddie. Viper realizes that *Eddie* killed his father so that Eddie and his *mother* could be together! After raping his mother, Eddie wonders what he should do next, and the Viper guns her down and buys Eddie a beer. With "Viper," there's a sense that young Spiegelman was chuckling to himself as he drew each panel, cognizant of the taboos he was busting and thinking, "They won't see *that* coming!"

After this early period, Spiegelman began to more clearly find his voice, veering away from sophomoric pastiches like "Viper" and creating more personal, meaningful stories. Even the 1974 hard-boiled private eye parody "Ace Hole, Midget Detective" is less a genre parody of Dashiell Hammett–style yarns than an experiment in comic surrealism, as the diminutive detective's adventures get more and more dreamlike and his case more and more incidental (at one point there's an arrow pointing to an important clue reminding us that it's a "Plot device, remember?"). Picasso's ghost appears, and we suddenly find ourselves in other people's comic strips including Winsor McCay's *Little Nemo* and Chester Gould's *Dick Tracy*. Ace Hole finds himself dreaming that he's underwater, where he muses, "Reality wasn't a very nice place to visit."

But autobiographical elements are still very much in place even in such a bizarre strip: early on, Ace Hole is sent on a caper to flush out Al Floogleman, "a small-change underground cartoonist," who looks suspiciously Spiegelman-esque. At the end of the nightmare escapade, Ace Hole is literally kicked to the curb by a Gertrude Berg look-alike, an elderly Jewish hausfrau in a polka-dot dress with a specifically Yiddish accent who screams, "Heffens! A dvarf iss!" Even in his lighter works, Spiegelman infused the stories with personal touches that referenced his own background: as an underground cartoonist, as a child of European Jewish immigrants (even in "The Viper," the characters are clearly Jewish, with names like "Solly Putz" and the parents' constant declarations of "Oy!").

Spiegelman's surreal detective spoof, "Ace Hole, Midget Detective."

Spiegelman's major accomplishment from this period was a three-page strip that he created for a 1972 comics anthology, *Funny Aminals* (misspelling intentional), called *Maus*. Spiegelman was friends with Terry Zwigoff—future director of comic book–centric movies like the adaptation of Dan Clowes's *Ghost World* and the documentary *Crumb*—whose only mandate was to deliver a strip featuring anthropomorphic animals of some kind. Spiegelman almost didn't contribute, but after receiving a letter of encouragement urging him to submit a strip, he realized that he could use the idea of talking animals as a potent vehicle to say something serious. His first instinct was to parody early animated cat-and-mouse cartoons by having the mice be the oppressed black people and the cats be the white oppressors. But Spiegelman was afraid that such a strip would lack authenticity and smack of guilty white liberalism, so he decided to hit closer to home and talk about the Jewish experience during the Holocaust. The cats would be the Germans and the mice would be the Jews.

In the three-page story, Spiegelman's father is tucking young "Artie" Spiegelman into bed (both are drawn as mice even in the frame story) as he tells him bedtime tales of his experience in the concentration camps. We see flashbacks in which an attempt to help out a desperate stranger backfires as the stranger leads "Die Katzen" (German for "the cats") to the hiding place of the mice. Later, in a move of swift and unrelenting justice, the mice exact revenge on the traitor, murdering him, and Artie's father remembers burying the turncoat. Not exactly the story of Rapunzel, as bedtime stories go. This is the sort of yarn Vladek Spiegelman would tell his son at bedtime, and Art Spiegelman rightly figured that there was something fascinatingly odd about the fact that he grew up being ushered off to dreamland accompanied by these disturbing true tales. But this was sober stuff compared to many of the raunchier underground comics then circulating.

How was the three-page version of *Maus* received? "Oh, . . . I don't know," Spiegelman laughs. "I don't think my editor liked it very much But editors there were just people gathering material together and bringing it to the printers. And whatever you did, they published. It wasn't oriented toward response. It wasn't like, 'If people like this I'll do more of it, or if people don't like this I'll do less of it.' It was more like, 'I found something. I found something that brought out a better strain in me.' By the standards of the underground comics surrounding it, even many of the other stories in that issue of *Funny Aminals*, it was very restrained. Like, the visual style was restrained. Although, not nearly as restrained as what became the *Maus* book after. And doing that three-page strip, I realized that I had a lot of unfinished business. It was a three-page strip and there was much more here that I could tap back into, although that's not where I went immediately after the three-page strip." For the time being, a longer version of *Maus* would have to wait, as Spiegelman's attention was diverted by the creation of a couple of new groundbreaking comics anthologies.

POSTPONED SUICIDES

In 1975, Art Spiegelman undertook his most ambitious project yet: *Arcade* magazine, which he cocreated and coedited with *Zippy the Pinhead* creator Bill Griffith. Published by the Print Mint, *Arcade* featured the work of Spiegelman and Griffith's fellow underground cartoonists, such as Robert Crumb, Mark Beyer, Michele Brand, Spain Rodriguez, Aline Kominsky, M. K. Brown, and Kim Deitch. S. Clay Wilson was at his grotesque best delivering features like "Vampire Lust," which takes the vampirism-as-sexual-metaphor motif to its most disturbing extreme (a comely female vamp drains a male's "essence" by biting into his "nocturnal erection"). And Diane Noomin indulged her penchant for autobiographical cartooning with stories like "Some of My Best Friends Are," in which she reminisces about childhood pals, marveling at how her life's changed and wondering what became of those who were once so close to her. The magazine also welcomed the work of contributors from outside the underground comics world, including *Naked Lunch* author William S. Burroughs, *Playboy* gag cartoonist Bernard Kliban, and *Village Voice* columnist Jim Hoberman.

Spiegelman himself, like his fellow contributors, used *Arcade* to indulge in experimental comics such as "As the Mind Reels / A Soap Opera," which, like "Ace Hole," starts out with straight genre parody (in this case spoofing an *As the World Turns*–style soap opera), and then dives right into straight surrealism. We start out with a cuckolded husband playing with a children's toy as his wife tries to get him to communicate with her; the snow on the television screen then becomes actual snow, as a blizzard overtakes the television studio in which the show is being shot. We cut to the bored housewife who's watching this show as she gossips endlessly on the phone. Then we're back to "As the Mind Reels," where two characters dole out dreary, soap opera–style exposition while one of them pours so much coffee that soon they're both drowning in the stuff. The whole thing is more of a disciplined exercise in narrative flow than "Ace

Hole," and here Spiegelman's work takes on the cinematic air of a surrealist auteur such as Luis Bunuel, one image melting into another seemingly unconnected image. One can see that Spiegelman is trying different ideas out, flexing his storytelling muscles, perhaps gearing up for a bigger, more ambitious comics project . . . but what?

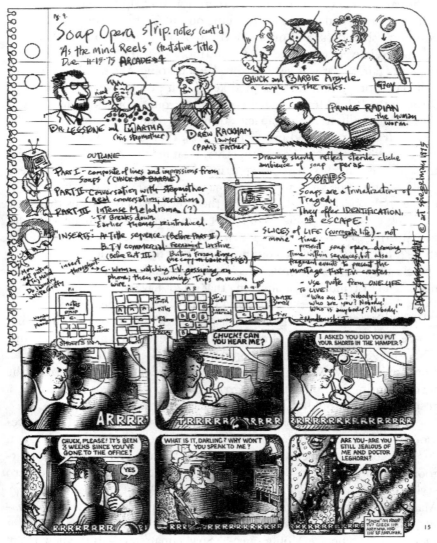

AN EXCERPT FROM SPIEGELMAN'S SURREAL SOAP OPERA PARODY "AS THE MIND REELS."

Arcade lasted just over a year, an astonishingly short life-span considering that it was a magazine boasting top-notch talent from the twin worlds of underground cartooning and subversive literature. It was a hipster's bible. But not, alas, a profitable one. "I was delighted with the stuff *in* the magazine," Spiegelman recalls. "[But] the business of running it was nightmarish. There was no money, there was no help to speak of, except volunteer labor, and it was mostly falling on Bill Griffith's shoulders, Diane Noomin's shoulders, and mine. With my moving back to New York for business relatively unrelated to *Arcade*, more of it fell on their shoulders than was fair, and it was very hard to keep it going. We didn't really have a distribution system that justified keeping it going. We [distributed it] through the Print Mint, which was an underground comics publisher. And they didn't really have the capacity to publish a quarterly magazine. The way their system worked pretty much was, they had a comic like *Zap* 1, and then whenever *Zap* 2 came together, it sat next to *Zap* 1, *Zap* 3 sat next to *Zap* 2, and that was based on putting them out so seldom. But we were really trying to become a quarterly magazine. And so by the time we got to the sixth one, the head shops and the alternative bookstores that were carrying them were going, 'We've got enough of these things! Why are you putting out more?' You know? Because like every three months there'd be another *Arcade* coming along, and by the time we got to five and six they were beginning to get punchy. And we hadn't quite found newsstand distribution for anything that might have made more sense. So, I was dissatisfied with the real world interfering with the dream."

After 1976, Art Spiegelman was happy doing his own comics, and "there was a long time in which I swore I'd never do a magazine again." Then in 1980, he coedited and copublished *RAW* magazine with his wife, Françoise Mouly. Mouly helped keep *RAW* afloat with the money she made printing and publishing *Streets of SoHo and Tribeca Map Guide*, a respected tourist publication.

RAW was a step up from *Arcade*, in that it was something new, fresh, previously unseen: even though *RAW* contained the occasional contribution from notables like Robert Crumb, it eschewed established underground cartoonists in favor of newer, unknown cartoonists just starting out, like retro stylist Charles Burns (*Big Baby*), "King of Punk Art" Gary Panter (*Jimbo*), Mark Newgarden (*The Little Nun*), political cartoonist Sue Coe (*How to Commit Suicide in South Africa*), and Drew Friedman (*MAD, Persons Living or Dead*). And Françoise Mouly opened Spiegelman's eyes to the new talent emerging in Europe, many of whom made their way into the pages of *RAW*, including Joost Swarte of the Netherlands and France's Jacques Tardi. *RAW* called itself a "graphix magazine," using the word "graphix" to distinguish itself from underground "comix" (which carried sex-and-dope connotations from which Spiegelman wanted to distance himself).

RAW #1 was subtitled, "The Graphix Magazine of Postponed Suicides," and Spiegelman says that far from being a hopeless, depressing sentiment, "Postponed Suicides" is a life-affirming term; after all, every moment you don't commit suicide is an affirmation, a decision to live some more, an act of faith. Spiegelman was quoting Romanian author E. M. Cioran (as he revealed in the inside front cover of *RAW* #1), who said, "A book is a postponed suicide." Spiegelman calls this attitude "provisionally optimistic."

So how did Mouly convince Spiegelman to work on *RAW* with her, after the mortifying experience of doing *Arcade*? "She wanted to, and I wanted her, so we did it," he laughs. "There was a need for it. I just wasn't sure I was up to the task of having to argue with cartoonists again. It's like, when you're editing at *The New Yorker* it's not so bad, because everyone wants to climb aboard, and if you throw [the artwork] aside and don't use it, so be it! People have gotten paid. And there's enough money involved so it can happen. But when [something like] *Arcade* is working on a real shoestring, and being probably more demanding than *The New Yorker* in some ways, it's easy to get into rough patches with people that are your friends and peers. And I wasn't sure I was ready to do battle. On the other hand, I'd learned something from *Arcade* that helped put *RAW* over. For one thing, nailing down how we might distribute such a thing, what might make it more noticeable, like the scale of it, the size of it.

"And like I said, there was a crying need, there's some really great work around that nobody's interested in having, including what was left of the so-called 'underground comics.' There were people who were coming along who should have been in the underground comics, but they were just a few years too late to kind of be grandfathered in. I mean, from the old underground comics we did publish work by Bill Griffith, by Crumb. It's not like we tried *not* to use the underground cartoonists. There were people who just had no place to publish that were very good. Like Charles Burns, Ben Katchor, and to a degree Mark Beyer, although he'd appeared in *Arcade*. Sue Coe, she was seen elsewhere, but she changed and developed through her appearances in *RAW*. And Gary Panter was already appearing in *Slash* magazine, but I would suspect that it amplified the world that knew about him. [There was] pretty much a generation of artists who made themselves known through their work in *RAW*. The people who were coming along, coming from slightly somewhere else, like the ones I just mentioned. And a lot of great work was beginning to appear in Europe and had no place to appear here! So it just sort of felt like an unwanted abandoned child on our doorstep to take care of."

RAW was a biannual, and was published on an exceedingly odd schedule. "We called it a biannual," Spiegelman says, "because we didn't know what a biannual meant, twice a year or once every two years, so that gave us some latitude. I don't think we ever managed to get two out a year. Although there was a year in there someplace where we might have put out two, plus a one-shot or two of individual artists' work as books."

A fusion of comics and fine art, *RAW* was instantly recognized as something different. What gave Spiegelman and Mouly the confidence that this would work? "Well, we didn't have any confidence, we just knew it was worth doing," Spiegelman says. "I mean, what it was really is that it seemed to have worked. We'd put it out on the table and show people that came over to our house. Then you'd put the stuff away! People'd come over, you'd take it out again! I was hired as a consultant at some point for various magazines, like some kind of *High Times* knock-off called *Daily Dope* wanted comics, *Playboy* hired me as a consultant for awhile for their comics section. And in all those instances, nobody was really interested [in *RAW*-type material], because all they really wanted was in one instance comics about dope, and in the other comics about sex. The last thing *Playboy* really wanted to hear is, 'Well you know how you publish fiction by Nabokov, why don't you have comics by the comics equivalent?' It's not what editors want to hear. So it's kind of frustrating. So we did *RAW* primarily just to show what it should be. Not even with the belief that we would have a second issue. It was just like, 'Oh, this is how *RAW* would look if it existed.' And then the response was better than we thought. We sold out of our five thousand copies! And the artists wanted more, and we figured, 'What the heck, let's do it again!' And it built from there."

For a small-press magazine with virtually no PR or advertising budget, *RAW* was an instant success, selling five thousand copies in 1980 based solely on word of mouth. By 1987, with *RAW* #8, that number had ballooned to thirty-five thousand copies. "It wasn't enormous," Spiegelman admits, "but we'd gotten some [cartoonists] whose work nobody else was doing! It did get attention. And it wasn't like we had a publicist, and it wasn't like I knew what I was doing, it's just we'd get people who were interested in it asking us questions. And then there was a lot of press."

By this time Art Spiegelman was teaching at the School of Visual Arts along with his cartooning heroes Will Eisner and Harvey Kurtzman, and Spiegelman found some of his contributors—some of these "abandoned children"—right on the doorstep of his classroom. He notes that "Kaz, Drew Friedman, and Mark Newgarden came from my course." Drew Friedman first published his notorious "Andy Griffith" strip (written with his brother Josh Alan Friedman) for *RAW*. "Andy Griffith" depicts with brutally satirical honesty what it would really be like for a black motorist to pass through a small Southern town like Mayberry in the 1950s; the motorist is lynched by Andy Griffith and his loyal stooge Barney Fife, who turn out to be Klansmen. It's a commentary on how *The Andy Griffith Show* conveniently avoided any of the discussion of racial strife that was overwhelming the South at the time the show was airing. "Drew Friedman originally did the Andy Griffith strip for an [SVA] student assignment first," Spiegelman says. "And it first appeared in a small circulation newsprint magazine [*Kar-Tunz*] that came out of Harvey Kurtzman's class [the year before]. But a lot of the work drew out of class assignments. Certainly the first stuff we had of Kaz's that I remember was first [done for class], and I think that was true of Mark Newgarden as well."

COVERAGE

One of the primary things that set *RAW* apart from other alternative comics anthologies is that Spiegelman and Mouly made each copy of the magazine into an art object. The cover of *RAW* #1, by Spiegelman himself, boasted a full-color "tipped-in" image glued by hand onto the black-and-white cover. *RAW* #7 featured a cover (also by Spiegelman) where the right-hand corner was torn off, but each copy of the magazine was torn by hand, and thus was torn slightly differently. Therefore, each issue was a slightly differently prepared art object, as opposed to a mass-produced product.

This was exactly the message Spiegelman and Mouly wanted to impart with their new magazine. "We were both, Françoise and I, interested in books for their objectness as well as their content," Spiegelman recalls. "The way they just felt tactilely, what kind of paper they were on, what they were! And in the very first *RAW*, we didn't have much money for color, and so I designed this cover that could have one little patch of color that you could paste off using a small printing press. Even though the rest of the magazine was printed on a larger press. So we already had a tip-in on the first issue. Françoise had gone to printing school, because we said we wanted to be publishers. So, we had a smaller-sized press in our loft. The magazine required a larger size. This allowed us to do certain inserts, things that would add color to the book. And the wanting to make something that was both hand-made and mass-produced at the same time led us down to those kinds of odd alleyways. We did books with individual artists [called] *RAW One-Shots*, and [for *RAW One-Shot* #3, 'Jack Survives'] we did a book with a really great comics artist named Jerry Moriarty. The color was printed on paper, and the black line, the holding line, was on the acetate over it."

Readers of *RAW* #4 were treated to a die-cut Charles Burns cover with a second, full-color cover beneath it. " 'Die-cut' is where you get a punch made," Spiegelman explains. "You punch a hole into a piece of paper, and they're not just holes, but whatever shapes you wanted. So there's one cover that was a black-and-white cover that had strategically placed shapes that had been cut out, that allowed one to make the letters *RAW* and part of an image in color. And it became a totally different image when you opened it up." The die-cut cover also came with a "flexi-disc," a record titled "Reagan Speaks for Himself," consisting of a Ronald Reagan audio-collage by Doug Kahn. The record appeared opposite a full-page Sue Coe illustration of Reagan in which the then-president appeared as a grotesque porcine creature, his corpulent figure festooned with dollar signs. Other *RAW*s came with giveaways that were more frivolous, such as issue 2's package of trading cards (by Mark Beyer), accompanied by a stick of bubblegum. Here in Spiegelman's world, high art and low art met and made a baby called *RAW*, where gum cards and astute political satire shared the same stage.

Then there was the notorious "ripped" cover for *RAW* #7, subtitled "The Torn-Again Graphix Magazine." This issue was one that Spiegelman remembers as being particularly confusing to the printer, who had no idea what he and Mouly were going for . . . or why they'd tear up their own magazine *on purpose*! "That was one issue where the printers were kind of aghast at what we were doing, where we did that ripped-off corner," Spiegelman admits. "We did so much weird stuff that there were times when the printers were just confused by us. Here, it was after working with these printers to get exactly the quality we were after, we asked the binder to let us set up in his place, to rip corners off [each one]. And there was a cover design that had been inspired by magazine returns where they just lop off the logos, and so we got a bunch of people together to rip the right-hand corner of the covers off of all—whatever it was by then—fifteen-, twenty-thousand copies. And Françoise had designed a contents page that made use of the torn-off corner, so it had to get taped back in inside. But not necessarily the same one got ripped off of one sheet, it might get put into another book. But we used all the things we ripped up, as part of the contents page, all of which was designed that way [on purpose].

"And definitely the binder was baffled by us, but he was very friendly, he was willing to let us be there. And it turned into a kind of science experiment, because over the course of two or three days, we had various friends of the artists, the artists' models, and the artists' husbands coming by. And very quickly, they could take on any job they wanted. All the males were at the table ripping cover corners off, and all of the females had sorted themselves out as being the ones who rescued and saved these corners by taping them up back again. Every group we started with, people would just say, 'I'm going to go over there for awhile,' it'd sort itself out by gender!"

A SURVIVOR'S TALE

RAW #2's status as the "gum card" issue is eclipsed by the fact that it was also the issue with the first installment of Art Spiegelman's more ambitious, long-form version of *Maus*. The first six chapters, which appeared in *RAW* from 1980 to 1985, would be collected in the 1986 graphic novel *Maus: A Survivor's Tale*. In 1991, *Maus II: And Here My Troubles Begin* was published, collecting the next four chapters (which also first appeared individually in *RAW* from 1986 to 1991), plus an all-new chapter added to wrap up and provide closure to the story.

No mere bedtime tale, this new *Maus* told two stories simultaneously: the full story of Vladek Spiegelman's experiences during the Holocaust, and the frame story of Art Spiegelman's attempts to interview his father about said experiences. In the process, we see how the horrors of the Nazi atrocities shaped Vladek into the damaged, broken old man he is in the frame story, a miserly soul with as many dysfunctions as he has prescription pills. We see Art Spiegelman's attempts to reach out to his father, which constantly backfire. A prime example is a scene in which Vladek wants Art to fix a leaky drain pipe. Art, not good at that sort of thing, offers to pay for a handyman, at which point Vladek barks, "Never mind! Forget I said anything," and changes the subject.

Maus was by far Spiegelman's most mature and extravagant work to date. In many ways it was a culmination of all his other work, incorporating many of the storytelling elements he'd experimented with in the past. Like the *Funny Aminals* version of *Maus*, this version also depicted the Jews as mice and the Germans as cats. But here, Spiegelman expanded the metaphor by portraying Poles as pigs, Americans as dogs, and the French as frogs. Just as he did in "As the Mind Reels," Spiegelman used rough diagrams and pages torn from notebooks to help tell the story, as when Vladek sketches out a drawing for his son depicting the coal bin in which he hid from the Nazis. As in "Ace Hole," there are psychologically revealing moments of pure dreamlike surrealism, as when Spiegelman is being hounded by the media about *Maus*, causing him to revert to a childlike state. Only when he visits his psychiatrist, who is an Auschwitz survivor like his father, can he puff himself back up to the status of a mature adult. As in many of his earlier works, in *Maus* Spiegelman uses himself as a character, recognizable through his ever-present "costume": a cigarette and plain black vest. Even "Prisoner on the Hell Planet" makes a cameo appearance in *Maus*, during one scene in which Vladek accidentally stumbles across his son's old underground comic strip, which brings back painful memories to the old man, making him even more ornery. (Although in the end, Vladek concedes that it's good that Art got the experience of his mother's suicide out of his system.)

Art Spiegelman says that the genesis of *Maus* as a long-term project goes back to at least 1977, when he moved back to New York from San Francisco. "I moved back to New York in '75, I confessed to my father that I'd moved back by about '77," he laughs. "And so some time in '77, I went back to talk to him with the idea that something might be there that I could work on, and I guess I officially started in '78. I had just turned thirty. And I figured, 'OK, you can't trust anyone over thirty, I'm supposed to be dead in a motorcycle accident by thirty,' and I'd never learned how to ride one. So I was taking on this project that I'd had somewhere in my head [thinking], 'OK, it'll be a very long comic book, and one that was more narratively propelled than some of the stuff that had immediately preceded work on that book.' Because, by God, if people wanted stories out of comics, I was going to have to tell a story that had to do something worth bothering with, 'cause my work habits make me a rather slow cartoonist."

Spiegelman attributes the slowness of his work method to his being dissatisfied with almost everything he does. "[It involves] just a lot of reworking, or rethinking," he admits. "So it didn't seem like it would be worth doing a long story that would be some kind of science fiction / fantasy thing, or something that would be 'amusing.' But like I said, the first impulse really was a *long* comic book story. Something that would be worth bothering with, to me and to the ostensible reader on the other end. And that became this *Maus* thing.

"The goal was to tell [my father's] story," Spiegelman says, conceding that he also talked to Vladek's second wife, Mala, while writing *Maus*. "And in the course of that, I suppose I did talk to various friends of theirs, but it wasn't a concerted effort. I mean, the main goal for me was to try to understand his story, so that led me to ask other people questions sometimes, but really the only in-depth interviewing was interviewing my father for years. Like, specifically going over with a tape recorder and interviewing him. That lasted at least from '78 to '81. He died in '82. I did a lot of reading, and at a certain point, I went to see a shrink who had been a Holocaust survivor of Auschwitz [as depicted in *Maus II*], who helped me get past some blocks into the second volume. And I'd put him on the list of people I interviewed as well."

Spiegelman's Holocaust memoir was one of the first graphic novels to make a regular showing in chain bookstores like Barnes & Noble. What made it possible for *Maus* to overcome the stigma of "low art," paving the way for future graphic novelists like Chris Ware (*Jimmy Corrigan*) and Daniel Clowes (*Ghost World*)? One reason was that Spiegelman didn't go through the normal comics distribution channels. Instead he bypassed comic book specialty shops and comics distributors like Diamond and

landed the book immediately in bookstores through a major publisher, Pantheon. "Well, the simple answer of course is mere distribution, by going with one publisher [rather] than another, but that would be of course naive," he explains. "*Maus* specifically was thought of as a book at a time when those kinds of books didn't exist in Diamond and related kinds of distribution and in those comics stores. And its premises weren't oriented there either. There's always some sight you're aiming at, some destination. And definitely the destination I had in mind wasn't the

© Art Spiegelman

THE COVER OF THE COLLECTED FIRST SIX CHAPTERS OF MAUS.

same audience that would read a superhero comic book. That it would actually make its way into those bookstores that I wanted it to land in was actually more than I'd expected or dreamed would actually come to pass."

A SERIES OF GOOD FLUKES

But *Maus*'s journey from serialized *RAW* feature to graphic novel certainly took some doing on Spiegelman's part. "The book publishing world in the early eighties was hardly receptive," he reveals, "and I think every publisher on the East Coast and beyond sent me either a form rejection or a four-page, soul-searching rejection, but still a rejection. And even the publisher that ultimately published it, Pantheon, took it on a second submission when it made its way in through a back door. So I knew that's what I wanted, that that's where it belonged, but that I actually managed to see that happen was a series of good flukes."

These flukes began when Spiegelman was called by a representative from the Scott Meredith Agency, asking to see *RAW*. "A Greek client was interested in *RAW* magazine's rights for Greece," Spiegelman explains. "The only agent I'd ever heard of, being rather outside of the book publishing world, had been Scott Meredith. So I went, 'OK, I'll send you some *RAW*s to look at.' The person who received it wasn't an agent, he was a foreign rights guy there who would have liked to be an agent. So I sent it to him, he sent it to the Greek publisher, the Greek publisher was pissed off, because what he was expecting was a sex magazine! The foreign rights guy gets back in touch with me and says, 'Well, they didn't want it, but um, there's this booklet that's in here called *Maus*, do you have a publisher for that?' And I said, 'No.' He said, 'Can I be your agent?' And [I said], 'Well, why not? Let's give it a try.' I wasn't quite ready to shop it around, I was just in the midst of making it. But he took it around, got it rejected from everybody, including Pantheon, where there were two editors who were especially antipathic to the material. One was an editor whose mother was a survivor of the camps, and in fact knew [my stepmother] Mala somewhat. And I think she was horrified by the project. Although, now she runs around taking credit for the book! But I know from various editors who were up there that that has nothing to do with the reality. And [then there was] another editor who also wasn't very sympathetic to it, and the whole thing just came flying back to me, and continued to wade through this guy's list.

"Then, a friend of mine, this art director at Pantheon, asked why I hadn't sent it to Pantheon. I looked through my rejections, and said, 'No, no, we were there!' She said, 'Do you mind if I show it again?' So the art director kind of made an end-run around the editors and went to the publisher. And he got interested, and found an editor at the house who *was* sympathetic, whose father had been a cartoonist in fact. So that's sort of how come it landed there, it's really just flukey. I just assumed I'd self-publish this thing and be on the side of finishing it whenever that was gonna happen.

"*Maus* was a big enough success from when it came out to create the expectation of more books like it in bookstores, so that somewhere between *Maus*, *Dark Knight Returns*, and *Watchmen*, all of which had only [word] balloons in common, there was a flag set up going, 'OK, graphic novels! Whatever! Comics! Whatever you want to call it, we'll set up a section for it!' But what came in its wake wasn't sufficient to make that section stick in the bookstores, and that the whole thing just became the repository of Dungeons & Dragons kind of stuff. And it took a long time for there to be a lot of solidly conceived work that would fit in those hypothetical sections. And that's what started happening maybe ten years after. And at this point, all the bookstores seem to have a comics / graphic novels sections again. And now there's other stuff that might go there for some reason or another, besides gaming books."

Spiegelman says that the reason it took about ten years for the graphic novel sections of bookstores to grow and ripen beyond glorified role-playing game repositories to places where a Chris Ware can display his wares (pun intended) is that graphic novels achieved critical mass. "In the sense," he says, "that there were critics looking at this stuff, *and* there was enough stuff to look at. I keep coming back to these phrases like 'critical mass,' like there's enough material that it's now harder to ignore.

"But also, I think it was [Marshall] McLuhan who said it, or maybe it's me who said it thinking McLuhan said it, but he said, 'When a medium loses its centrality, it either becomes art or it dies.' For instance, woodcuts. Woodcuts were the way things got printed, they were central to a medieval culture. Eventually, that wasn't the main way things got reproduced anymore, but woodcuts survived as something artists were interested in doing. Theater lost its centrality with the development of movies, radio. It wasn't the only way you could get dramatized narrative anymore. And yet, movies—first for a while called photoplays, and then just being their own language—moved to center stage, and theater had to sort of reinvent its reason for existing. And it managed to do so, so that there is such a thing still as live theatrical performance, because artists are making that happen.

"And I think that comics at this point have totally lost their franchise, even though there's still money to be made for cartoonists working it the right way, I suppose. But it ain't nothing like what was happening in the forties or fifties for comic books, or what was happening in the twenties and thirties for comic strips. When they *were* the central ring of our culture, you know? And so that process of redefinition has finally taken root. Why it happened now rather than 1985 I really can't say. Except certain things including *Maus* happened that allowed other people to say, 'Oh you know we can do a long book for grown-ups that don't usually read stories about caped crusaders!'"

Maus's publication in 1986 was met with critical and popular kudos. Authors such as Umberto Eco (*The Name of the Rose*) and fellow cartoonists like Jules Feiffer (*Tantrum*) praised Spiegelman's work, as did major magazines like *Esquire* and *Newsweek*, and it soon became used as an educational resource in school libraries. As with any American success story, a sequel was mandatory. But Spiegelman always considered both *Maus* books two halves of the same whole. "Oh, it was [all] one book," he explains. "As I explained, I wanted part one to get published so it would beat the animated film *An American Tale* [which also featured anthropomorphic Jewish mice] in the public's consciousness. And it did. They had union problems making the cartoon. Strikes, trying to use skilled laborers. The movie got slowed down, the book got speeded up, so part one came out before *American Tale* made it to the theaters. There was even one op-ed kind of piece in I think the *Boston Globe* that said, 'Don't see this movie,'—with a picture of a cel from *American Tale*—'Read this book,'—with a frame from *Maus*. But at that time it was always meant to be one work. I just kind of got sort of halfway through [by 1986]. But it got out to the planet because of the review in the *New York Times Book Review*!"

Maus II's publication in 1991 was arguably an even bigger success than its predecessor. With both *Maus* books finished, Spiegelman was awarded a "special" Pulitzer Prize for the complete Holocaust memoir in 1992, an unprecedented honor for a comic book. Spiegelman received the National Book Critics Circle nomination in both 1986 and 1991 for *Maus*, and his artwork (including images from *Maus*) was the subject of a 1991 show at the Museum of Modern Art in New York City.

However, for all its near-universal accolades, *Maus* was not always understood. The stigma of a comic book being frivolous children's literature still made some uncomfortable about the idea of turning such a chapter in Jewish history into one. This sentiment was espoused when Spiegelman was asked to be a part of a conference for children of survivors. "[This was] where children of survivors and children of Nazis were supposed to get together and have a public exchange," he recalls. "And there this one poor child of the Nazis came and she was just such a neurotic mess. So it wasn't as advertised. There were primarily survivors in the audience. And unlike a lot of the other things I had done up to that point, the other events I had been at had a more self-selecting audience who had come because it was *me*. And here, they were there because of the subject, and they were appalled by the very notion of what I had done. It was very hard to even talk about it without grumbles from the audience. It was like I had three hundred Vladeks in the audience! You know, [they were saying], 'Couldn't you wait until we were dead to make fun of us!' They weren't getting what I had done. You know? But other than that, I've spoken over the years, I've gotten a couple of letters from a number of survivors who were impressed or taken with or interested in what *Maus* was per se."

NO TOWERS

After *Maus* won a Pulitzer Prize in 1992, Art Spiegelman largely retreated from comics for the next ten years. From 1992 to 2002, most of his energy was focused on his new gig: illustrating provocative covers and occasionally writing essays for *The New Yorker*. *RAW* magazine had ceased publication in 1991. Tina Brown, then editor of *The New Yorker*, gave Spiegelman the chance to use the venerable metropolitan magazine as a forum to say something beyond the standard *New Yorker* cover image, which was often intellectually stimulating but hardly controversial or even culturally relevant. Art Spiegelman would change all of that, with Françoise Mouly by his side as the magazine's newly appointed art editor.

All told, Spiegelman created twenty-one covers for *The New Yorker* from this period, all of which stand out as being particularly daring. The February 1993 Valentine's Day cover featuring a Hasidic man and a black woman entangled in a loving embrace drew the ire of both the black and Jewish communities of New York, coming as it did on the heels of rising tensions between both ethnic groups. But Spiegelman had designed the cover as a way to plead for an end to the animosity both communities had expressed toward one another. The September 24, 2001, cover Spiegelman created for the *New Yorker* provoked the exact opposite reaction, featuring austere, stark black-on-black silhouettes of the World Trade Center's recently obliterated twin towers. Spiegelman summed up the national mood of sobriety and pain in a tasteful, understated manner.

In the wake of this national tragedy, Spiegelman often felt like he was in a state of sustained panic, as though he was "waiting for the other shoe to drop." On seeing the first tower fall, Spiegelman and Mouly raced to their daughter Nadja's school to collect her, and Spiegelman remembers that his nervousness actually made his daughter *more* apprehensive about the situation. Needing a release for these feelings—and for his anger at what he saw as the Bush Administration's jingoistic hijacking of the tragedy to promote their own agenda—he created a ten-part series of oversized one-page comic strips titled *In the Shadow of No Towers*. *No Towers* also uses classic comic strip characters for satirical effect: in one strip, George Herriman's *Krazy Kat* plunks away on the guitar with a zombie-like stare, droning, "Freedom's just another word for nothin' left to lose." In another, Rudolph Dirks's *The Katzenjammer Kids*—who have the Twin Towers jutting out of their heads—are bathed in crude oil by a foaming-at-the-mouth Uncle Sam, until there's nothing left but charred Katzenjammer corpses.

Spiegelman himself is seen in these strips as just barely holding on, operating as a vessel for national anxiety; every now and then he even draws himself as his *Maus* persona, an anthropomorphic mouse, drawing parallels between the helpless victims of Auschwitz and the helpless victims of 9/11. But Spiegelman was surprised to learn that *The New Yorker* wasn't interested in running the series, most likely because of its edgy, overtly political bent. The series was published from 2001 to 2003 in the Jewish magazine the *Forward* and in a handful of foreign publications including Britain's the *Independent* and Germany's *Die Zeit*, and then collected in graphic novel form in 2004 along with an essay by the author.

"I don't remember how the editor [of the *Forward*] got wind of the fact that I was doing them," he remembers. "I must have met him in some other context, and mentioned that I was doing some broadsheet-size comics page for a German newspaper called *Die Zeit*. And I said, '[*No Towers*] is not about Jewish issues per se.' And he said, 'It's OK, *you're* Jewish!' It was like this very intensive thing that I'm only climbing out of now, it was only ten pages, but each one took me forever. And like I say, they were my American publisher. It was seen in the wider circles in England and Germany and France and Italy as about the hijacking of September 11, and the hijacking of September 11 by the politicians that came in its wake. And it's about my own particular brush up against that feeling of disaster when your personal sphere is invaded by political exigencies which require that I put on a Maus mask every once in a while in the course of those pages. When I finally finished, it was a ten-page adventure, but each one took me about a month."

Art Spiegelman says that the events of September 11 have reinvigorated his desire to make comics. "It's definitely an outgrowth of what felt like a near-death experience," he offers. "We were down in the epicenter of it when it happened, getting our daughter out of Stuyvesant, where she started going to school three days before or so. At that point, I realized that I hadn't done enough comics. And even though comics take forever and I felt I wasn't going to live forever, it definitely refocused me. And I wanted to try and digest what had happened to me, it took me a while to figure that out enough to begin working on such a series of pages. And it made me impatient with my gig at *The New Yorker*, so I pretty much walked from that, for now, so I could really focus on the *No Towers* thing without having to keep a sort of genteel mask on, through which everything in *The New Yorker* is seen. So that's how it affected me.

"How it affected the rest of comics, I don't know. I can't tell to what degree it's all coincidence or interconnected to specific events, but comics have actually hit some kind of tipping point in so many areas recently, so that if there were such a thing as a high/low divide, I think comics have crossed it. It becomes more clear as more and more museums willingly embrace comic art as some of the things that they're willing to show, the Whitney Biennial being a pretty clear example, where Chris Ware's work was one of the fifteen or twenty artists in the show. And libraries are eager to have comics, graphic novels, whatever they want to call them, on their shelves, because it actually gets kids past the computer terminals. The publishing industry is in the doldrums, but one of the only areas of growth is the graphic novel section. The amount of attention that's paid [to comics] in academia has grown a lot also. At the same time, Hollywood's become interested because now [through special effects] it can make people fly almost as easily as a cartoonist can. So all those things happened at once. Whether any of those things have a connection to September 11, I don't know—I doubt it somehow. But maybe comics have achieved a kind of cumulative force."

Spiegelman's more politically sensitive work isn't *all* he's been occupying his time with since he finished *Maus*. He's also indulged his fun side. Since 2000, he and Françoise Mouly have published (through their RAW Junior imprint) the hardcover children's book series *Little Lit*, comics anthologies where a dream team of writers and cartoonists team up to tell children's stories in comics form. Among the contributors for the first book, *Little Lit: Folklore and Fairy Tale Funnies* are Spiegelman himself, famed children's book author William Joyce (*Rolie Polie Olie*, *Dinosaur Bob*), and Bruce McCall (contributor to such shrines of grown-up-hood as *National Lampoon*, *The New Yorker*, and *Saturday Night Live*). In 2001, Spiegelman and Mouly's next collection, *Little Lit: Strange Stories for Strange Kids*, had contributions from *Where's Waldo?* creator Martin Handford; *Where the Wild Things Are* author Maurice Sendak; and a collaboration from *Me Talk Pretty One Day* author David Sedaris and *New Yorker* artist Ian Falconer. The third *Little Lit* collection, *Little Lit: It Was A Dark and Silly Night . . .* was published in 2003, featuring Halloween-themed stories from such luminaries as *Sandman* creator Neil Gaiman and *Playboy* cartoonist Gahan Wilson; *A Series of Unfortunate Events* author Lemony Snicket's collaboration with *Evil Eye* cartoonist Richard Sala; and a contribution by *Underworld* cartoonist Kaz.

By recruiting some of the greatest talents in comics, prose fiction, and commercial illustration to work on the *Little Lit* anthologies, Spiegelman is creating a treasure trove of family friendly, high-quality stories that will stand the test of time. His mission statement is clear: to get kids interested in comic books from an early age, so that they'll understand the power of comics storytelling throughout the rest of their lives. And of course, in this day and age of dark and conflicted angst-ridden superheroes and adults-only alternative titles, it's nice to have comic books that are actually appropriate for kids. It's as though Spiegelman and Mouly are saying, "Hey, kids! Comics aren't just for *adults* anymore!"

HERE MY TROUBLES END

In the 1960s, in the pages of a particularly lighthearted issue of *Fantastic Four*, writer Stan Lee jokingly announced that he and cartoonist Jack Kirby should be considered by the Pulitzer Prize Committee for their work on the *FF*. At the time, it was a joke: a *comic book* winning the Pulitzer? How ridiculous! With *Maus*, it's no joke. Art Spiegelman has brought a new awareness of the storytelling power and artistic potential of comic books to the American public. In creating a work as psychologically probing, dramatically gripping, and artistically ambitious as *Maus*, he's done what so many others—including Will Eisner, Jack Kirby, and Harvey Pekar—spent their lives attempting. He's made comic books that can be labeled art with a capital A (that wasn't the hard part; Eisner, Kirby, and Pekar all did this), and he's made the non-comics-reading world sit up and take notice (*that* was the hard part).

Like the Moses of comics, Spiegelman shepherded comics into bookstores and schools, and he inspired a new generation of cartoonists, including Marjane Satrapi (*Persepolis*), Ho Che Anderson (*King*), and Joe Sacco (*Palestine*). Thanks to Spiegelman, the very idea of a serious graphic novel being designed for consumption in bookstores—thus bypassing comic book specialty store distribution—is less often the exception, and more often the rule. Of course, thanks to *Maus*, comic book stores are also now stocking more books *like* the groundbreaking *Maus*. And with subsequent projects like *In The Shadow Of No Towers* and his *Little Lit* anthologies, Spiegelman has made sure not to rest on his laurels.

Today, Art Spiegelman is working on a variety of projects, most of which are related in some way to either creating comics or spreading the word about the importance of comics as a valid form of both art and literature. An advocate for comics literacy, Spiegelman has carved out a niche as both a master of the form and a sort of diplomat teaching potential readers that comics can be art, touring the country and giving a lecture he calls "Comix 101." In this lecture, he takes his audiences on a chronological tour of the comics medium, tracing its evolution and history while explaining why it's too important to be ignored. Spiegelman believes that in our post-literate culture, comics echo the way the brain works, and so the importance of this art form is on the rise. He is also currently working on a comics memoir, *Portrait of the Artist as a Young Nerd*, which will incorporate reprints of his most important underground comics work. And in what little spare time he has, he's been working on the libretto and set design (with composer Phillip Johnson) for an upcoming stage musical about comics history entitled, *Drawn to Death: A Three-Panel Opera*.

Clearly, dentistry's loss is cartooning's gain.

GILBERT HERNANDEZ

BETO
05

© Gilbert Hernandez

SELF-PORTRAIT.

"Or perhaps it began when Luba came into town. You see, Chelo had been the only banadora in town, and was not prepared for this upstart from the North to take a good portion of the bathing business from the veteran bather."

—From the story "Sopa De Gran Pena," *Love & Rockets*

Gilbert Hernandez is the cartoonist who brought magical realism to comics. Before him, comic books had embraced straight-up fantasy, but it usually involved orcs, dragons, and wizards. Or, if a comic book *did* involve ordinary, everyday folks encountering ghosts, the undead, and other aspects of the supernatural, it was often in a pulpy, *Tales from the Crypt* manner. Hernandez broke from tradition by crafting refreshingly realistic, sophisticated stories that simply happened to include a dose of the paranormal. He did it in the pages of *Love & Rockets*, the critically acclaimed gold standard of the so-called independent comics movement. The first wave of "indie" comics was initiated in the late 1970s and early '80s by comic book publishers such as Pacific, Dark Horse, Fantagraphics, Eclipse, and Comico. These companies' catalogues of material was a middle ground, not *purely* mainstream (superheroes, science fiction/fantasy, action/adventure), but also not *wholly* underground (slice-of-life/autobiography, social satire, porn).

Created by brothers Gilbert and Jaime Hernandez in 1981 (other brother Mario occasionally contributes as well), *Love & Rockets* was uncategorizable, and so it created its own unique category. These were stories where the art was so engaging, the writing so full of ideas, the characters so likeable, and the storytelling so clean, that even if someone didn't gravitate toward "indie" comics, they'd have to admit this was pretty damn good stuff. Soon, other cartoonists such as Dan Clowes (*Ghost World*) and Bernie Mireault (*The Jam*) were being influenced by Gilbert and Jaime Hernandez, and a British pop group even appropriated the name *Love & Rockets* (without bothering to ask the Hernandez Brothers' permission first).

Every issue of *Love & Rockets* contains several long-running features, the most popular being Jaime's "Hoppers 13" stories (also known as the "Locas" or "Maggie" stories), and Gilbert's "Heartbreak Soup" stories (a.k.a. the Palomar stories). The "Hoppers 13" stories concern a complex group of pre-dominantly Hispanic young women. Among them are the ostensible pro-tagonists of the stories, best friends and sometime lovers Hopey and Maggie. Over the course of the series, we've followed them from the early days of the L.A. punk scene into the present as they've grown and evolved.

Gilbert Hernandez's Palomar stories are something else entirely. Set in the fictional Central American town of Palomar (Spanish for "pigeon coop"), they involve a rich conflagration of characters, from the local sher-iff, to the *banadoras* (bathers), to the gigolos, to the village idiot. Every-one's opinion is heard, everyone gets in his or her two cents in this intensely involved narrative with a novelistic scope. In fact, many critics have noted the similarities between Hernadez's work and the literary genre of magical realism, and he's frequently compared to authors such as Gabriel Garcia Marquez. All of which is fairly high-brow for someone who still considers one of his primary influences to be *Archie* comics.

THE OXNARD YEARS

Gilbert Hernandez was born in 1957 in the small, agricultural town of Oxnard, California, about sixty miles north of L.A. "It was basically a really nice town to grow up in," he remembers. "It was really safe. Kids could walk down the street by themselves, [or go] down to the park and play baseball or whatever. I'm afraid to say it, but [it was] the good old days."

And while most kids' parents were throwing away their children's comic book collections, Hernandez's mom was doing anything but. A fer-vent comic book fan in her own right, the Hernandez matriarch introduced her children to comic books, sparking a lifelong passion in Gilbert. "I started reading comics because it was OK for me to read them," he remem-bers. "As far as I can remember, comics had always been laying around the house. Mom thought it was OK because she read them as a kid. She was reading *The Spirit*, and *Captain Marvel*, you know, all the great comics of the forties. So we thought, 'Well that's cool!' The fact that our mom was just really into it and really loved comic books was really really inspiring."

Hernandez's most prevalent influences were 1960s Marvel artists like Jack Kirby and Steve Ditko. "Kirby and Ditko, and over at DC guys like [*Flash* artist] Carmine Infantino and guys like Dick Sprang were doing *Bat-man*, a real cartoony, real simplistic style of comics. A couple of artists over at Archie Comics, Dan DeCarlo and Harry Lucy, were just terrific artists. It's just a mishmash of basically everything that was coming out at the time."

Another big influence that would find its way into both Gilbert and Jaime's *Love & Rockets* comics was old school rock 'n' roll, with its edgy mix of teenage rebelliousness and raw sexuality. "Rock 'n' roll was like comics for us, it was always around in the house," Hernandez explains. "The radio was always on! This was the Golden Age, with the Beatles and the Stones and the Beach Boys. So we grew up with that, and at the same time we were reading comics, so that kind of came together. High school was boring, but it wasn't that terrible for us, like it was for a lot of comic book fans. We weren't isolated, we knew girls. We partied, we were just regular rock 'n' roll guys in high school. We were just bored out of our skulls, [because] we didn't agree with the whole jock/cheerleader thing."

While purposefully alienating himself from pep rallies and the "in crowd," Hernandez also didn't gravitate toward the "nerd herd." In fact, at the time, he didn't know comic books had any sort of geek stigma. "Because we didn't know other kids that really liked comics!" he explains. "I mean, a few of them would buy one and get rid of it, whatever. But you know, we *collected* comics. We were *into* the artists, we were *into* the characters, we were *into just everything* about comics. We just thought of it as our particular interest, we didn't know about the geek status, because nobody really talked about it in our house!" Regardless, when he was in grade school, the other kids didn't think of him as a geek. In fact, if anything, they seemed to admire his drawing ability. "Yeah, they were impressed," he admits. "Most of them were pretty nice. They'd go, 'You should draw superhero comics!' I'd go, 'No way, no way man!' I mean, I loved comics, I loved reading them, but I didn't want to draw Spider-Man! I've always been pretty narcissistic when it comes to my art, where it's like I want to do what I wanna do and that's it. I think I'm more creative—I think I'm at my best—when I'm doing my own thing."

And for the teenage Gilbert Hernandez, "doing his own thing" often meant making late-night excursions out of town and journeying into Los Angeles, with its promise of excitement and danger. He was starting to feel the pangs of wanderlust, starting to wonder about the big bad world out there and what it had to offer that Oxnard did not. "What happens is," he explains, "growing up in these nice little towns when you're in your teens, you go nuts! You want more. And the town, it basically gives you the same thing it gave you when you were a little kid. And so that's when you start partying, and going nuts, and making trips to L.A. to go see rock 'n' roll bands. We had no outlet for our interest in storytelling. So we just basically started doing comics seriously, just to keep from getting bored!"

A MUCH-NEEDED GROTH SPURT

By the time the brothers reached their early twenties, Hernandez noticed an interesting development. "We'd been drawing comics for ourselves since we were kids," he recalls. "And having done them for so many years, by the time we were teens, we got pretty good! And by the time it came to doing something with our lives, cartooning was the best thing we knew. So, we put together almost a fanzine of the first issue of *Love & Rockets*. We spent all our money doing that. Basically we handed them out at [comic book] conventions, and got some kind criticism here and there. But we still had a bunch of issues laying around the house that we didn't know what to do with! So, since we had a couple of issues left, one of the issues was sent off to the *Comics Journal*. We figured, those guys are the biggest pricks in comics, so we figured if we could take their punishment, we could take anything! And they reviewed it, and we got a little free press. Well, as luck would have it, [*Comics Journal* and Fantagraphics Books publisher] Gary Groth read it and liked it, and said, 'How about if we publish it?' It was that simple! It wasn't an overnight hit or anything like that. But, us becoming professional cartoonists, was pretty quick. We went from amateurs to professionals overnight. Even though technically we weren't professional."

The Hernandez Brothers created and distributed that first self-published issue of *Love & Rockets* in 1981, but the first Fantagraphics-published issue of their comic didn't come out until the following year. Why did it take a year for the team to make their professional debut? "Because our [self-published comic] was originally thirty-two pages, and Gary Groth wanted a sixty-four page comic," Hernandez explains. "He just said, 'Add some pages,' and we said, 'Sure!' It's a little like rock 'n' roll bands. It takes your whole life to do your first album, then takes you a year to do your second! Well, it took us all our lives to do the first issue of *Love & Rockets*, the version we made. And when it came to adding pages to it, in a reasonably short time, it was difficult. It took us a long time to finish it."

YOUNG LOVE

When *Love & Rockets* first started appearing from Fantagraphics in 1982, it certainly went through its share of growing pains. Early on, Hernandez told not only stories about the mythic town of Palomar, but also stories set in alternate realities, stories with a distinctly sci-fi bent. In fact, for a comic book that was ostensibly an independent comic, early on *Love & Rockets* had one foot in the science fiction/fantasy camp, thoroughly embracing the Jack Kirby and Stan Lee comics that the Hernandez Brothers devoured as children. Gilbert Hernandez's early non-Palomar stories included "Radio Zero," a decidedly Orwellian and definitely adult tale about a futuristic dystopia right out of a *Flash Gordon* strip, with elevated walkways, gleaming cityscapes, and futuristic technology. But *Flash Gordon* would never feature stories about the heroine of "Radio Zero," Errata Stigmata, a put-upon child-woman who (as her name indicates) bleeds from the hands. What Hernandez was doing here was clearly using the trappings of old-fashioned, cheesy superhero comics to tell stories that transcended them, in a quintessentially postmodern manner. "One of the things we were conscious of when we were starting *Love & Rockets*," he explains, "is that superhero comics for us, we had outgrown them. But we still had an interest in them, because we grew up with them. There was a sort of a Jekyll and Hyde thing going on. But *Love & Rockets* was basically the comic book to read *after* you read superheroes. It was kind of a juggling act there in the early days [of *Love & Rockets*], and [after awhile] we just dropped it altogether, because we basically outgrew them."

But for a while in the early eighties, Hernandez's non-Palomar *L&R* stories occasionally featured characters who wouldn't be out of place in a superhero comic. This is specifically evident in his early multi-part epic, "BEM." Those familiar with Stan Lee and Jack Kirby's monster stories of the late 1950s and early '60s know that BEM—or Bug-Eyed Monster—is Stan Lee's nickname for the slimy radioactive bog beasts and mutated dinosaur creatures featured in those now-quaint comic book stories. "BEM" concerns a rampaging Bug-Eyed Monster and Castle Radium, the stalwart Flash Gordon/Superman/James Bond–style hero who tries to stop the monster. Gilbert says that Castle Radium was inspired by Gene Kelly. "I was watching Gene Kelly movies at the time, so I made Gene Kelly a superhero," he reveals.

But then about halfway through the story, "BEM" takes an unusual twist! We find out that BEM isn't the Bug-Eyed Monster; rather, the Bug-Eyed Monster is merely an agent of BEM, a.k.a. "The Horror," an all-pervasive evil force who seems akin to the biblical Lucifer in terms of his power and influence. "The story was just poorly written, that's why there's all that confusion," Hernandez laughs self-deprecatingly. "I should have just made it simple and said, 'Yeah, the Bug-Eyed Monster *is* BEM, and that's it!' But no, it had to be something else! I had to get too clever for my own good! I just winged it. I had thirty-two pages of story, and when Gary Groth approached us to do a sixty-four–page comic, I had to finish thirty-two more pages!"

WHERE MEN ARE MEN

The Palomar stories also had a touch of the fantastic in them. Two qualities endeared them to audiences and made the "Heartbreak Soup" stories Gilbert Hernandez's magnum opus from 1982 to 1996: the touch of magical realism sprinkled throughout the series, and the engaging cast of characters whose complex relationships rang true with audiences from the first.

The literary genre of magical realism is defined by science-fiction novelist Gene Wolfe as "fantasy written in Spanish." There's some truth to this, as many practitioners of the genre are Latinos and use Latin folklore and spirituality in the stories. More accurately, however, magical realism is a branch of serious fiction set in the real world, in which said reality is invaded or intruded upon by nonlogical elements, such as witches, premonitions, or apparitions from the spirit world. Gabriel Garcia Marquez's novel *One Hundred Years of Solitude* is frequently pointed to as typifying the magical realist school, and it features such magical realist images as a woman so beautiful that wherever she goes, a cloud of butterflies follows. One can see imagery such as this in Gilbert's various Palomar stories. In the second installment of "Heartbreak Soup" (from 1983), we learn that the quiet, bright, nonconfrontational child Heraclio can see the ghosts of three dead townspeople. He seems to be the town's link to the spirit world, as when he's asked by his (living) friend Satch, "Are all three of 'em there today, Heraclio? Are they waving back?" Heraclio can only matter-of-factly reply, "Yeah, I guess they're in a good mood today."

Magical realism, with its observation that the fantastic exists within the realm of mundane everyday life, is a literary tool often used to explore the realities of communities that exist outside the cultural mainstream. And this applies specifically to Gilbert Hernandez's town of Palomar, which to the typical American observer couldn't be more outside the norm.

Palomar, described by one local as a town "Where men are men and women need a sense of humor," is a rustic Central American community, one that exists independently of the modern technology and rampant consumerism that so pervades big city life. Hernandez purposely made Palomar the ultimate iconic small town. "I wanted to do stories that were similar to my own growing up in a small town," he says. "I created a fictional town,

AS WE SEE HERE, GUADALUPE HAS INHERITED HER FATHER HERACLIO'S ABILITY TO SEE THE GHOSTS OF DEAD PALOMARIANS.

and [thought that] if I peopled it with fictional characters, then I can apply my experiences and my imagination into those characters' stories." Palomar, as a town, is so small in fact that in one "Heartbreak Soup" story, sheriff (and former midwife) Chelo voices her concern about the advisability of installing phone lines in Palomar. Chelo wonders if this modern form of communication will corrupt the city. "I created the town of Palomar to be a very simple place so those kinds of things could come from it," he explains. "My thinking was just to make [Palomar] so primitive, [to take it] as far as I could go, just to make it as simple and direct [as I could]. [Hopefully] there would be a certain sympathy for the characters living that way. That stuff simply evolved from those beginnings. I don't know how I pulled it off, but I trusted my instincts and went with that. I knew in the near future that I would be able to do things like [Chelo's] phone conversation. Of course I couldn't project exactly what it was, but I got a good feeling about it, [as if to say], 'Well, if I just keep it like this and progress, I'll make something of this.'"

MEET THE HEARTBREAKERS

Indeed, Hernandez not only made "something of this," he made an intricately thought-out cast of characters that quickly became one of the most fascinating dramatis personae in comics history. Readers typically flock to superhero titles for the action-packed set-pieces. Often, they read underground comics for the shock value or titillating subject matter. However, readers came to the Palomar stories to see what happens to the *people*, much as television viewers tune in to their favorite sitcom or soap opera to see what the characters will do next.

And when one thinks of Palomar, one's thoughts immediately turn to mild-mannered, sensible Heraclio, and buxom, brash Luba, two of the most iconic personalities in the series. As with all the other characters in the strip, we see both of these people age and grow throughout the years. "Heraclio and Luba, the one voluptuous character in the cast, are both equal parts based on my personality," he admits. "Heraclio is more an inquisitive, more open-minded, more even tempered, very observant of things, more of a face in the crowd. Whereas Luba is the id."

Heraclio seems distanced from the other Palomarians. Much of this comes from the fact that he went to college "up North," and as an adult he gets a job teaching music at a school outside of Palomar. "Yeah, he gets on the bus and he works outside of town," Hernandez says. But he's quick to point out that Heraclio "comes back to Palomar because he loves it!" Heraclio certainly seems to be someone with a greater sense of the world at large, even if some of the other locals don't appreciate him and mis-pronounce his name as "Hercules." He's more literate than the other Palo-marians, and as such is a fitting contrast to the other characters' more provincial attitudes. "They are not aware of [the outside world]," he says of the other Palomar residents. "I mean, in one of the early 'Heartbreak Soup' stories, ["Sopa De Gran Pena,"] some of the kids talk about Dis-neyland as this strange, magical place. They're not even sure what it is, but to them, it's like, 'Well, someday you go to Disneyland!' You don't go to heaven, you go to Disneyland. And I just thought a naive quality to the characters was something engaging."

Luba is a creature of wild extremes. Constantly wielding a claw ham-mer and equipped with disarmingly enormous mammaries, Luba is one of the most memorable figures in modern comics. We first meet her in "BEM," where she tries to stand up to the slimy creature that we're led to believe is the title character. Even in this early, vestigial phase of her life on the comics page, we get a sense of Luba's strength, her passion, and her unwillingness to ever back down. The monster bats her around like a rag

THE ICONIC AND VOLUPTUOUS LUBA, ROMANCING HER PARAMOUR, ARCHIE.

doll, and for a time we think she's been killed, but she keeps coming back for more! Later we see Luba in the opening "Heartbreak Soup" story arc, "Chelo's Burden," in which she first comes to town and sets up shop as a bath giver, immediately stealing resident bath giver Chelo's business.

Hernandez says that Luba, who drifts from relationship to relationship and can't seem to stay in one place, is a sort of wandering character. "She's displaced," he explains. "She doesn't belong anywhere. I never thought about it too much, it was just a storytelling device that Luba just doesn't belong. She doesn't even belong in her own skin! She doesn't belong in that body, but she's forced to deal with it. She's uncomfortable. She never relaxes, she can never one hundred percent trust people. She's been used so many times! But at the same time, and this is true for real people, at the same time she's very vain. She doesn't hide herself, she doesn't back off, she's pretty proud of who she is, and of what she looks like. But at the same time, she's wary and has to keep moving, or feels that she does. I really like Luba, she's real complex." And how does Hernandez explain her ever-present hammer? "She's always working, she's always defending herself," he says. "That's another part of her vanity. She likes to be an enigma. She's totally schizo. One half of her says, 'Leave me alone! I'm normal!' The other one says, 'Look at me! I'm in this fix!' And that's the same person."

Gilbert Hernandez created Luba to be an empowered character, one whose physical charms distracted you from the substantially thoughtful person on the inside. The concept behind Luba was that if you took the time to get to know her, you'd see that she isn't quite the frivolous floozy she appears to be. However, he's up-front about the fact that her . . . excessive endowments have caused trouble for *Love & Rockets*'s audience. "The trouble with a character like Luba is if you emphasize a character like that too much, you start to alienate readers, [because of] her physicality," he reveals. "Some readers would prefer not to look at somebody who looks like that. There's a period [when she was] in her twenties and thirties where she's still very pretty, very attractive. But I really upped the ante with the voluptuousness, and that was part of the story. But over the years, I still get the sense of [people saying], 'Well, if you didn't have this character it'd be a lot more popular strip!' You open up an issue of *Love & Rockets*, you see Luba, you're not thinking, 'Well here's an empowered character!' They're going to think, 'This guy's drawing cheesecake and I'm not interested.' And that's happened so many times, and so many times I've heard people go, 'I finally read an issue of *Love & Rockets*, and I really liked it! I didn't think it was going to be like this.' So there's preconceived notions just from thumbing through a magazine. But you know, that's part of the character as well. People have preconceived notions of Luba as well."

Luba's voluptuousness also signals something else about her. "The fertility goddess thing is applied to her," Hernandez points out. "She's basically a woman who grew up looking this way, and she does have this nurturing quality to her personality, but at the same time, she didn't ask for it. She's never happy with what people apply to her, even if it's positive." And if another woman saw Luba walking down the street, she might regard the curvaceous hammer-wielder as the village tramp and not know anything about what she's really like. "We have these preconceived notions, whatever bad training we get growing up," he adds. "Luba is my best character! Luba's all these things, but this is comics. Be a grown-up, and accept the way she looks, and understand the character!"

Not that Heraclio and Luba are the only characters in Palomar worth talking about. Not by a long shot. There's the town sheriff (and former midwife/bath giver), Chelo, who even after she ages considerably and loses an eye, is still always recognizable by her ever-present star-shaped badge. Gilbert Hernandez says that Chelo's as much of a symbol as she is a person. Aside from being the law, "[she's] the matriarch," he explains. "But I try to infuse a lot of humanity and humor in such characters. I've had trouble with the police in my youth, so do I have a certain major prejudice toward the police? Sure. So what do you do? You create a character who's a policeman, you know? You deal with certain aspects of your personality, and you go against them sometimes. With Chelo, I humanized [my ideas about] the police. What better way to challenge your preconceived notions than doing the opposite of how you feel about certain people?"

And then there's Pipo, Hernandez's longest-running character. "Interestingly enough, the character that is usually the least brought up is Pipo," he shrugs. "I don't know why that is. She's the most attractive of all the women and she's the only character that's been from the very beginning to now. She was born in Palomar, and now she's a wealthy business woman, and she's still in the series, and yet she's talked about the least. Luba is actually a newcomer to Palomar when I first started the story. Other characters have fallen by the wayside, but Pipo's still here, and I just think that's funny. I think it's taken for granted that she's always there." He attributes Pipo's lack of popularity to the fact that Luba takes center stage in such a major way. "Oh, absolutely," he nods. "I mean, if Pipo's standing in the room, and Luba is standing in the room, you're going to notice how pretty Pipo is *after* you look at Luba. That's just the way it is."

Pipo also has a fascinating character arc. She starts out as a really beautiful little girl, and all the little boys have crushes on her, and then she turns out to be an almost preternaturally beautiful woman and grows up really fast. By age fourteen, she's fully developed physically and a single mother to boot. Desperate, she marries an abusive jerk, Gato. She's very insecure, but after investing in the stock market and divorcing Gato, she starts dating his ex–business partner, who helps her set up a successful sportswear business. She then becomes more confident and less codependent, finally taking control of her own life. Hernandez finds Pipo to be a more down-to-earth character than Luba, and therein lies her appeal.

"The advantages of Pipo over Luba," he explains, "is that readers will enjoy looking at Pipo. They prefer looking at Pipo over Luba, whether male or female. Pipo is so attractive, she's thin, and she never ages! That's a little secret that's, well, no longer a secret. And it's a lot more subtle what's going on with her than what's going on with Luba, who's fire and brimstone. [Pipo] grew up too fast and she became a cynical businesswoman way before she should have. At the end of the first 'Heartbreak Soup' story, you'll notice that she becomes a crafty businesswoman right away. She's fourteen, she gets pregnant by [Manuel], who gets killed. And so immediately, she goes right after the guy who's been in love with her since she was a kid [Gato], and marries him. This is all done very subtly, but the clue is that right away she's interested in a guy that she's never been interested in before; she's got a baby coming, she's got to take care of it, and so it begins there. Of course, she just knows that if she can bat her eyelashes that she can get her foot in the door, so she's really very intelligent. Her instincts for getting things done her way are just very good, other than just her good looks. Anyway, her [character] arc is more subtle, [she's] more able to stretch and change. Already I've mellowed her out. She's tired of being a cynical businesswoman. That's not who she is. She's still the little girl sweeping the steps [in front of] the house."

But the characters in Gilbert Hernandez's stories are about many things under the surface. If Luba and Pipo are metaphors for the way women can be overlooked due to their appearance, the whole cast can accurately be read as an antidote for the lack of Hispanic representation in pop culture. "It actually goes deeper than that," Hernandez explains. "My brother [Jaime] and I are Mexican American. Growing up we realized that, at least in America, that [the thinking was], 'OK, you Latinos are OK, we just don't want to have to deal with you.' Well, our comics were our revenge! [We were saying], 'This is what people look like. This is who they are, and now you've gotta look at them! And we're going to make the best comics we can, and if that works, you're screwed. Because we're just going to do it! We are going to do it more and more!!' I mean, that's pretty arrogant, but we were thinking along those lines, like, 'We'll show you!'"

If *Love & Rockets* was partially conceived as a response to the lack of Hispanic role models and images in American popular culture, it was also a response to the lack of Hispanic characters (well, positive ones, anyway) in comic books specifically. "That was one of many, many things that we were aware of," Hernandez nods. "[Why not] do Hispanic characters? Because we weren't one hundred percent sure of anything in the first issue of *Love & Rockets*. I had done Castle Radium, he could be any ethnicity. You know? But we got pretty good notice right away, and in the first issue I wanted to emphasize the Hispanic part, because there wasn't anything else we could see that was going on in pop culture was satisfactory to us. We were basically filling a need—our own need—in our comics."

Gilbert Hernandez filled this need by making Palomar as populous and diverse as any real small town. Many of the other

© *Gilbert Hernandez; published by Fantagraphics Books*

CARMEN'S QUOTE SAYS IT ALL.

Palomarians, while not as iconic as Luba, Heraclio, or Chelo, are no less multifaceted or colorful. There's the repulsive businessman Gato, a sleazy creature with shifty catlike eyes who somehow manages to marry Pipo. When they divorce, it comes as a surprise to no one. There's Carmen, who eternally looks like she's twelve years old, even when she's pregnant with husband Heraclio's child. Carmen, who resents Heraclio for his bookish qualities, is symbolic of the provincial mentality of Palomar that so many Palomarians are anxious to escape.

Then there's shallow Yankee photographer Howard Miller, who in the "An American in Palomar" storyline arrives with the intention of using Palomar as the subject for a picture book. Howard Miller is symbolic of the American interloper with a massive sense of entitlement who barges into the relative tranquility of an unspoiled wilderness and unintentionally wreaks havoc among the indigenous peoples. Miller has a relationship with naive Tonantzin, a local seller of *babosas* (edible slugs), during which he fills Tonantzin's head with dreams of Hollywood glamour; it's clear that this will end horribly.

There's Israel, whose twin sister disappeared during a solar eclipse when they were both children, an event which haunts him forever. Later he leaves Palomar, going out into the big city of San Fideo, though he does come back to help his—and Heraclio's—friend Jesus in the "Ecce Homo" storyline. After he has an affair with Carmen behind Heraclio's back (revealed in the story "For the Love of Carmen"), Israel promises never to set foot in Palomar again. In a way, Israel becomes a staple of the big city, and more than that, a symbol *of* the big city.

There's Maricella, Luba's daughter, whom we first meet in "Chelo's Burden." More of a peripheral character that we see from time to time, Maricella is nevertheless also someone who can't wait to get out of Palomar and explore the world at large. This is something that we come to understand fully in the "Human Diastrophism" story arc.

Perhaps the richest and most moving of the "Heartbreak Soup" storylines, "Human Diastrophism" is a complex narrative in which we find out that one of the locals (at first we don't know who) is a serial killer, his acts of cruelty witnessed by Humberto, an intense young artist who's slowly driven mad by what he's seen, and too terrified to tell anyone that he knows who the killer is. Meanwhile, the villagers are driven to distraction by an epidemic of loudly chattering monkeys, and Tonantzin is emotionally unraveling after her relationship with Howard Miller went sour in "An American in Palomar."

Against all of this, we see that Luba doesn't really know anything about her daughter Maricella, as when she incorrectly guesses that Maricella is sweet on her friend Riri's brother Hector. This couldn't be further from the truth because of two simple facts: First, Hector is eight years old. And second, Maricella is a lesbian, and Riri is not only her friend, but also her lover. This points out another aspect of Gilbert Hernandez's *Love & Rockets* stories (also evident in Jaime's stories): the characters' fluid sexuality. Many of the characters in Palomar are gay, lesbian, or bisexual. Riri and Maricella have steadfastly positioned themselves in the closet, Maricella in particular being particularly frightened of incurring her mother's wrath. And Israel (like many of the other former and current Palomarians) is bisexual, having both male and female lovers.

Hernandez says that creating gay and bisexual characters was a response to another chip on his shoulder, the homophobia so prevalent in American society. "Growing up, we perceived gays as normal," he explains. "You know, different but equal. And where that came from, I'm not really sure. But we just saw it that way early on. It's a completely normal thing in the real world. I grew up with a childhood friend, he was my best friend. And later on, not until we were adults, I found out he was gay. But looking back, I remember how much grief he got. For being different, for being a sissy, whatever you want to call it. And I really regret probably going along with a lot of that. But at the same time, when we weren't bothering him, when we weren't teasing him, he was just a friend. He was just a regular guy. So that's how we perceived it. We just looked at the characters that way, too. We went, 'You know what? In the real world, people just kind of live that way! They're just living their lives and that's how we are going to portray [them].'" Although, the very fact that Maricella is afraid to come out as a lesbian until she's left Palomar indicates that some of the other characters in Hernandez's stories aren't quite as nonjudgmental as their creator. "It was just kind of a different take on the way Jaime was handling his stories," he explains. "Basically, Jaime handled it as a day-to-day life for these characters, and I just decided to go with the angle where it was difficult for the characters."

LOVE & GENDER

The fact that *Love & Rockets* has always embraced all forms of sexual orientation is one indicator that this wasn't your typical testosterone-driven comic book. Another indicator, perhaps related to the realistic portrayal of gay women, was its realistic portrayal of female sexuality in general, and of female characters, emotions, and experiences of all kinds. As opposed to many other underground and independent comics written by men, where women are the love interests or the objects of desire (especially in autobiographical comics like Chester Brown's *Yummy Fur* and Joe Matt's *Peep Show*), here women comprise most of the main characters, and in a sharp role reversal, the *men* are often the love interests. For this reason, *Love & Rockets* has always had as many female readers as males, something of an anomaly for a comic book written and drawn by men. Hernandez says that when he and his brothers get fan mail for *Love & Rockets*, "Usually half of it's women. If not more."

Speaking of women, Palomar is a matriarchy. This is typified by the fact that many of the women in the town seem to symbolize various societal institutions and ideals: Chelo is the law, Pipo is big business, Luba's cousin Ofelia is responsibility, Luba is the home and hearth. Hernandez says that the strong female characters in his comics come from the women in his family. "I guess it goes back to mom and grandma," he elaborates. "We grew up in a house pretty much with mom and grandma running things, because dad was never around. And he died at a young age, [when] I was in the fifth grade. We grew up without a father figure, which has its own problems, but at the same time we learned to look at women as leaders. My mother had a bunch of sisters, so it was my mother, her sisters, her grandmother that we were living with when our father died. And none of them were you know, 'paint your nails, eating bonbons all day' [kind of women]. You know? These were working women. So that was lacking in other pop culture, so we basically filled a lot of holes in pop culture, because we had a different experience."

A HEARTBREAKING HIATUS

In 1996, *Love & Rockets* ceased publication for what looked like an indefinite period of time. This was the end of the Palomar stories, which made sense, since many of the locals had moved out of the picaresque town. In the final storyline, also called "Chelo's Burden" as a way of bookending events from the first story arc of the same name, a reunion of sorts is staged when many of the characters who've left Palomar over the years return to help out after a devastating earthquake rocks the town. Luba's buxom sex-bomb of a daughter Doralis, who'd since left town to become a television star, has returned, as has her friend and fellow celebrity Pipo. Howard Miller also returns, taking pictures of the ruined city and visiting Tonantzin's grave in the process. At the end of "Human Dias-trophism," we'd learned that Chelo punished Humberto for his silence by forbidding him to draw anyone. So now, to satisfy his artistic urge, he carves sculptures of the other characters out of rock. Aided by fellow artist Augustin, he buries said sculptures underwater. We see many of the series' major characters immortalized in stone, a fitting epitaph to the "Heart-break Soup" series. And finally, after Luba's elderly guardian Gorgo is hunted down by hit men (sent by his enemies, who have been trailing him for decades, as we saw in the previous story arc, "Luba Conquers the World"), Luba and Gorgo realize that it's no longer safe to remain in town, and everyone gathers to see them off. This is most appropriate, as the series began with Luba's arrival in Palomar, and it ended with her exit.

As comic books are a perfect medium for serial fiction, there is often the temptation to keep running a comic book series long after it's lived out its welcome. Gilbert and Jaime Hernandez both realized this and decided to stage a preemptive strike by cancelling *Love & Rockets* in 1996. "I just didn't want to spoil it," Hernandez explains, "I just didn't want to keep going on and on and on. [I hate comic books where] the artist doesn't know his own decline, so I just stopped it before that could happen, before I was alerted of my decline. I don't mind now slipping into the void, but then it was important for me to finish it when I thought it was still cookin'. I do miss some of the old Palomar characters, but since I'm not going to go back there it's difficult to come up with reasons to bring them back."

However, just because Hernandez had closed the book on the city of Palomar, that didn't mean that he would never again tell the continuing stories of the various Palomarians themselves. For now that they were away from their quaint, provincial hometown, what would Luba and company do now? Good question, and one that he's answered in a variety of spin-off titles in the late nineties.

The most prominent of these spin-offs was *Luba*, a ten-issue series that began in 1998 and chronicled the title character's post-Palomar life, filled with all the sexual intrigue that made the original *Love & Rockets* series so potent. There was also the series *Luba's Comics and Stories*, which focused on what might be called Luba's "satellite characters": her put-upon cousin Ofelia; her equally curvaceous sisters Petra (a lab assistant) and Fritzi (a lisping psychiatrist); and Petra's spunky towheaded daughter, Venus.

And then there was the unfortunately short-lived children's comic book anthology *Measles*, edited by Gilbert Hernandez, with stories by *The Magic Whistle* cartoonist Sam Henderson and *Nickelodeon* magazine cartoonist Johnny Ryan. Also included were Hernandez's own stories about Venus and Petra, this time geared specifically to a family audience. (Brothers Jaime and Mario were also frequent contributors.) But what an interesting change of pace to see G-rated *children's* stories featuring characters like Petra, who in titles like *Love & Rockets* would be dealing with complex issues like infidelity and betrayal. But here in *Measles*, the drama in Petra's life was limited to tending to Venus when the latter came down with the measles. It's a convincing demonstration that the *Love & Rockets* characters were some of the most *human* people seen in comic books, and therefore adaptable to the full range of human emotions and experience.

ROCKETING TO THE FUTURE

Since Gilbert and Jaime Hernandez stopped *Love & Rockets* in 1996, Gilbert Hernandez not only continued chronicling the adventures of various former Palomarians such as Luba and Venus in spin-off titles, he also worked on various non-*L&R*-related projects. One such project was the short-lived 1999–2000 DC/Homage Comics series *Yeah!*, created and written by cartoonist Peter Bagge (of *Hate* and *MAD* fame), which Hernandez illustrated. "It was about a teen girl rock band who performed in outer space," he explains. "They were famous in outer space, but on Earth, nobody had ever heard of them." *Yeah!*, a family-friendly comic book for preteen girls, was also something of a change of pace for Hernandez in that it was the first series he illustrated that he didn't create and own. For once, he wasn't his own boss. "I was trying sort of a neo-*Archie* style, so that was a learning experience," he reveals. "You know, working with somebody else on the script, and basically having to hammer out three pages a day, three careful pages a day. It was really difficult for me. I've known Peter for years, and when he approached me with the project, you know, I'd enjoyed his work for many years so I felt comfortable in going along with him. I've been asked to illustrate other writers [where] I just didn't gel with it. And with Bagge, I'd just known his work for so long, I knew that it would be a relatively loose experience. It turned out to be different; not with Bagge or anything, all that was fine. Just that my new, professional speed really wore me out. I was still doing my own stuff at the same time and it was kind of hard." Also difficult to bear was the poor reception the whimsical, bubbly series received. "It was supposed to be a regular monthly but it only lasted nine issues," Hernandez shrugs. "It just didn't connect with the audience that it should have."

But in the years since *Love & Rockets*'s demise, Hernandez found that he missed delineating the adventures of his lovably flawed characters. So in 2001, like a legendary rock group announcing that they're "putting the band back together," Gilbert and Jaime Hernandez relaunched *Love & Rockets* to universal acclaim. Not burdened by the rigorous publishing schedule of mainstream comics, the series comes out an average of four times a year. "It's actually coming out more than it ever has," he says proudly. "There's no end in sight! Unless the readers and the retailers say so. If it just doesn't sell anymore, we'll stop."

And what's on the horizon for the architect of Palomar? "With *Love & Rockets* right now," Hernandez reveals, "I just sort of want to finish the story arc I've been working on for years and return to what I was doing earlier, a few years ago, where I'm just going to do a single story, an issue that [isn't beholden to] continuity. Basically a few short stories that I've been itching to do for a while. That, and I'm actually working on a comic for DC/Vertigo, my first [non-*L&R*] graphic novel. Completely original material, no continuing characters, just for this one-shot. It's like a hundred and twenty pages, and it's a new experience because I realized I've been working in comics for over twenty years now, and I realized I haven't done a graphic novel yet. A real one [that wasn't] a collected edition." What made him take the plunge into the world of original graphic novels? "It was time," he nods. "I hadn't done it, and there was a space open at DC for those interested in creator-owned publications. You know, 'Let's let the creator do what he does on his own.' It's called *Sloth*. It's about teenagers living in a small town, oddly enough, and one of the teenagers basically wills himself into a coma for a year, and wills himself out of it. It's about how he did it, why he did it. Because he's not really sure why he did it, and so we just dig into his mind throughout the story to [find out]. It's about bored youth, bored teens in a small town."

Another one of Gilbert Hernandez's more recent projects isn't even a comic book. It's the self-produced DVD *The Naked Cosmos*, a parody of old-time kids' shows, in which both he and his wife, Carol Kovinick, play multiple roles inspired by classic kids' show hosts and late-night performers like Vampira, Captain Kangaroo, Uri Geller, and Soupy Sales. The show centers around phony television prophet Quintas, played by Hernandez himself in a Captain Kangaroo wig, as he promotes his "Cosmic Connections to the Collective Mindstream" through his no-budget television show. "It's basically sort of a mix," he explains. "In the old days, they used to have horror hosts. Usually just some goofy weatherman who just put on a wig and stuff, and they became real cult figures for kids in those days. So we basically did a parody of that, my wife and I. But I also mixed in [a parody of] those psychic infomercial guys. So it's about a guy who's basically a fraud. He [pretends to] connect to the cosmos, and he introduces other characters. We did it as a lark, and a guy got a hold of the tape, saw it, loved it. He's a professional editor in films and he said, 'I could re-edit this and we could get it out there.'"

The *Naked Cosmos* DVD, composed of four twenty-two-minute episodes of the faux kids' show, made its professional debut at the Alternative Press Expo in San Francisco during the Spring of 2005 (with a free companion comic book by Gilbert), and is currently available through some of the more discerning comic book specialty shops nationwide, as well as over the Internet through distributor Bright Red Rocket.

Clearly, Gilbert Hernandez is branching out into new worlds and new media. The restless, easily bored kid from Oxnard was able to turn his pop-culture obsessions and fascinations into a career, garnering a cult of hard-core fans in the process. His "Heartbreak Soup" stories have enticed a generation of readers, and given much-needed representation to Latinos, the gay and lesbian community, and women. Today, even the earliest stories don't seem dated, and they still stand as some of the only comics stories in which both Hispanic characters and gay characters are non-judgmentally portrayed; they're not a symbol for anything, they just *are*. His sprinkling of *brujas* (witches), ghosts, wish-granting trees, and other magical realist elements into his stories set the "Heartbreak Soup" tales apart from virtually anything else being done in comics. And in all the years he's spent crafting stories of everyday people and their quest to find love and redemption in a cruel world, the main lesson he's learned is that Gilbert Hernandez is happiest when he's doing his own thing.

KYLE BAKER

SELF-PORTRAIT.

"Look at Humphrey Bogart! We live in a society which permits an ugly man named Humphrey to be a sex symbol! How many ugly female stars are there?"

—From *Why I Hate Saturn*, 1990

The phrase "comic book" was first coined because it was the easiest way to describe the magazine-length reprints of newspaper comic (as in funny) pages. Think *Thimble Theater*, *The Katzenjammer Kids*, *The Yellow Kid*, *Li'l Abner*. Even serious adventure strips like *Little Orphan Annie* and *Terry and the Pirates* had the requisite comic relief supporting characters. And today that tradition continues, as most newspaper strips are of the humor variety, from *Garfield* to *Cathy* to *Boondocks*. Comic books, on the other hand, couldn't take themselves more seriously, and therefore the term has become something of a misnomer. You can't swing a dead mutant in comic book land without hitting a dark knight swearing to avenge his murdered parents or a hideously misshapen hellspawn trying to redeem himself. Humor comic books have a history of selling very badly; witness DC's *'Mazing Man* and *Plop!* or Marvel's *Comix Book*. And this makes Kyle Baker's career all the more fascinating.

Kyle Baker is the cartoonist who put the "comic" back in comic books. In an industry where graphic novels concern either brooding, jaded super-heroes or brooding, jaded Gen-X (or Gen-Y) loners, Baker tells defiantly funny stories. There's no hidden agenda here, there are no existential musings on whether we're alone in the universe or the fact that with great power comes great responsibility. His graphic novels like *Why I Hate Saturn* are about everyday people falling in love, fighting, screwing, stabbing each other in the back, and generally making the audience guffaw with their infantile shenanigans. The fate of the world isn't at stake; the only thing at stake in a Kyle Baker book is often the protagonist's rent check, which may or may not bounce. His stories are a welcome breather from the all-too-dramatic fare normally found in most comics, and their relata-bility and lightness of tone make them not only welcome, but necessary.

But like a film or television comedian who's decided he needs to broaden his range, he's used his growing clout to found his own publishing company and divide his time between frothy, humorous fare like *The Cowboy Wally Show* or his *Plastic Man* series for DC; sprawling biblical epics like *King David*; and serious works with political and historical significance, like his breathtaking self-published *Nat Turner* miniseries, or the political satire graphic novel *Birth of a Nation*, his collaboration with *House Party* director Reginald Hudlin and *Boondocks* creator Aaron MacGruder. And somehow the polymath workhorse has found time to write and direct various animation projects for film and television, often overseeing every aspect of each production in true auteur style from his studio in Manhattan's SoHo district. As a renaissance man and a storyteller with an innate sense of the theatrical, Kyle Baker is more than comics' court jester; he's its Woody Allen.

THE UNINTERESTED YEARS

Kyle Baker was born in 1965 in Queens, New York. From an early age, he knew what he wanted to do for a living, and what he *didn't* want to do was draw comic books. He really set his sights on becoming a newspaper strip cartoonist, like his hero Johnny Hart, of *BC* and *Wizard of Id* fame, and he much preferred comic *strips* to the staid, humorless world of comic *books*. "When I was a kid comic books were lousy," he laughs. "And all the good cartoons were in the newspaper. I [also] liked a lot of magazine [gag] cartoonists. That was what I really wanted to do, and comics was really just a job that was easier to get. In the eighties, it was not a good business. There was no profit-sharing, they wouldn't give the [original] art back sometimes. And so, a lot of the really good people just passed through, like [legendary cartoonists] Neal Adams and Berni Wrightson. When they became successful, they got out and got some paying jobs in advertising or Hollywood. Berni ended up doing [conceptual design for] *Ghostbusters*. And Frank Frazetta got out and started doing commercial art, [*MAD* legend] Jack Davis quit, so it was an easy job to get."

Another problem with the comic book industry was its aversion to humorous subject matter, something that irked the young Baker on a very personal level. "They just weren't making any funny comic books. I liked *MAD* magazine, and when I was just starting in the early eighties *MAD* didn't want anybody. I dropped by [their offices] one day, and they said, 'We like writers, but we've got plenty of artists.'" Ironic words, since a decade later, Baker would be among the new generation of *MAD* artists.

But at this point, circa 1983, Baker took the first industry gig that would have him, a high school internship at Marvel Comics. He quickly segued from interning to apprenticing as a background inker for a couple of established pros, like inking veteran Josef Rubenstein. And then in an unprecedented move, the Marvel editors—who normally never printed gag cartoons—published gag strips by Baker spoofing their established characters like the X-Men. "Because I still wanted to do gags," he explains, "Marvel would have me do little one-shot gags about Marvel characters." How did he, a comics neophyte, land this admittedly rare gig? "It was because I was around the office," Baker reveals. "And I was trying to break in. Things were a lot looser back then, and [it was] easy for them to say, 'Kyle's a nice guy, he's a little kid, and he's trying to get a break! Let's make some room in this comic book for a little gag by Kyle.' Back then, it was not a business where anybody was killing themselves. It was an entry-level job. The money was lousy."

Also during this period, Kyle Baker graduated to his first credited comic book inking work, on top-tier titles like *New Mutants*. Heady stuff for a high school kid. "I was surprised I stayed in it as long as I did," he shrugs. "I didn't really take it seriously. The first few years I started doing comics to pay for college. I was going to the School of Visual Arts, again to learn a useful trade. Even though they had a cartooning program with Will Eisner, Harvey Kurtzman, and guys like that, I didn't take any of those classes, because I was already drawing [professionally] for Marvel and I was hoping to get out. So I was taking classes like Marshall Arisman's magazine illustration [class]. And I worked for [famed illustrator / graphic designer] Milton Glaser for a little while, as part of an alumni thing, he used to hire recent graduates. I drew books for him, for pay. And I wanted something like Milton Glaser was doing. I thought maybe I could do that." After a couple of years at SVA, Baker was forced to drop out, due to the overwhelming amount of work he was getting inking comic books.

THE COWBOY WALLY LEGEND

But while he was stuck in what he then saw as the comic book ghetto, Baker did something extremely savvy. Still an inker for Marvel, he took control of his career by moonlighting on a personal project that showed the industry just what he could do. This project featured the wacky exploits of a bumbling, unscrupulous children's show host named Cowboy Wally. Eventually, his Cowboy Wally project gestated into the acclaimed 1988 graphic novel *The Cowboy Wally Show*, completely written and illustrated by Baker himself. But it didn't happen overnight.

"What happened was, I was [still] trying to get in the newspaper," he reveals. "And it's hard. I tried to put together some strip samples. I did a funny animal thing that went absolutely nowhere, and then I did *Cowboy Wally*, which was supposed to be a strip. So I did however many months of strips you had to do to get the samples package together, and sent them to the syndicates and they didn't want it. It's just hard to get a strip [in the newspaper]. They only pick up one strip a year, and you really pretty much have to wait for somebody to die. Literally. That still largely [happens]. They're still not picking up any new strips, and you have to wait for, you know, the guy who's drawing *Blondie* to die. And then, once you're in, they are more likely to look at your submission, so that's what *Cowboy Wally* was."

Since it didn't seem like anyone was dying anytime soon, Baker was convinced that *Cowboy Wally* was going to remain a fondly remembered pipe dream. And then in 1986, the comic book industry was rocked by a trio of graphic novels: Frank Miller's *The Dark Knight Returns*, Art Spiegelman's *Maus*, and Alan Moore & Dave Gibbons's *Watchmen*. Suddenly, comic books were thought of as bona fide literature, critics and the news media sat up and took notice, and major publishers were starting to look for works to package in graphic novel format. Baker's Cowboy Wally project was a perfect fit for this new arena. "In the late eighties, everyone started to think, 'Woo! Graphic novels, might be some money in 'em!'" Baker confirms. "So a lot of publishers, like Doubleday, started getting into graphic novels. But they didn't know anything about producing them, and didn't have any budget. So Doubleday couldn't afford any real [famous] cartoonists, because they didn't want to pay for them. So they ended up with me and [*American Splendor* writer/creator] Harvey Pekar as the graphic novel line. We were both cheap. And for me, it was just because this editor had been asking for cartoonists. And a friend of mine, who worked in the bullpen at Marvel [in the production department] was talking to an editor at Doubleday, and he said, 'Oh, I know a kid who needs a break, and he's got this big stack of strips that are really funny, and he can't get rid of them. Maybe he'll let you have them.' So *Cowboy Wally* ended up being a graphic novel. The format was designed so that I could use whatever gags I had. Like if I had a hospital gag, I could have Cowboy Wally make a hospital show. Once I ran out of hospital gags, I could move onto the next thing. It's random, and that's why. It was a newspaper strip that was re-edited to make a book."

The Cowboy Wally Show is a mockumentary-style shaggy dog story that follows the obnoxious-yet-guileless huxter Cowboy Wally as he goes from

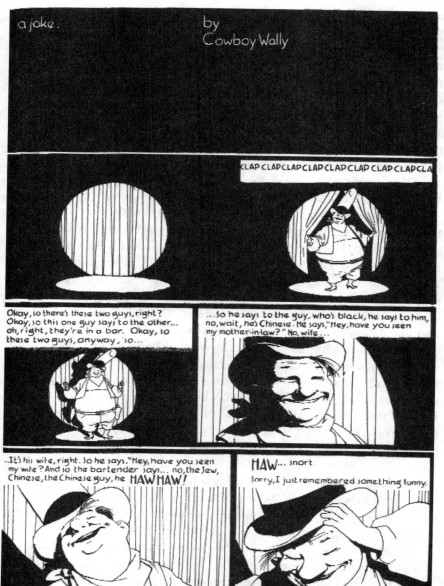

THE GRAPHIC NOVEL THE COWBOY WALLY SHOW PROVED BAKER'S METTLE AS A WRITER/ARTIST.

blackmailing his way into a career in children's television to his abysmally mediocre, grade-Z foreign legion epic, and his attempt to film a remake of *Hamlet* while still in prison. It's like watching an expensive sports car plow into a police blockade. Yet Baker packs the loosely plotted narrative with so many jokes and gags, many of them culled from his sketchbooks, that the reader can't help finding these pathetic characters hilariously endearing in their ineptitude.

And because Kyle Baker had intended to use *The Cowboy Wally Show* as a writing sample to get work in the film and television world, the protagonist's sheer idiocy was Baker's commentary on the worst that the showbiz world had to offer. In fact, the character of Cowboy Wally evolved after Baker had spent time reading books on the entertainment industry; he thought it would be fun to conjure up the most blissfully ignorant sort of pandering sleazeball. "Because I was interested in that business, I was reading up on it," he explains. "Anything I'm interested in doing, I'm always reading about successful guys in that field. So I was reading about filmmakers and TV producers that I was interested in. I read [*Happy Days* and *Laverne & Shirley* executive producer] Garry Marshall's book, and stuff like that. And I was watching a lot of TV at the time, and just wondering who was making this incredibly bad TV, and what kind of meetings you'd have to make awful stuff like that."

The character was also inspired by some of Baker's own dealings with the high mucky-mucks of the comic book world, who shall remain nameless. What he read about in his research on the world of film and television, it turns out, "was very similar to what I was going through in comics. Before I'd established myself in comics, they'd tell me to change everything. Every time you'd come up with something new, everybody thinks you must've made a mistake. You bring something in that doesn't look like Neal Adams, and they're like, 'Oh, you've messed up! Let me show you how to make it look more like Neal Adams!' And you're like, 'No no, it's *supposed* to look like that!' So I was familiar with how corporations just destroy artists' work. And that's kind of what *Cowboy Wally* is about, where you have that screenwriter [character], Lenny, who's very interested in doing something good. [Lenny wants to do] Shakespeare, and Cowboy Wally turns it into a piece of crap. I understood that thinking. They're like, 'Let's do *Hamlet*! Oh, what if we changed everything about *Hamlet*?'"

Today, *The Cowboy Wally Show* has gone through several successful reprintings and is remembered fondly by critics and audiences alike. The book is something of a benchmark, and it occupies the same place in Baker's oeuvre that *Take the Money and Run* did for Woody Allen; that is, it's his debut as a writer/artist, and in that way, it set the precedent for all the graphic novels he was to produce thereafter. But in 1988, at the time of *Cowboy Wally*'s release, it was something less than a blockbuster. Although people today seem to have conveniently forgotten this minor factoid, the book was actually a flop. Kyle Baker surmises that *Cowboy Wally*'s lack of success was due to it being the first of its kind: a humorous graphic novel. It took a few years for people to catch up to a product that was ahead of its time. "A lot of my books are like that because they're new," he shrugs. "With something like *Cowboy Wally*, there wasn't even a graphic novel format really. This was back in the eighties. *Cowboy Wally* was just a disaster. Nobody had ever heard of me, nobody had heard of the format, there was just [the general consensus of], 'What the hell is this thing?' There was just no precedent! There was no such thing as an original graphic novel. If you did a humor book, it was a collection of newspaper strips or something that was [culled] from [an existing comic book series], but this was like a new product by a guy nobody knew! Now, there's such a thing as the 'Kyle Baker graphic novel,' I put a completely different one out every year, and they say, 'Oh, this is another one of those books, that's like the last ten books.' But at the time, people didn't know what to make of *Cowboy Wally*. And it didn't do well. And the same thing with *Why I Hate Saturn*."

Why I Hate Saturn was Kyle Baker's follow-up to *The Cowboy Wally Show*. Even though *Cowboy Wally* wasn't a success, it had amassed a modest following, and Baker was also becoming even more well known for his work on titles like DC's *The Shadow* and *Justice, Inc.* He was gaining marquee value, so he was allowed to create a sophomore effort. Maybe this one would break through. No dice. Even though *Why I Hate Saturn* is now deemed a classic, on its release in 1990 (through DC's now-defunct sister line Pirhana Press), it was considered somewhat less than successful. "DC was trying to introduce a new format to a new market," Baker explains. "And *Why I Hate Saturn* was part of a line of books that was designed for the bookstore market. Because of the success of *Maus*, DC, just like Doubleday, said 'Oh, we've gotta get into graphic novels! We've gotta get into the bookstores!' But again, that was because it was a start-up, they didn't know what the hell they were doing, they couldn't get it into the stores."

In *Why I Hate Saturn*, Anne is a freelance writer with a fondness for procrastination, booze, and her platonic male friend Ricky. Anne and Ricky routinely get together in dive bars and bitch about how pathetic their sex lives are. After a night spent not working on her new novel (of which she has yet to write word one), Anne drunkenly staggers to the door to see her nutso sister Laura, who's proclaimed herself "Queen of the Leather Astro-Girls of Saturn," and who's on the lam from her all-powerful, megamani-acal billionaire boyfriend Murphy. Murphy has the authorities in his pocket, and there's no way to escape him. Naturally, Anne and Laura go on the run, and the wackiest road movie in comics history ensues. And so goes *Why I Hate Saturn*, a sort of *Thelma and Louise* meets *The Odd Couple*, told in sketch-comedy-size vignettes that riff on everything from gender discrimination to homelessness to mental illness, all in a distinctly satirical, laugh-out-loud way rarely seen in the comic book medium. Like *The Cowboy Wally Show*, *Why I Hate Saturn* is very loosely plotted. As in Baker's previous book, emphasis is not on dramatic structure, but *Saturn* is a more character-driven work than its predecessor.

As with many of Baker's later works, it's also got serious themes on its mind. *Saturn* isn't afraid to take to task institutionalized racism or homophobia, as long as it does so with tongue firmly planted in cheek. Consider the scene where Anne meets up with Mike, her editor at *Daddy-O* (a spoof of magazines like *SPIN* and *Details*), and she finds out that Ricky—who isn't a journalist—is on his way there as well. Turns out that Mike wants Ricky (who's black) to write a "black column." They got Ricky to do it because they wanted an outsider's perspective. "I hate to tell you this, Mike," Anne says, "but Ricky's black." Ricky explains what Mike's afraid to divulge; that any black man who's educated and speaks articulately is not considered "really" black. "It's the same reason people think you're a dyke," he offers. "People think I'm a dyke?" Anne asks, shocked. Ricky shrugs, "Take it as a compliment. I've learned to." As arguably the most prominent black cartoonist working in mainstream comic books, Baker has taken it upon himself to deal with the issue of race in many of his works, and in a less didactic, less predictable way than would be expected in this often formulaic medium. *Why I Hate Saturn* was his opening salvo in discussing the issue of race. Even if the issue is only mentioned fleetingly in that book, it would be explored in further detail in Baker's later works.

Baker also used *Why I Hate Saturn* to turn certain overly serious issues on their heads. For example, by 1990 he'd found that American culture had ceased to find the humor in the comic drunk, formerly a staple in the repertoires of comedians ranging from Charlie Chaplin to Jackie Gleason. And Baker thought that this was a shame. "I try to think about stuff that's not being done at the time," he explains. "*Why I Hate Saturn* was an attempt to bring back the funny drunk. You never see a funny drunk anymore! You know, [these days] the drunks always have a [serious] problem, but in [the movie] *The Thin Man*, Nick was always drunk, and it was very funny. I'm a big W. C. Fields fan and that was his whole routine, was that he was always drunk, or needed a drink. That stuff's funny!" Another politically correct cliché that Saturn tried to shatter was that the mentally ill need to be treated with kid gloves. You certainly can't laugh *with* them, let alone laugh *at* them. Anne's sister Laura is crazy; she thinks she's from Saturn. But she's crazy in a harmless, fun way that's reminiscent of screwball comedy characters of the 1930s. "[*Saturn*] was also sort of like a *Harvey* rip-off," Baker offers, referencing the classic play and film about a gentle loon and his invisible rabbit pal. "In *Harvey*, Elwood P. Dowd could be the crazy guy, but maybe he's *not* crazy! In *Why I Hate Saturn*, Laura thinks she's from outer space and you know, maybe she is! And who's she hurting? That's the whole thing about *Harvey*: OK, the guy thinks he's got a giant rabbit, but who's he hurting?"

THE SITCOM FROM SATURN

Why I Hate Saturn was Baker's last graphic novel for almost a decade, as he spent the majority of the nineties working very steadily in the world of commercial illustration, drawing caricatures, spot illustrations, and covers for some of the staples of the magazine publishing world, including *VIBE*, *MAD* magazine, *Esquire*, *Rolling Stone*, and *New York* magazine (for the latter, he drew the weekly *Bad Publicity* strip for three years). He was also doing some very distinctive comic book work, like his 1991 adaptation of Lewis Carroll's *Through the Looking Glass* for First Comics, or the Dark Horse Comics *Instant Piano* humor anthology (which he produced with fellow cartoonists Evan Dorkin, Mark Badger, Stephen DeStefano, and Robbie Busch). By all accounts, his star was on the rise, and in the nineties he finally made good on his long-held goal to work on film and television projects.

Ironically, Baker's first job in television was writing the pilot of *Why I Hate Saturn*, which was then (circa 1990) in development as a major network sitcom. "What happened was, DC Comics sold it to Warner Brothers, their parent company, for three thousand dollars," he reveals. "Of that, I got half of it, but they didn't want me to work on it. I asked them, 'Let me work on it!' Otherwise, I'm only going to make fifteen hundred. They said, 'Well, write a treatment.' They weren't going to let me write a whole script, they figured my issue was that I wasn't getting enough money. So I wrote a treatment, and my stuff is unpitchable. A lot of what makes my stuff work is the execution. If you describe *Why I Hate Saturn* it's not that interesting. I actually had a lot of problems with that book because nothing happens in it, so if you try to describe it, it's like, 'And now they talk, and sit around, and they've got no job, really. She complains a lot.' So I tried to describe my idea for the pilot and they turned it down. They turned down my treatment, and to write this treatment I had to join the

"Hey, there's flowers in the fridge. Aren't you taking this herbivore thing too far?"

"Those are your flowers. I put them in there so they'd stay fresh. Like I said, I wasn't sure when you were coming home. You're never here any more."

"I came home once last week. Didn't recognize it, so I left. Flowers, that's nice. You never get flowers from your boyfriends."

"I tell them not to."

"I can't wait to hear this one."

"It's just--well, why is it that when we see something beautiful, we want to possess it? We end up killing it, destroying the beauty that made us want it in the first place."

"You fool! That's the whole *point* of relationships!"

© Kyle Baker

THE FRICTION BETWEEN SISTERS ANNE AND LAURA DRIVES MUCH OF THE COMEDY IN BAKER'S <u>WHY I HATE SATURN</u>, A GRAPHIC NOVEL THAT ALMOST LED TO A SITCOM.

union, because Warner Brothers is a union job, and that cost me fifteen hundred dollars! Then I decided I should probably get an entertainment lawyer, because my graphic novel got an option, but I didn't make a dime! I got this entertainment lawyer, and he needed a retainer of fifteen hundred bucks. So I had lost fifteen hundred bucks on this deal."

Knowing that this could be his last chance to wrangle any creative control over the television version of his comics brainchild, Baker asked for and won another opportunity. "I said, 'Give me one more chance,' so they said, 'OK, bring something in on Monday,'" he explains. "They were just trying to get rid of me, and I knew that I just wasn't going to get a decent treatment together by Monday, that it was never going to work. So, I wrote the entire pilot script over the weekend, and it was really funny, so they gave me a two year deal." So, what was the plot of the pilot episode of *Why I Hate Saturn*? "Anne didn't have any money for the rent," Baker explains, "and she's trying to get a story in by the deadline so she can get her money for the rent. And her sister Laura shows up, and she spends the whole show trying to get rid of her. And somehow something ends up going wrong with the story, so she's not getting it in by the deadline, and just when the landlord is about to evict her, her sister comes up with the money, which sets up why they're going to be moving in together." And there's a reason we still have yet to see *Why I Hate Saturn* on television; it never got past the script stage. "They couldn't cast it, even though they had a couple of people attached," Baker laments. "Parker Posey was attached for about five minutes. The reason [the project] ended, and the reason that CBS and NBC passed on it, was because it was 'too narrow of a demographic.' They thought everybody was the same age, [they said], 'It's a little too New York-y,' so in other words nobody wanted to watch a show about young people in New York. This was before *Friends*, before *Seinfeld*."

However, not all of Kyle Baker's adventures in Hollywood were this frustrating. He's also worked on productions of which he's justifiably proud. A prime example is the 1994 HBO made-for-cable movie *Cosmic Slop*. This sci-fi anthology film was masterminded by the producing-directing team of Reginald and Warrington Hudlin, a.k.a. the Hudlin Brothers, who together had worked on such films as *House Party*, *Bebe's Kids*, and *Boomerang*. Funk mastermind George Clinton (after whose 1973 album the film was named) served as the Rod Serling–style narrator of the multicultural *Twilight Zone*–type show. Kyle Baker's segment, "Tang," concerns a couple on the dawn of the "Black Revolution," who discover that the *real* enemy comes from within. Baker's involvement with *Cosmic Slop* began with a phone call from Reginald Hudlin. "He asked, 'Know any good short stories that we can option?' I said, 'Oh, I remember reading this Chester Himes story, "Tang,"' and then he called me, 'OK! I optioned it! When can you start writing it?' And then I picked up the book, and I hadn't picked up the book in about ten years. I didn't realize the story was only three pages long! It was a good story, it had a good ending, and a good beginning. And I just had to sort of add twenty minutes in the middle. And it was fun!" The three-tier, hour-and-a-half movie that aired on HBO was supposed to be the pilot for a regular *Cosmic Slop* series, in the vein of earlier HBO anthology series such as *Tales from the Crypt*. However, after its first airing, *Cosmic Slop*'s racially charged social satire sparked controversy among viewers, and HBO shelved plans to serve up regular helpings of *Slop*.

But even though *Cosmic Slop* didn't go to series as planned, it was an attempt to do something smart, insightful, and different. And unfortunately, many of the projects Kyle Baker was getting offered didn't have similarly high intellectual standards. "I sold two shows accidentally one day to Warner Brothers," he recalls. "The network had turned down *Why I Hate Saturn* because it appealed to too narrow a demographic. And my producer told me this and I asked, 'What do they want? Something that appeals to the broadest possible demographic?' He said, 'Well, yeah!' So I'm like, 'Well, what? *Ghost Chimpanzee*? And he's like, 'How would that go?' So I pitched *Ghost Chimpanzee* and he bought it! The other one was *Bounty Hunter Dad*."

Kyle Baker didn't feel like he would make his mark telling stories about ghost chimpanzees. And even though he was still working as a writer, an illustrator, or both on various comic book titles, he needed to get back to the more creatively satisfying world of graphic novels, and he needed to do it soon. He would do so with a graphic novel that would let the comic book industry know he was back—with a vengeance.

HERE YOU ARE

Even though Baker still has one foot in the world of film and television, starting in 1999 he began to plunge back into the world of graphic novels. He missed the creative autonomy of writing and illustrating his own stories without studio interference. So, by utilizing what he'd learned thus far about dramatic structure while hunkering in the showbiz trenches, he created *You Are Here*.

He readily admits that his frustration with the Hollywood machine spurred the development of *You Are Here*. "I'd just gone back to comic books with *You Are Here*, and was having a much easier time doing that than the Hollywood stuff, where they make you change everything, water it down and make it lousy," he confesses. "Because I had found that while I was going to make a good living out of Hollywood, there was nothing I could point to that was any good! Like when I do a [graphic novel], the books—because I have total control—come out good! And then you can show it to somebody and say, 'See this *good* piece of work? I did this, and I can do this for you too!' And it leads to other things, either other books or other kinds of jobs. Whenever I've done a Hollywood thing, it's been rewritten and redone so much, and ruined, and it either doesn't come out, or it comes out totally changed with your name not on it, or it comes out totally changed *with* your name on it but it sucks! I mean, you could give it to somebody as an example of your work, but then you'll be asked to do more of that same awful work." By contrast, Baker can point to *You Are Here* and his other graphic novels as undiluted Kyle Baker productions.

You Are Here was Baker's first full-color graphic novel. It was also the first Kyle Baker graphic novel to make a profit. By 1999, when *You Are Here* was released by DC's adult imprint Vertigo, graphic novels had become far more commonplace than they were when *The Cowboy Wally Show* was first printed. They even had their own section in bookstores, and that accounts partially for the success of *You Are Here*. But the book was also a bit of a departure for Baker. Like actor-filmmaker Mel Brooks, who scored a hit with his third directorial effort *Blazing Saddles* (after *The Producers* and *The Twelve Chairs* had bombed), Baker put his all into the certified crowd-pleaser *You Are Here*, and it shows. This is him at his best; the characters are relatable as always, but unlike his previous two books, which are largely episodic, this is a book the reader will want to finish in one sitting. *You Are Here*'s success can be attributed to the fact that the stakes for the characters are considerably higher than those in his previous graphic novels.

The story might be best described as an action movie with the soul of a romantic comedy: Noel Coleman, a likeably compassionate ex-convict, has reinvented himself as a commercial illustrator, and he's tried desperately to hide his shady past from Helen, his refreshingly naive, unflappably chipper fiancée. But when serial killer Vaughan Dreyfuss begins stalking Noel because of a past indiscretion, Noel's seedy past threatens to catch up to him, tearing a gunshot-sized wound in the idyllic, pastoral life he has planned with Helen.

In *The Cowboy Wally Show*, all that's at stake (if anything can be said to be at stake) is the title character's career, and as Cowboy Wally's a blithering idiot, it's hard to care. In *Why I Hate Saturn*, the lives of Anne and Laura are jeopardized when they're hunted down by Murphy, but Murphy's so comically larger-than-life that even though the characters are in peril, you know everything's going to be OK. However, in *You Are Here*, the reader has absolutely no idea how things are going to turn out. This is evident when Noel's friend and confidant Oscar is brutally murdered by Dreyfuss about halfway through the story. By showing us this gruesome act, Kyle Baker is signaling us that we're in for a different sort of a trip than in his previous books. And because the threat is real and brutal, and uncompromisingly so, we can't wait to see what happens next. Everything might *not* be OK. We have to turn the page to see whether Noel lives to see tomorrow, whether his relationship with Helen will survive the revelation that he's not the man she thought he was, whether Oscar's stripper girlfriend, Tracy, will discover the fate of her gruesomely mangled beau. It's still a comedy, but a comedy about real people with real problems who really might not all be alive by the end of the book.

EPIC PROPORTIONS

Now that he had a bona fide hit on his hands with *You Are Here*, Kyle Baker had even more lofty goals that he wanted to explore. He had a couple of biblical epics in mind, one intended for the screen and one designed for the page.

The first biblical epic that Kyle Baker wanted to explore was *Noah's Ark*, which he'd been thinking of adapting as a graphic novel in 2000. He was approached by an independent film producer who wanted him to do *Noah's Ark* as an animated feature instead. But Baker felt the producer wanted him to compromise his vision in such a way that the finished product would have given audiences a watered-down, uninteresting adaptation of this potentially thrilling epic, so he did something he never does: he walked off the project.

The next biblical epic Baker had in mind, the story of King David, would be done the way he'd originally envisioned *Noah's Ark*: as a graphic novel. And it would be done his way, with complete creative control. In 2001, Vertigo published Baker's *King David*. The sweeping epic recounts all the high points of David's life: his beginnings as the peasant boy who slew the giant Goliath; his days playing the harp for King Saul, who grew increasingly jealous of this new champion of the people; and his life as King, when he exhibited his most human failings, including the adulterous affair that led to the murder of one of his soldiers. Clearly, Baker had waited until he had a few other graphic novels under his belt before he crafted this, his most ambitious, sprawling graphic novel to date. And perhaps most importantly, here he was able to create a full-scale biblical epic, uncensored, and without any interference.

"When the *Noah's Ark* movie didn't work out," he admits, "the *King David* graphic novel was a response to that, because I have more control over the comics. I have the power to take the comic book away basically." He also reveals that rather than creatively limiting him, working for a big corporation like DC frees him up to a certain extent. "Working on *Noah's Ark* for an independent producer was worse than working for a [major Hollywood] studio," he explains. "The thing about a studio is they can lose the money. Like even when I'm doing something with DC, I can be a little bit more experimental in the work than I can with self-published stuff. Because self-published stuff has to sell immediately! When I do something like *King David*, that's going to take a couple of years for people to catch up to. And a lot of my books are like that because they're new."

King David is a perfect example of this, as comic book fans are used to seeing the King David story told in a bland, painfully reverent style meant for young children (as in the well-regarded Silver Age comic book series *Classics Illustrated*), not the glaringly adult narrative Kyle Baker stresses, wherein his characters embrace colloquial speech, and the harsher moments are leavened with smidgens of comic relief. Baker's version of the venerable Bible story might be a bit jarring for readers not used to his style, and it goes without saying that it's *not* for the kiddies.

Kyle Baker also sees *King David* as a way to combat a disturbing trend in pop culture; the underrepresentation of black people both in front of the camera and behind the scenes. The characters in *King David* are markedly not white. But *King David* is only one book, and there are still notably few black characters or creators in the comic book industry. Baker feels that to truly have more black representation in comics, "You need more black publishers. The reason I started drawing comics is, I was interested in animation but it was too expensive for me; you have to buy film, you have to buy cameras and lights and develop it. Whereas with a comic book, I only need a pencil! It's really low-tech. That's the biggest way to change that. At my age, rather than complain about what's on TV, I'll make a TV show that people should be watching! Like with *King David*, every time I see an adaptation of the Bible there's always these blue-eyed English people, and I always find that confusing. Any of those movies, it's always Gregory Peck or something. So, rather than complain about it, and saying, 'How can Cleopatra look like Elizabeth Taylor?', write *your own* Cleopatra!" And to put his money where his mouth is, Kyle Baker started his own publishing company.

A KYLE BAKER INSTANT PERENNIAL

By 2003, Kyle Baker had spent a year directing Bugs Bunny shorts for Warner Brothers. Before that, he'd also served as a script doctor on the 2003 release *Looney Tunes: Back in Action*, starring Brendan Fraser, Heather Locklear, and Steve Martin (as well as a certain Wascally Wabbit). He'd even done conceptual designs for 2000's blockbuster hit *Shrek*. And he was still publishing graphic novels like Vertigo's *Undercover Genie* (2003), a collection of short takes, some of which had been inspired by his Hollywood experiences, such as "Bounty Hunter Dad." By any standard, he was doing well, but there was still one venture he hadn't tried: self-publishing. So he put together a sample self-published comic book, largely consisting of autobiographical strips about his family, and sold it at the famed San Diego Comic-Con, the most hotly anticipated American comic book convention of the year.

"When I first started self-publishing I wanted to do comic books, and that was the plan," he reveals. "I published one comic book—*The New Baker*, which was a *New Yorker* parody—and I realized that was a terrible way to make money, a dollar at a time. This was my first try at printed comic books, and it was just a test. I wanted to start small before losing a bunch of money. I said, 'Let me just try to print a tiny comic book and sell it at a convention.' But you'd sell ten books and you go, 'Wow! I just sold ten books and I made ten dollars, and it took me an hour to make ten dollars!' Whereas I was also at a table selling all my old graphic novels, *Cowboy Wally* and stuff like that. If you sell five copies of *You Are Here*, you make a hundred bucks. Comic conventions are interesting places, too, because the recognition is not as connected to the sales. Like, in the regular world outside of comic conventions, people are most familiar with my best-selling graphic novels, or the jobs that had the biggest circulation. You know, like *VIBE* magazine had a huge circulation, so, you say, 'I did the cartoons in *VIBE* magazine,' and they say, 'OH! Yes, I've seen that.' But at conventions, You get the guys who know you because you worked on *Spider-Man*, or the guys who liked my [comics adaptation of the 1990 film] *Dick Tracy*, because that book sold a lot."

Baker learned much from this experience, and the first lesson was that his new self-publishing venture, Kyle Baker Publishing, would largely court the "regular world outside of comic conventions," where people mostly knew him for his graphic novel work. Using *The New Baker* as a template, in 2003 he published *Kyle Baker Cartoonist Volume 1*, a collection of short comic strips and gag cartoons, many of them about the trials and tribulations of being a husband and father. One strip in *Volume 1* features Baker's adorable daughter Lillian gesturing in what looks like an attempt to scratch herself. She goes on like this for a couple of panels, never quite satisfied, then marches over to her father, who gamely tickles her, scratching her itch as it were, causing her to erupt in a fit of blissful, satisfied giggling. The following year, he published *Kyle Baker Cartoonist Volume 2: Now with More Bakers*, which also largely featured autobiographical gags about his wife and kids (between *Volume 1* and *Volume 2*, his third child was born, hence the subtitle).

With such focused subject matter, why choose an ambiguous name like *Cartoonist* for the project? "The reason the book is called *Cartoonist*," Baker explains, "is that I had to have a title for

© Kyle Baker

BAKER HOPES THAT HIS AUTOBIOGRAPHICAL SERIES OF HUMOR STRIPS, THE BAKERS, WILL ONE DAY BE AS UBIQUITOUS AS PEANUTS OR FAMILY CIRCUS.

this book, and I didn't know what was in the book. But I had to put the ad in the catalogue, so I figured I'll call it *Cartoonist* because I know it'll have cartoons in it! I don't know what the cartoons'll be, because I was just going to throw a bunch of random stuff in there and if people laugh it goes in the book, if people don't laugh I throw it in the garbage. And I have the luxury of learning as I go; like, the second *Cartoonist* book I think is better than the first one, because the first one I really had no idea what I was doing."

Now that the strips in *Cartoonist* about the Bakers have proven such a hit with readers, the next book of autobiographical family strips, published in 2005, was appropriately entitled *The Bakers*. And Baker has big plans for these characters, whom he hopes will become beloved characters in much the same way as Bil Keane's *Family Circus* or Charles Schulz's *Peanuts*. "*The Bakers* is something I'm going to retire on," he explains. "My plan for all of the self-published stuff is keeping the stuff going forever. My goal is that in like twenty years I'll have twenty or thirty books in print and doing like all these companies did, like Disney or Hanna Barbera, just keep moving stuff around and putting out different formats. Like, I'd like to color in some of *The Bakers* stuff, put them out in smaller hardcovers for children, put them in more of a 'Golden Books'–style format—stuff like that. Same material for different audiences."

However, not all of Kyle Baker Publishing's comics are laugh-out-loud funny. He's also explored more serious subject matter, such as his recent four-part series *Nat Turner*. Based on the actual prison confessions of Virginia slave Nat Turner, who led an 1831 slave rebellion before being arrested, hanged, and mutilated, this series is an unflinching look at the cruelty and violence that shaped a true freedom fighter. "With *Nat Turner*," Baker points out, "people might think, 'Oh, it's probably like those other boring black history books I've seen.'" The gripping manner in which the series is paced ensures that Baker has proven these naysayers wrong. Before we meet Nat Turner himself, we follow his mother as she's kidnapped from her home in Africa and made to endure the rigors of the Middle Passage. We see how another African woman who was packed into the same boat threw her baby to the sharks, rather than have the child grow up in this living hell. This series is the antithesis of a dull, academic treatise; it's living history.

Kyle Baker also points out that it's important that the *Nat Turner* series is

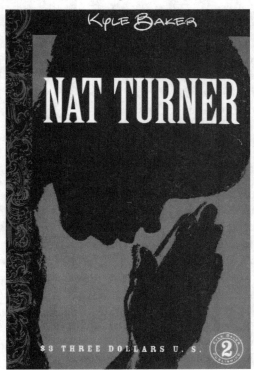

© *Kyle Baker*

A BRUTAL DEPARTURE FROM HIS OTHERWISE COMEDIC OEUVRE, BAKER'S NAT TURNER MINISERIES IS BASED ON THE VIRGINIA-SLAVE-TURNED-FREEDOM-FIGHTER'S OWN PRISON CONFESSIONS.

based on Turner's actual confessions, rather than a second-hand account of the events. "I think when you're dealing with this touchy a topic it's important to keep it factual," he says, "because I'm guessing, just based on the African American response to *Nat Turner*, that people are going to get on my case about the book [if I have factual errors]. If you start fabricating facts, then that gives them more ammunition: 'Oh, not only is this man bad, but he's lied to make his point! He's exaggerated the situation and skewed facts.' Like what they said about Michael Moore's last movie [*Fahrenheit 9/11*], 'Oh! It's very one-sided, he distorted things!' So I'm basically just sticking to historical fact, and it's a good enough story that I don't have to really puff it up." With *Nat Turner*, Baker has indeed turned a corner creatively, demonstrating that he can tell a serious dramatic story with the same ease and mastery as the comedic yarns he's famous for concocting.

QUALITY, JOLLITY, BUT NO FINALITY

Even though Baker is involved with his own personal projects like *Nat Turner* and *The Bakers*, he's still got one foot anchored in the world of mainstream superhero comics for companies like DC and Marvel. In fact, two of his more recent mainstream comic book projects have proved to be somewhat controversial. *Truth*, his 2003 miniseries collaboration with writer Robert Morales, told the tale of the unknown first Captain America, a black man the U.S. Army experimented on, in a blatant reference to the infamous Tuskegee experiments conducted on unwitting black soldiers during the 1940s. Some Caucasian comic book fans, used to their Captain America sporting a lily-white countenance, screamed bloody murder on Internet chat rooms all over the country. Similarly,

© Kyle Baker

EVEN AFTER ALL HIS ACCOMPLISHMENTS, THE PROLIFIC KYLE BAKER IS STILL VERY MUCH A WORK IN PROGRESS.

Baker's recent *Plastic Man* series, arguably the only version of *Plastic Man* to successfully duplicate the spirit of whimsical mayhem epitomized by the character's creator Jack Cole, outraged some comic book fans weaned on the character's watered-down 1960s and 1970s incarnations, who didn't expect a fully comedic take on the character.

In both these cases, Baker isn't surprised by the outcry, given the current state of comic book fandom. Still, he isn't about to change for a few irate fans. "If you're going to review *Captain America* [on the Internet], it's because you're way into *Captain America*," he points out. "And if you're way into *Captain America*, you have to like the way they're already doing it. *Truth* is designed for people who aren't [already] reading *Captain America*. Marvel said, 'We're trying to attract a different reader, we're trying to broaden our audience.' Same thing with *Plastic Man*. If you want kids to read it, you have to make it for kids. But then the five guys that were still reading *Plastic Man* get very upset that you changed it, but you're just going to have to lose those five guys to pick up the thousands [of new readers]." It's Baker's confident attitude and willingness to color outside the lines that have made a Kyle Baker comic book—be it something that he's created or a work-for-hire effort—an object of cultish devotion.

Baker's pathway toward becoming part of the pantheon of modern comic book masters has been an unexpected one. The apprentice inker who tried for years to get out of the "comic book ghetto" now regards the comics medium as the one in which he has the greatest amount of creative control. Graphic novels such as *The Cowboy Wally Show*, *Why I Hate Saturn*, *You Are Here*, and *King David* are classics. His film and television work—like the "Tang" segment he scripted for HBO's *Cosmic Slop*, or the "Break the Chain" music video he directed for rapper KRS-1—has won the respect of industry peers and tastemakers alike. And with Kyle Baker Publishing, he's turned his life as a husband and father into a comic book sitcom in the pages of *The Bakers*, while exploring more serious historical themes in series such as *Nat Turner*. The scary thing is, he's still relatively young, and true Kyle Baker fans realize that he hasn't even gotten started yet.

NEIL GAIMAN

"And then, fighting to stay asleep, wishing it would go on forever, sure that once the dream was over, it would never come back . . . . . . you woke up."

—From *The Sandman*: *The Wake*

By all accounts, the so-called British Invasion that rocked the American comic book industry in the 1980s raised the bar for comics storytelling and made the argument for "comics as literature" that much more convincing and palatable to a non-comics-reading public. And one of the fiercest arguments for comics as literature usually came in two words: *Neil Gaiman*.

Neil Gaiman, more than any other comic book writer, demonstrated what you could do with the canvas of mainstream comics. No, you didn't have to tell superhero stories; yes, you could tell deeply felt, powerful, emotionally resonant fantasy or horror stories, or even (heaven forbid) straight dramatic stories about normal human beings that didn't involve gods or demons; and yeah, OK, if you had to, you could even tell super-hero stories, but you could also bend and twist the superhero genre in ways that made the superheroes more human, stories that took them to the next level of relatability beyond what writers like Stan Lee, Chris Claremont, and Denny O'Neil had done in the 1960s and '70s. Stories that took into account other forms of dramatic storytelling such as theater or cinema, or the long-form novel, and incorporated those other forms into the comics medium. Yes, you could do all of this, even within the limits and dictates of a mainstream American comic book publishing company. And you could even get *girls*—actual females—to read comics (imagine!).

In accomplishing all of the above with his acclaimed DC horror-fantasy series *Sandman* (1988–1996), Gaiman inadvertently started a minirevolution in comics, one that led to the creation of DC Comics's sister division Vertigo, the Miramax to DC's Disney. By turns whimsical, moving, disturbing, and hilarious, *Sandman* incorporated a range of emotions and a cast of well-drawn characters rarely seen in the world of work-for-hire comics. But *Sandman* was only the beginning, and since then Gaiman has pushed the boundaries of the comics medium, dragging this seminal twentieth-century art form kicking and screaming from out of the darkness and into the twenty-first century.

POSTCARDS FROM OZ

Neil Gaiman was born in Portchester, England, on November 10, 1960. From an early age, he found himself interested in reading, and particularly in reading comic books. "I don't honestly remember a time that I wasn't interested in comics," Gaiman says. "Just as I don't really recall a time that I wasn't interested in books. When I started reading, all books had pictures. And I don't think I made any kind of distinction in my head between books that were text with occasional big pictures and books that were comprised of small pictures. I just loved stories. And then *Batman* happened."

Young Gaiman, then about five years old, had discovered the *Batman* television show starring Adam West. "My father mentioned to me that in America they had a *Batman* TV show," Gaiman recalls. "And I said to him, 'What is Batman?' And he explained that it was somebody who dressed up as a bat and fought crime. And I had never encountered any kind of bat at that age except a cricket bat. And that was a very strange thing—you know, 'Why would anyone dress up as a cricket bat and fight crime?' And then it came on television, and then I just remember being incredibly excited, I was finally going to get to see this guy! And he didn't look anything at all like a cricket bat, which puzzled me." The *Batman* television show became a way for Gaiman and his father to bond. "My dad at the time was working for a property company, I think it was, in Portsmouth, which meant that he was away during the week and home on weekends," he explains. "And his way of sort of making it up to me was he knew that I loved Batman, and there was an English comic at the time called *Smash* which had Batman on the cover."

Gaiman admits that *Smash* was the one that did it, that first opened his eyes to a whole new world of comics literature, proving that there was more out there than just the caped crusader. There were entire universes in these little multipanel pages! *Smash* was a mixture of English comics and reprints of American comics. These reprints were Gaiman's first exposure to the works of Stan Lee, Jack Kirby, and Steve Ditko, and titles like *Amazing Spider-Man*, the *Fantastic Four*, and the *Incredible Hulk*. "My first encounter with the *X-Men* is Jean Grey turning up at the school," he recalls wistfully. "It's not full color, it's black, white, and red. But it's actually rather larger than the original comics. And I wind up in these conversations with people like Alan Moore. We were reading the Marvel stuff as it came out." Gaiman was hooked, and he wanted to know where these strange superheroes came from. "And being an observant kid, within about a year, I then found American comics," he says. "I remember just lying in the hall and reading them, and they were the *Batman*, *Brave and the Bold*, and the *Justice League of America* and [their predecessors] the *Justice Society of America*." The roster of the Justice Society included the original 1940s Sandman, a.k.a. Wesley Dodds "who fired these sand guns, and wore a gas mask and a suit."

Neil Gaiman has fond memories of those days, and he recalls that reading American comics was "like reading postcards from Oz. [In American comics,] there were all of these cultural assumptions that were being made that meant nothing, and thus were really, really, really cool. For example, I remember to this day a comic in which Superman has gone into some kind of alternate universe. Perry White's now a pizza chef and Superman is staring at him, [using] x-ray vision or whatever, staring through a wall. And Perry White is throwing something round and sort of doughy into the air, and he's tossing the pizza dough. There were no pizzas in England in 1967. And they really didn't turn up until 1979–1980. So, pizza was something that you simply didn't see, and the idea of somebody tossing dough and wearing a funny hat was every bit as strange as the idea of somebody using their x-ray vision to look through a wall and see this thing. There were no fire hydrants in England. So [in Superman] there are all these fire hydrants everywhere, and I was never able to quite figure out what a fire hydrant [was], 'What are they? They squirt water and no fire comes out of them, and what's the deal with them?' Everything was as unlikely as everything else."

THE DREAM BEGINS

In his teens, Gaiman started becoming seriously interested in a career in comic books. One day during high school, he thought that his chosen profession was about to receive the encouragement it so sorely lacked. He couldn't have been more wrong. "When I was about fifteen going on sixteen, we had our school's careers counseling day," he recalls. "And I was very excited. 'Cause finally I was going to find out how to get into comics! I go in, I sit down. I'm very excited, and he says, 'Well, young man, very interesting results of your tests. Amazing vocabulary, numerical skills are very good, and so . . .What do you want to do?' And I said, 'I really, really want to write American comics.' And he said, 'Well, how do you go about doing that, then?' And I said, 'I have no idea. You're the outside careers adviser. You tell me.' And he just kind of sat there for a bit, looking very very uncomfortable. And then he said, 'Have you ever thought about accountancy?' And I said, 'No, I've never thought about accountancy.' And then we sat there and stared at each other for a while and then I said, 'Shall I show the next boy in?' And he said, 'Yes, you may as well.' And that was my careers counseling. After he said that, there was a real level on which at that point I gave up [on comics]. I mean, I just assumed that you couldn't get there from here."

In retrospect, Gaiman feels no sense of remorse that he gave up on comic books at that juncture. "To be honest," he explains, "I think if I had gone out of school and started working in comics at the age of twenty-one or whatever, I just would have written some crap comics, because I didn't have anything to say. I would have copied the style without actually having any content."

His desire for a career in comic books extinguished, Neil Gaiman decided to become a freelance writer. Starting in 1980, he took a few tentative stabs at fiction writing, even writing an early draft of a children's book, and after eighteen months of collecting rejection slips he steadied his resolve and switched to journalism. And suddenly, he had a career. Lying about his experience, he quickly landed the first of many high-profile assignments and began writing for such varied publications as *Time Out*, *Sunday Times Magazine*, *Penthouse*, *Knave*, *City Limits*, and the *Observer*. He also wrote a biography of the rock group Duran Duran. "Looking back on it," Gaiman reveals, "I'm really pleased with the way that things happened. I got to be a journalist, which is an incredibly good thing for a kid to be who doesn't really know the way the world works, but wants to know. And you talk to people from all sorts of social strata, you move through all sorts of different worlds, you know, all of that kind of stuff."

THE MOORE THE BETTER

Even though he'd begun a successful freelance career and had decided against pursuing a career in comics, Gaiman still continued to read comic books, albeit in moderation. He limited his comics consumption to reprints of Will Eisner's classic 1940–1952 comic strip *The Spirit*, which in the early 1980s were being reprinted in comic book form by various independent publishers both in the United States and abroad. "*The Spirit* stuff I remained fascinated by," he admits. "They were wonderful. So I'm reading and loving *The Spirit* but have this theory that I was probably wrong about comics!"

But then Gaiman started taking notice of Alan Moore's radical revamping of the DC Comics series *Swamp Thing*. Created in 1971 by Len Wein and Berni Wrightson as an atmospheric but fairly run-of-the-mill horror title in the "beauty and the beast" vein, *Swamp Thing* concerned scientist Alec Holland, who had been turned into the titular bog beast and separated from the woman he loved. The core story had been completely cracked open and put back together by Moore, who refashioned this saga of a monstrous plant creature as a theater of ideas replete with psycho-sexual overtones, existential musings, and a cinematic sense of pacing. Moore's Swamp Thing was the latest in a long line of "plant elementals" who only *thought* he was scientist Alec Holland; he was really just a walking vegetable with the late scientist's memories. Gaiman was fascinated from the get-go. "I was reading this Alan Moore stuff," he recalls, "and [I was] going, 'You know what? Comics are a medium that have as much potential as any other, and this Alan Moore stuff is as interesting as anything that I'm seeing on the stage or seeing at screenings of films or getting to review with books! This is the real thing!'"

Gaiman decided to use his clout as a freelance writer to meet this burgeoning comics icon. "In '85, when my first book came out, *Ghastly Beyond Belief*, I sent a copy to Alan, with a note just saying, 'I love your stuff, here's something I did,' and got a phone call maybe three days later from Alan saying, 'You bastard, I've lost a writing day because of you!' We started talking on the phone, we became sort of telephone pen pals. And Alan was a big fan of [horror authors] Ramsey Campbell and Clive Barker, these sort of people that I knew, and there was a convention in Birmingham. Alan came to the convention, 'cause he wanted to meet those guys, and I said I'd introduce him and look after him. And at one point during the weekend I said, 'Look, can you show me what a comic script looks like? I have no idea, and I've always wanted to write comics and I don't know how you write comics.' And he said, 'Sure.' And I went away and wrote one script and sent it off to Alan, and he said, 'Good! It's got problems, but it's getting there.' And so I wrote another one, and sent it to him, and he said, 'Yeah, that's a proper story.' So that was cool. This was early '85-ish. And that story eventually got published in an anthology called *Midnight Days*, drawn by [*Swamp Thing* artists] Steve Bissette and John Totleben. It was a *Swamp Thing* story, 'Jack in the Green.'"

Once Neil Gaiman started writing comics, he desperately wanted to continue. He sought out anyone he knew who had any connection to the comic book industry. "So the next thing that happened was bumping into a guy at a pub," Gaiman laughs. "And we got chatting and he said, 'What do you do?' I said, 'I'm a journalist, what do you do?' He said, 'I write comics.' I told him about these two scripts that I'd written. And the phone rings about three days—maybe a week—later. He explained that he was doing a comic with young, untried new talent. Brave new talent. Slowly it became apparent that things that we were being told had perhaps a rather more tenuous relationship with reality than we were at first led to believe. You know, the offices were actually the offices of a telephone/telemarketing company that he'd been fired from, and the money to put this thing together wasn't really happening. I don't think there was any harm in him—but there were definitely sort of delusions of grandeur. Or delusions of competence.

"But on the other hand, there were people like me, and [artists] Dave McKean and Mark Buckingham, and a bunch of good young talent there. And we started putting together a comic. The trouble was, it was now starting to happen, and this guy wasn't actually in a position for it to happen. And then suddenly he's trying desperately to sell this stuff to [independent U.S. comics publisher] Eclipse, and we're going, 'Hey, hey, what's happened to this brave new comic you were doing?' And this comic sort of went down. But Dave McKean and I had now met, and we liked each other's work very, very much. Adverts have been taken out for this new comic in Paul Gravett's magazine, *Escape*, and he came down to see what was going on. [Gravett] was never actually paid for the adverts, but did not hold that against the talent. He asked me and Dave if we'd be interested in doing a five-page story for *Escape*. And then to his credit, when we came back a week or so later and said, 'Can we do a forty-eight-page graphic novel called *Violent Cases*,' he said yes."

VIOLIN CASES

The graphic novel *Violent Cases*, written by Neil Gaiman and illustrated by Dave McKean, was published in late 1987 by Titan Books (in association with *Escape*). The book is a meditation on time and memory, how one's memories of childhood events change and distort as one gets older. The book was an attempt by Gaiman and McKean to do something that had nothing to do with superheroes or science fiction, to tell a completely adult story in graphic novel form. It was the beginning of a long and fruitful creative partnership.

Violent Cases starts with a present-day Neil Gaiman facing the viewer and telling us, "I would not want you to think that I was a battered child." He then goes on to tell us about an incident that occurred when he was a child: Gaiman's father accidentally sprained his son's arm while trying to drag him upstairs to bed. He takes his son to an osteopath who is rumored to have treated Al Capone. The kindly old doctor tells young Gaiman about gangsters who carry "violent cases," which is the way the seven-year-old Gaiman mishears the phrase "violin cases." The young Gaiman finds himself at a friend's birthday party with an odd magician, and he escapes from the party to a pub next door, where he finds . . . the osteopath! The child's imagination spins out of control as the old physician tells him stories about his younger days in mob-infested Chicago.

From there, however, the story begins to get fuzzy: Did the kindly old osteopath look like Albert Einstein, or rather like Humphrey Bogart's partner in *The Maltese Falcon*? Did gangsters really come to take the old man away? How reliable is one's memory? How do you separate truth from fiction when too much time has elapsed, and the intervening years have muddled the two together into a sort of mess? "*Violent Cases* is such an odd story," Gaiman explains. "People would say, 'Is it true or not?' And I'd try and explain that it's kind of like a mosaic table, all the little red squares are true, but the red squares aren't actually the picture. They're just things that make up the picture."

And what did Gaiman's father think of the rather frank portrayal he received in his son's book? "Yes, my father grumbled to hear that people would assume that he'd spent his entire life abusing me as a child," Gaiman laughs. "Which is really not the case. The weird thing about both *Violent Cases* and [my other semiautobiographical work] *Mr. Punch* is having created these weird little fictions that then go off and live in my family memory, to the point where I had an aunt asking me about some of the stuff in *Mr. Punch* and saying that she thought it was a bit puzzling because wasn't I too young to remember some of this? And I had to point out that actually I was too young to have remembered pretty much all of this. That at the point where my grandfather actually *did* own an amusement arcade with a mermaid in it, I was barely born. I was never actually there. I think there are elements of that in *Violent Cases*. Although I'm really pleased.

"*Violent Cases* for me was all about being the father of a three-year-old. And it all came out of throwing Mike, my son, on my shoulders and walking him up to bed, carrying him off because he wouldn't go to bed at that time. And just remembering doing exactly the same [thing], being carried up to bed by my dad, and banging on his back trying to get him to put me down. Then remembering as well that I thought, 'If I had a kid I'd never do this,' and here I am doing [it]. This was the place that *Violent*

Cases began for me. It was the idea of just remembering what it was like to live in this world sort of occupied by giants, in which everything was incomprehensible. Every single piece of information was new!"

BLACK HAWK KID AND OTHER TALES

Violent Cases gave Neil Gaiman what he desperately needed at that point: a reputation. And rather than having a reputation for being a workman-like spinner of superhero tall tales, he was in the enviable position of occupying a rare place in the comic book pecking order, that of a writer with a unique, distinctive voice. It didn't hurt that the British Invasion was by then in full swing, with various British comics creators working for DC Comics. During the mid-1980s, Alan Moore was writing *Swamp Thing* and various one-shot *Superman* and *Green Lantern* stories, *Judge Dredd* artist Brian Bolland was illustrating the twelve-part Mike W. Barr–scripted maxiseries *Camelot 3000*, and artist Dave Gibbons was working on *Green Lantern* with writer Len Wein and *Watchmen* with Alan Moore. Clearly, British talent was seen as having a new and different sensibility, one that the Powers That Be at DC were keen to exploit. "When Dave and I started working on *Violent Cases*, people from DC Comics were coming over on a little talent scouting expedition," Gaiman reveals. "I found out where they were [staying] from Alan Moore, and dragged the rather protesting and grumbling 'they-don't-want-to-see-us' Dave McKean up to the hotel room of [DC editors] Dick Giordano and Karen Berger, and that was where it all began. We walked out of there with an agreement to put together a proposal for Black Orchid."

Black Orchid, a magenta-clad superheroine created in 1973 by writer Sheldon Mayer and artist Tony DeZuniga, was a fairly nondescript character, one who boasted arbitrary superpowers such as flight and super-strength, neither of which plays off any sort of "orchid" motif. In fact, given the lack of excitement she inspires, one might question why Gaiman and McKean opted to reboot such an unmemorable heroine. But Black Orchid wasn't the first pick on Gaiman and McKean's list of characters they wanted to revive for DC. They pitched numerous, more popular characters that others were already in the process of revamping. "And I just started pulling DC characters out of my head and trying to get more and more obscure. Finally I said, 'Uh, Black Orchid.' And Karen Berger said, 'Black Hawk Kid, who's he?'

"And Dave and I go down to the bar, and he looks at me with his lugubrious long-suffering sort of what-have-you-got-me-into-now face, and he says, 'Great, you're going to get me drawing cheesecake for two hundred pages.' I said, 'No, honestly not.' He said, 'I wanted to do something noble. I wanted to do something with an ecological theme about the death of the Amazon rainforest.' I said, 'I'll put that in there!' He said, 'Oh, OK.' And I went home, plotted *Black Orchid* on the way, phoned Dave McKean the next morning at arts college and told him the plot, pitched him the entire story. It was about a forty-five-minute phone call. And Dave still tells me about how he took the phone call in the corridor, where the phone was. And just stood there, listening to me while I told him the story. Slowly, a line of people who wanted to use the phone lined up behind him, and they couldn't work out what he was doing because he never said anything. He was just standing there. It was like some strange piece of performance art: Man Holds Phone to Ear."

Neil Gaiman and Dave McKean's three issue *Black Orchid* miniseries was a radical departure from the 1970s version of the character. Whereas Alan Moore's take on Swamp Thing was a loving tribute to the original Len Wein and Berni Wrightson concept, here Gaiman kept only the name Black Orchid and scrapped virtually everything else. At the start of the first issue, Gaiman has Black Orchid killed off, clearly wiping the slate clean. We learn, among other things, that the Black Orchid wasn't human at all! When Dr. Philip Sylvian's childhood friend Susan Linden was murdered, he took her genetic material and used it to grow a plant/human hybrid known as the Black Orchid. (It's implied that this is the 1970s version of the Black Orchid, whose secret identity and origin were always shrouded in secret.) However, this plant hybrid wasn't the *only* Black Orchid! Dr. Sylvian created two other hybrids, and both of them hatch after the original's demise, one of them an adult, the other a child. Neither Black Orchid fully comprehends who or what she is. The two surviving Orchids attempt to evade both billionaire crime boss Lex Luthor's team of thugs and ruthless killer Carl Thorne, while encountering various longtime DC characters along the way, such as Swamp Thing and Poison Ivy, both of whom accentuate the "plant" motif that runs throughout the series.

After Gaiman was given the green light and started writing the series in earnest, the DC brass had an alarming epiphany. "We were sort of halfway through it," Gaiman laughs. "I had written #1, and Dave was working on it, when the people at DC suddenly went, 'What the fuck are we doing?' And Karen phoned me up, and she said, 'Look, we're not actually sure this is a very sensible thing to do, because we've been thinking about this. You're two guys nobody's ever heard of, doing a character that nobody's ever heard of. And a female character at that! Female characters don't sell. We think that this may be a huge mistake.' And we said, 'OK, well, what do you suggest?' And she said, 'Well, maybe you guys should make some kind of name for yourself, so if you did a monthly comic of some kind, and if Dave did a *Batman* comic, then you guys might have some kind of name." Dave McKean's "*Batman* comic" was the acclaimed inmates-take-over-the-booby-hatch graphic novel *Arkham Asylum*, on which he collaborated with writer Grant Morrison. And Neil Gaiman's "monthly comic of some kind" was a little thing called *Sandman*.

PAPER GODS

In late 1988, DC released *Sandman* #1 (cover-dated January 1989), written by Neil Gaiman, penciled by Sam Keith, and inked by Mike Dringenberg. Sandman is many things, but first it's best to establish what he *isn't*. He *isn't* a revamping of any of the previous DC characters called Sandman, even if that's how he was pitched. He certainly isn't Wesley Dodds, the 1940s Sandman "who fired those sand guns and wore a gas mask and a suit." Even moreso than Black Orchid, the only thing that this Sandman truly has in common with the previous characters of the same name is just *that* . . . the same *name*. And rarely does anyone in the *Sandman* series even refer to this character as "Sandman." This character isn't a superhero, like previous bearers of that sobriquet. This "Sandman" goes by many names. One *could* call him Sandman, but the other characters in the series *usually* call him Morpheus, Oneiros, Lord Shaper, Nightmare King, or simply . . . Dream. Neil Gaiman's Sandman is the physical projection, or rather the personification, of dreams. He inhabits and rules "the Dreaming," the place where we go when we sleep, the place where we spend a third of our lives.

The major DC superheroes almost never appear in the pages of *Sandman*, except in minor cameo roles. It's a commonly held assumption that the reason so few well-known characters from the established DC Universe pop up during the run of *Sandman* is that Neil Gaiman insisted on it. Originally, in fact, Gaiman wanted to insert *even more* established DC characters into the series! "What's interesting is that when I began it, I really did try to implement lots of DC characters," Gaiman reveals. "But it proved to be such a pain in the ass! I started [writing] *Sandman* #5 with the Joker instead of the Scarecrow, which is why it's an April Fool's joke. 'Cause he's pretending to be dead, and Dr. Dee's escaping from Arkham [Asylum], and it was going to be a Joker encounter. Except that I'm writing this, and suddenly I'm told,

'No, no, you can't use the Joker this week! We just decided that the Joker's been overused, so we're not using him for another six months.' Honestly, it was that kind of thing, [and] I just decided at that point that probably over-all I would be better if I just only ever used DC characters that nobody ever cared about or had forgotten. So, that's why I used [obscure 1960s super-hero] Element Girl. I could write an Element Girl story because she hadn't even made it into the [official guidebook] *Who's Who of the DC Universe*. They'd forgotten about her. And I could do a story about [teen president character] Prez because nobody cared about him! Prez hadn't been around for fifteen years! Nobody cared and nobody was going to go out and rewrite my dialogue."

By setting Sandman inside DC's official continuity, and yet rarely hav-ing him encounter the other major DC characters, Gaiman ensured that everyone was happy. Sandman existed in his own world, apart from the capes-and-cowls set. And unlike most DC superheroes, Neil Gaiman's Sandman is far from the most likeable character you'll ever encounter. Dream is often portrayed as an unfeeling jerk, unable to have a healthy, long-term romantic relationship with the various Graeco-Roman deities, African princesses, and Faerie queens he falls in love with during the series' run. And yet, he's eerily relatable. He has his foibles, his gaffes, his screw-ups, which we as an audience can see as a mirror of our own flaws. And because of this, he's entirely sympathetic. This too was a conscious decision on Gaiman's part. "If I was going to do something that was going to turn into a monster-of-the-month [series], then I would go mad. I knew that I couldn't do that, so I wanted something that would go all over the place. I remembered what [sci-fi writer] Roger Zelazny had done, in several of his books from the sixties, particularly a book called *Lord of Light*, where he sort of turned men into gods and got a thing that was kind of close to [a] comic book out of it. I thought, 'Well, I bet you could do more or less the same with gods!' At the same time, John Byrne had gone on explaining why he'd had to de-power Superman because comics with all-powerful charac-ters could only be boring and problematic. And I thought, 'No, actually, comics with all-powerful characters seems like an amazing place to start!' Because then what actually drives things is the personality and the foibles and the problems of the person doing it, of the all-powerful character! That seems like a really interesting place to go and live. And beyond that, I guess some of [Dream] was me, and most of him was himself."

The first *Sandman* story arc—collectively called "Preludes and Noc-turnes"—consists of the series' first eight issues, in which Dream is captured by an Aleister Crowley–style magician named Roderick Burgess, who performs a ritual to capture death, but accidentally captures Death's brother, Dream. Burgess traps Dream in a glass bowl and strips the Nightmare King of his helmet, his amulet, and his pouch of sand—symbols of his power that are also potentially powerful weapons if used in the wrong hands. All of this happens in 1916, and for the next several decades, bizarre sleep-related

© DC Comics

This portrait of the Endless by Sandman artist Mike Dringenberg was subtitled "Still Life With Cats." Clockwise from left: Dream, Death, Destruction (with helmet), Desire, Destiny, Despair (with harp), and Delirium (sitting).

phenomena begin to crop up all over the world. Finally in 1988, Morpheus is accidentally freed by Burgess's son Alexander. Dream punishes the younger Burgess by trapping him in a continuous loop of never-ending nightmares. Dream then goes on a quest to recover his helmet, amulet, and pouch, and to reclaim his kingdom, the Dreaming.

We eventually meet Dream's siblings, the Endless. The membership of the Endless includes the hooded, blind Destiny, who shuffles around with a *grimoire* attached to his wrist; Dream's sister/brother Desire, who is like an androgynous Patrick Nagel print come to oddly seductive life; the psychedelic Delirium, who used to be Delight untold ages ago, before an undisclosed tragedy shook her up and changed her into her present state; Despair, a fanged, self-mutilating she-beast who certainly lives up to her name; and Destruction, a member of the group who resigned his post as part of the Endless some time ago, and now appears from time to time as a rowdy, good-humored hitchhiker with a bag slung over his shoulder. Oh yes, and there's also Death, perhaps the most popular member of the Endless.

Neil Gaiman's concept of Death—a beautiful, good-humored young woman who's so delightful and charming that you almost look forward to meeting her—flew in the face of so many previous comic book interpretations of the Grim Reaper that from the moment the character first showed up in *Sandman* #7 to cheer up her depressed brother Dream, many readers felt the then-fledgling series had truly found its voice. Death seemed to ground the series and lend it a welcome measure of comic relief, all of which is quite ironic considering that Death is usually someone people live in constant dread of seeing. But fans clamored for Neil Gaiman's Death, and she eventually won her own series.

The popularity of Death is in equal measure due to Gaiman's talents as a writer and the superb draftsmanship of artist Mike Dringenberg. "The really big thing that Mike in particular brought to the table was Death," Gaiman admits. "In my original proposal [for *Sandman*], I said that we'd probably either base her visually either on Nico, from the [1960s rock group] Velvet Underground during her glory years, or perhaps on [silent film actress] Louise Brooks. And those were the two visual places that I thought we'd probably go for Death. And Mike looked at the outline and did this drawing. He knew a girl called Cinnamon, who had that sort of look, the ankh and big black hair thing, going on at that point. And he did this drawing, the one that's been on all the T-shirts. The 'How would you feel about life if Death were your older sister?' one. And he sent it over to me, and I went, 'Oh, well, that's Death!'"

A DREAM TAKES WING

With such a vibrant, colorful, engaging cast of characters, one would think that *Sandman* was an immediate hit, but that wasn't quite the case. In fact, when Neil Gaiman began writing "Preludes and Nocturnes" he prepared himself for the possibility that this could be both the first—and last—*Sandman* storyline. "You have to bear in mind," Gaiman clarifies, "that with the sole exception of *Watchmen*—which was a limited series, it wasn't an ongoing thing—good critical response tended to be commensurate with poor commercial response in comics. Well-written comics were famously the kiss of death. Comics that the critics liked and comics that people bought rarely intersected. I didn't think I was writing something that people would buy!"

So when did *Sandman* become successful enough that Gaiman wasn't worried it was doomed? "Well, we didn't really take off in a big way, but we always took off in a very, very slow [way]," Gaiman explains. "We started selling more." Things radically started to change for *Sandman* once the early-1990s "comics glut" occurred, spurred by rampant fan speculation. In order to compete with each other, the companies were all instituting gimmicky storylines, such as DC's "Death of Superman" story arc, in which their flagship character was killed and then dramatically resurrected. Marvel was madly printing special covers, some of them sporting holographic images, some of them featuring silver-embossed designs. In the midst of this, a group of Marvel artists jumped ship to form their own company, Image Comics. Fans started buying up five and ten copies of every comic book published by DC, Marvel, and Image, hoping that these titles would become rare collectibles worth their weight in gold.

All this crazy competition by the "Big Three" actually helped *Sandman* move past its status as the little comic that could. "By the time that *Sandman* finally got to about one hundred thousand, suddenly the comics industry went into its mad overdrive thing and it was doom year and Image titles were selling in the millions," Gaiman explains. "Only they *weren't* selling to a million readers, they were just selling in boxes of twenty-five to collectors and stuff! But enormous quantities were going out, so we sat there. We were like #100 on the top one hundred [sellers] at that point. A year or so later, the comics industry went into freefall. *Superman* had sold two million with 'The Death of Superman,' and *Superman*'s now selling seventy thousand, sixty-five thousand, and then sixty thousand. And *Batman* is now selling seventy-five thousand, then sixty thousand. But I'm still selling my one hundred thousand! So month after month, I'm just steadily climbing the top ten. [Image flagship title] *Spawn* is collapsing, everything's collapsing, and by the time I got to the last two issues of ['Preludes and Nocturnes'], we were the best-selling DC comics title, and I don't know if we beat *X-Men* [then Marvel's top seller], but we were doing really well."

DRAWING DREAM

The *Sandman* story was initially interpreted by the creative team of penciler Sam Keith and inker Mike Dringenberg, who were assigned to draw the first few issues. And even though he created and wrote *Sandman*, Neil Gaiman is—to this day—flush with appreciation for the artists who first brought his then-fledgling comic book series to life. "It's possible to minimize the artist's contribution, but I think you're making an enormous mistake and sort of missing the point if you did," he points out. "And the point is that it's comics. The point and joy of comics is that it is a visual medium. If I'd written *Sandman* as a novel, it wouldn't have had anywhere near the impact because one of the strange and magical things about comics is everybody has the same visual experience. If you take a novel like *The Catcher in the Rye*, everybody who's read that novel has a different Holden Caulfield in their head. They could probably describe him to you, but whether he has dark hair or blond hair, whether he's tall or short, whether he looks like somebody they knew or looks like themselves or [whatever], so you have a million readers and a million Holden Caulfields. With *Sandman*, everyone has the same visual track, and that's something that really does unite readers." With this in mind, Gaiman solicited concept drawings of Dream from various artists, including Dave McKean and Leigh Baulch. But the illustrator who really seemed to nail it was Sam Keith.

How do you draw a Dream? The look that Gaiman and Keith agreed on for Dream gave the Prince of Stories a mop of unruly black hair, a chalk-white complexion, a spindly, spidery physique, and a limited fashion sense with a particular fondness for the color black. Dream was designed as a bold, dramatic figure in stark black and white, one who would stand out from the rest of the crowd on the comic book racks by virtue of his lack of graphic clutter, his noted absence of the garish, lurid, colorful accoutrements that normally adorn a comic book character's body. In other words, Dream stood out because a skinny pale guy in a black jacket was more relatable to a certain segment of the comics readership than a muscle-bound steroid case in tights.

In a move that might have shaken the group synergy of a lesser series, Sam Keith left *Sandman* after issue 5. Although he had contributed various visual concepts that Gaiman ended up using in the series, such as the wall of faces that Dream and John Constantine encounter in issue 3, Keith had begun to feel increasingly out of place working on the series. "We were the wrong gig for Sam at the wrong time," Gaiman admits. "And I think what I was asking him to do was very different to what he wanted to do, and it was very constricting for him I think. I was very relieved when he quit. Not because I didn't think he was brilliant and not because we weren't working better and better together, and I think by the time you get to *Sandman* #5, which he drew two issues after he'd quit, we really are working very well together. But because it made him miserable. He really wasn't happy doing it, and I'd get off the phone each day with him, going, 'Oh my God, I'm ruining this poor man's life!' "

Mike Dringenberg took over as penciler on *Sandman* #6, although he too had problems working on the series, and issue 11 was his last as *Sandman*'s uninterrupted regular penciler. After this, he worked on and off on the "Doll's House" storyline (which he'd begun with issue 9), his gaps being filled by various guest artists such as Chris Bachalo and Michael Zulli, before leaving his post as regular *Sandman* penciler for good after issue 16. "Mike was very different [than Sam]," Gaiman reveals. "Mike loved the work and loved doing the thing, and I would have happily kept Mike on as the artist of *Sandman* until the end of time. But Mike had real problems with the 'commerce versus art' and the 'deadlines versus not deadlines' nature of comics, and the weird sort of [process]."

With Mike Dringenberg off the series, Neil Gaiman had to find a replacement, and he soon found a rather inventive way to solve this dilemma. "Once it became apparent that Mike wasn't going to be coming back," Gaiman reveals, "we'd already worked with dozens of different [guest] artists because of places where Mike had gone off to get time to do stuff, and so forth. And suddenly I was like a kid in a candy store. The idea that instead of having to find artists and stay with them forever, I could just find the perfect artist for each storyline. Which was a completely new idea, you know, nobody had done that before." Gaiman soon found himself working with a dream team of comics' best and brightest artists, including Jon J. Muth, Kelley Jones, Jill Thompson, Matt Wagner, and Charles Vess. One artist would usually handle the art chores on the bulk of a storyline, with occasional gaps to be filled by guest artists here and there. With Gaiman carefully choosing each of the artists who would illustrate his various story arcs, he could be likened to a filmmaker casting a movie, a comics auteur using the artists most suitable to interpret each of his scripts.

A LOVELY SORT OF MIDDLE GROUND

One artist who has remained a constant throughout *Sandman*'s entire seventy-five issue run is cover artist Dave McKean. McKean is such a vital part of the *Sandman* family that he has designed the covers for all the collected editions, as well as the 1996 short story collection *Sandman: Book of Dreams* (coedited by Gaiman), Hy Bender's 1999 *Sandman Companion* (a book of interviews with Gaiman, alongside Bender's own analysis of the series), and the 2003 graphic novel *Sandman: Endless Nights*. However, in the beginning, DC wasn't exactly sold on McKean. After all, this was someone who was designing covers for a series called *Sandman* . . . and yet, more often than not, Sandman himself was nowhere to be seen on the cover!

"Probably the biggest editorial battle I ever fought was the one that we fought for the *Sandman* covers," Gaiman reveals. "Because up until that point, really the rule on covers for ongoing series was, the lead character's on the cover. And our perspective was, that was kind of a silly rule. Karen was really kind of worried about this. She said, 'But we don't do it like that. We've never done it like this! How will people know that it's *Sandman*?' We said, 'Because it'll say *Sandman* on the top!'" So how did Gaiman convince her that his and McKean's approach to covers was the right one? "I think really it was the quality of Dave's drawings," he shrugs. "He showed her these amazing sketches. And again, the

DAVE MCKEAN'S EVOCATIVE ARTWORK ILLUMINATED THE COVERS OF EACH ISSUE OF SANDMAN, MAKING HIM THE ONLY PERSON APART FROM GAIMAN TO CONTRIBUTE TO EVERY INSTALLMENT OF THE SERIES.

thing about *Sandman* was, by the time [we realized that] what we were doing was too weird to be allowed, we were selling so many copies that nobody was going to stop us doing anything. But we weren't selling so many copies that anybody was suddenly going, 'We should really play it safe here because otherwise we might lose some people!' It was a lovely sort of middle ground."

That "lovely sort of middle ground" gave Neil Gaiman the license to explore a wide variety of subject matter as fodder for *Sandman* stories. Soon he was tackling the Bard himself, implying (in issue 12's story "Men of Good Fortune") that William Shakespeare had made a deal with Dream, a.k.a. The Prince of Stories. When we meet Shakespeare in this story, he's a struggling playwright who wants more than anything to be a good writer. Dream offers to make Shakespeare a great writer, but asks something in return. Later, in *Sandman* #19, titled "Midsummer Night's Dream," we learn that Shakespeare's end of the deal was to deliver two plays, one at the beginning of his career (*Midsummer Night's Dream*), and the other at the end (we learn in the final issue of *Sandman*, issue 75, that this was *The Tempest*). Both "Midsummer Night's Dream" and "The Tempest" were illustrated by Charles Vess, who's also illustrated *The Adventures of Spider-Man* and *Swamp Thing*, and who has achieved a reputation for grounding fantastic characters in a foundation of realism while still allowing their more unearthly qualities to breathe freely.

In 1991, Gaiman and Vess's "Midsummer Night's Dream" became the first comic book story in the medium's history to win a literary award, in this case the coveted World Fantasy Award. However, the fact that a mere comic book won an award usually reserved for short stories and novels became a bit of a controversy. So much so that the morning after the award was given out to Gaiman and Vess, the rules for the awards were rewritten so as to exclude comic books! Therefore, "Midsummer Night's Dream" became not only the first comic book to win a World Fantasy Award, but quite possibly the last, unless this rule is further amended some time in the future. "I think it was absolutely stupid of the sacred masters or whoever it was who actually made that decision," Gaiman muses. "They got all confused, and when I talked to them about it, they all started to explain, 'It's all because I didn't know if they were giving out awards for the script, but [since] they gave it to me and Charles Vess, how could a short story be awarded if it was going to an artist, blah blah blah.' Yes, we got the World Fantasy Award, which was the big important cool thing— for a short story. Which I think is the first time a mainstream literary award had gone to a comic. And not the last time. I mean [Chris Ware's graphic novel] *Jimmy Corrigan*, for example, won the Guardian First Book Award [in 2001]. And I just think these things, they aren't going to happen often, but they just prove that we're up there with everybody else. That we can compete on our terms and we're good enough."

A STORY ABOUT STORIES

As implied by many of the *Sandman* stories, among them "Midsummer Night's Dream," *Sandman* was often a story about stories. In "The Tempest," the achingly lonely Dream confides to Shakespeare that "I am Prince of Stories, Will; but I have no story of my own. Nor shall I ever." Dream is someone who is averse to change, and that is his downfall. He observes the stories of others, but he's loathe to participate in them, to form a real relationship, to get close to another or to confide or lose himself in someone else. Of course, this is the ultimate irony, as dreams are what fuel our relationships with others, our passions, our desires, our pains, our very lust for life itself. All of these things Dream denies himself. As the Prince of Stories, the lord of the realm where humanity's dreams take shape, he sits on the sidelines like a pale sad clown, a tragic prince, unaware of the irony of his own existence. The fact that *Sandman* was a story about stories was "one of those things that sits in the back of my head anyway," shrugs Gaiman. "I mean it's probably at least one of the giant motifs that run through everything [I do]. It's there in everything. There's not much I can do about it. I didn't start out going, 'I'm going to do a story about stories!' I started out going, 'I'm going to tell a story about this person' and then just went off and did it."

In writing his "story about stories," Gaiman had decided very early on that he wanted his chronicle of the Dream King to end with the title character's death. This was an unprecedented move, as comic book characters routinely continue their existence after their creators leave the series. Spider-Man is still plugging away in his continuing crusade against villainy, several decades after his creators Stan Lee and Steve Ditko stopped writing and drawing his adventures. The *Spider-Man* comic book just got taken over by other people. Not so with *Sandman*.

"The biggest thing that I wanted to do with *Sandman* was take Morpheus off the stage before I stopped," Gaiman admits. "There are so many things that seem obvious in hindsight but had never been done before. And the biggest of those is just the fact that *Sandman* stopped when I was done.

That never happened before in comics. So it took us ages to get there. The first time we were maybe about two years in and I said to [former DC publisher] Jenette Kahn and then to Paul Levitz and then to Karen Berger, each of them individually, that I think it would be a good thing if *Sandman* stopped when I stopped. And each of them explained to me in their own way why this wouldn't happen, why this would be impossible. That was at the time as far as it went, and after that I just gave interviews, and people would say, 'What do you want to have happen?' and I would say, 'I would like *Sandman* to stop. My attitude on it is that I will keep working for DC if it does stop, and if it doesn't stop, then that will be that on my relationship with DC with no hard feelings.' "

How did Gaiman convince DC to actually cancel the series? "I don't know," Gaiman laughs. "By that point I wasn't really telling them what I was doing anyway. But they trusted me. It got to the point where I think they realized that whatever I was doing on *Sandman* was what I was doing on *Sandman*, and that it would have been really silly of them to go and get somebody else to write it."

ENDLESS

Sandman ended in 1996, and many readers thought that this was the last they'd ever see of Dream or his colorful family. Gaiman fans were somewhat placated in the years since the series' end by projects such as 1997's miniseries *Death: The Time of Your Life*, or 1999's *The Sandman: The Dream Hunters*, a short illustrated novel by Gaiman, in which he supposedly adapted an ancient Japanese folktale to encompass Dream. (In reality, he'd made up the "folktale," and the stunning brushwork by Yoshitaka Amano further succeeds in pulling off this ruse.) However, *Dream Hunters*, as a folktale homage/pastiche, depicted Dream as the King of Dreams found in so much folklore and mythology the world over, and didn't involve the greater backstory and mythology of the *Sandman* series; one never saw supporting characters such as the Endless. Moreover, *Dream Hunters* was an illustrated novel, not a comic book (at least not in the strictest, most commonly accepted definition of the phrase).

Readers hadn't seen a *Sandman* comic book in several years. Then, in 2003, that changed, with the publication of the graphic novel anthology *Sandman: Endless Nights*, seven short stories in comics form that each focused on a different member of the Endless. Gaiman wrote all the stories, each of which was illustrated by a different artist, none of whom (with the exception of P. Craig Russell) had ever depicted the adventures of Morpheus prior to this.

Gaiman's collaboration with artist Barron Storrey on the Despair chapter of *Endless Nights* was a particular change of pace from the ordinary *Sandman* tale, in that it was composed of "Fifteen Stories of Despair." In other words, it was composed of fifteen minitales—some would be classified as poems, some as monologues, some as very short short stories—that are all focused on the theme of Despair. "Originally I wanted to do something like twenty-five portraits of Despair with Barron and we were going to do it as a [separate] book," Gaiman reveals. "[But] somewhere in there I thought, 'That's going to get me so fucking depressed!' The idea of doing it in this book and doing it as fifteen portraits of Despair just seemed bearable. And even then I had people telling me that it's easily the most depressing thing that they've ever read. I love that story. But most of it was really loving the idea of doing a bunch of different stories in a bunch of different genres, a bunch of different places and ways.

"The thing I love about short story collections is that you're not meant to like everything. It was something that happened when [my short story collection] *Smoke and Mirrors* came out. The reviews for *Smoke and Mirrors* all said that there were some good stories in here and really bad stories that they should have never have allowed into this collection. And then they'd say what the good stories were and what the bad stories were. And if there had been any agreement on what the good stories were and what the bad stories were, I might have taken it to heart. And instead, all it told me is that different people like different things. And I think the same really was true of *Endless Nights*. Different people like different things. And that was really all I heard out of all the criticism of that."

Time will tell if there are more *Sandman* stories up Gaiman's sleeve. One thing his readers have come to realize is that, as in the *Sandman* books themselves, the end is never really The End.

THE WOMEN WERE THERE

Sandman evolved into much more than a mere monthly comic book; it was one of the rare mainstream titles that actually became a pop culture phenomenon. Gaiman's comic was also a pioneering publication in that it was used as the flagship series in a new imprint of DC Comics that editor Karen Berger started in 1992 to showcase DC's more mature, personal, provocative titles, usually (but not always) titles with a fantasy, horror, or science-fiction bent. That imprint was Vertigo, and to give you an idea of its content, imagine what would happen if David Cronenberg had decided to get into the comic book business instead of the film industry. *Sandman* may have emerged as Vertigo's flagship title, but as Gaiman remembers, "There was no first *official* Vertigo title. What you had was a point in 1992, where Vertigo was created, and at that point, all of the 'For Mature Readers' titles were hived off over to Vertigo, all the stuff that Karen was editing was hived off to Vertigo. And I guess *Sandman* was considered the flagship title of all of the stuff because it had the highest profile. *Death: The High Cost of Living* #1 [first in a miniseries that spotlighted Death, of the Endless] came out, I think, with the first Vertigo logo as well. I think that was launched when we were something like *Sandman* #41 or #42, something like that, when we went over to Vertigo."

Sandman also reached out to a broader swath of the reading public than other mainstream comics titles. From 1988 to 1996, one could always spot the kids at any given high school or university who were fans of the rather outré title. Gaiman's comic book resonated especially strongly among teens and young adults, including a large Goth fanbase, as well as any other kids who felt like outsiders or who identified with the lonely, sad-eyed characters within the series' pages. As everyone feels this way from time to time, and as the series was also buffered with hearty helpings of comedy and satire so as not to be weighted down with pathos, all of these elements made *Sandman* incredibly attractive.

And the series, with its immediately relatable stories and characters, and its user-friendly nature (it wasn't bound to fifty years of history and continuity like so many other comic books) was an instant hit among people who previously hadn't even read a comic book. This was especially true of women, a demographic that, sadly, hadn't been strongly courted by mainstream comics since the romance comics boom of the 1950s. But *Sandman* gave female readers two things that other titles didn't: a noted absence of steroid-addicted men in tights, and strong female characters who were far more than the mere wives and girlfriends (or, worse, the broadly depicted virgins and whores) seen in other comic books. "By the middle of [*Sandman*'s] second year, the women were there," Gaiman recalls. "And they'd all tell me exactly the same story, which was that their boyfriends had been trying to get them to read comics. Their boyfriends would say, 'No, comics are great,' and they'd go, 'I don't believe it,' and their boyfriends would have given them *Sandman*, and they'd go, 'This is cool,' and they'd start reading it."

Gaiman has a very specific idea as to why so many thinly written female characters prevailed in comics before *Sandman*. "I think that a lot of it had to do," he posits, "with the fact that many comics at that point were—and many these days still are—as far as one can tell, written by people who never actually encountered anybody of a female gender . . . ever, under any circumstances. [In their comics], women would all look like [Marvel Comics vigilante] the Punisher, but with melons tied to their chests. They'd be saying things like, 'Now you've really made me angry!' and they'd go and pose. They'd put on their posing thong if they were particularly angry. And I'd never met any women like that, so I just sort of wrote women sort of like the ones that I knew. I got an e-mail the other day from someone doing an interview about the gay characters [in *Sandman*], the transgender characters, why they were in there and what my agenda was. And I had to say that I didn't have much of an agenda other than there weren't many people in comics like the kind of people that I knew. I had a number of friends who were transgendered and there weren't any people like that in comics. I had a lot of friends at the time in London in the eighties who were lesbians, and I hadn't seen any relationships in comics particularly at that point that any way resembled any of the lesbians that I knew. The major agenda was just sort of like, 'I don't see the people I know turning up in comics, I think I'll put them in.'"

Another demographic that *Sandman* courted, however inadvertently, was the literati. Sandman quickly became a cause célèbre among celebrities like singer/songwriter Tori Amos (*Little Earthquakes*), filmmaker/novelist Clive Barker (*Hellraiser*), author Norman Mailer (*The Armies of the Night*), science-fiction novelist Samuel R. Delany (*Dahlgren*), and journalist Mikal Gilmore (*Rolling Stone*). Television writer/producer J. Michael Straczynski named an alien race on his sci-fi series *Babylon 5* "The Gaim" in honor of Neil Gaiman (Gaiman himself ultimately contributed a script to the show as well), and Tori Amos has inserted many references to both *Sandman* and Gaiman himself in her songs. "It actually happened fairly early," Gaiman says of *Sandman*'s love affair with the world of arts and letters. "Tori was '91, Norman was '90 or '91. Really the comic was coming out all through 1989, got the first twelve issues out, and it was starting to get read in odd places."

Through Gaiman's skillful writing and the storytelling gifts of his artistic collaborators, *Sandman* was able to earn the kind of clout and respect you just can't buy. And at the end of the day, that's more valuable than being the week's number one comic, because it represents something far more necessary: staying power. After the success of *Sandman*, Gaiman was one of comicdom's most in-demand writers, and various publishers were clamoring to put his unique stamp on their established characters. And that's exactly what Gaiman, ordinarily associated with DC, accomplished for rival publisher Marvel in his most recent major comics project.

INTO THE PAST AND THE FUTURE

Neil Gaiman first became interested in comic books by discovering reprints of American comics such as those that Stan Lee, Jack Kirby, and Steve Ditko created for Marvel in the 1960s. So it was only fitting that after *Endless Nights*, Gaiman's next major comics project was *1602*, a miniseries that he crafted—in collaboration with artist Andy Kubert—in homage to the Marvel Comics of his youth. Published by Marvel during 2003 and 2004 (and collected in graphic novel form shortly thereafter), *1602* poses an interesting question: What would

Stan, Jack, and Steve's creations have been like if they had existed in the year 1602?

Gaiman gives us some fascinatingly fanciful yet historically accurate hypotheses: Dr. Strange would have been the court magician for England's Queen Elizabeth, whose spymaster would have been secret agent Nick Fury; Fury's operatives would have included a young Peter Parker and a blind acrobat named Matt Murdock; Bruce Banner would have been working in the court of Scottish King James, Elizabeth's rival for the throne; The X-Men, branded "Witchbreed," would have been continually on the run from the Spanish Inquisition; Magneto would have assumed the mantle of

© *Marvel Characters, Inc.*

1602 was Gaiman's love letter to the 1960s-era Marvel Comics he fell in love with as a child.

Grand Inquisitor of said Inquisition; Dr. Doom, then as now a vain European monarch, would have captured the Fantastic Four. And into all of this, Gaiman has thrown an innocent in peril. Virginia Dare, the first child of British descent born on American soil, makes her way back to England to beg for assistance alongside her bodyguard Rojhaz, a monosyllabic, mysterious white man who has adopted Native American ways. Somehow *1602* finds time to explore classic Marvel themes such as prejudice (both metaphorical and literal), gender issues and sexuality, the idea that nobody is completely evil, and the awkwardness of adolescence. And it does it in a rollicking, rip-roaringly adventurous way that makes one realize that these classic Marvel characters fit rather seamlessly in this other era.

Gaiman says that the genesis of *1602* was a curious one. "That was immensely straightforward in that I wound up in a court battle with a very dodgy publisher who had made a lot of promises that he then hadn't kept," he explains. "He'd filed fraudulent copyright forms and all sorts of things. Fighting a legal case is incredibly expensive and I needed a fighting fund. I knew that I was in the right, and I also knew that the history of comics is littered with the bones of people who were in the right and couldn't afford to sue. And I had no intention of being one of them, so I put together a deal with Marvel whereby they would help me fund the legal case and I'd do a project for them. And that really was where *1602* came out of. The year was 2001, and I had to decide what I was going to do. And I had some ideas in my head, and then September 11 happened. And I said, 'You know, I don't think I can write something with explosions in it. I can't do something with skyscrapers, I don't want any of that stuff.' I wanted to see what would happen if you had started the Marvel Universe much earlier. [In a] pre-technological world, really."

Aside from his various other non-*Sandman* comics such as 1997's *Stardust* and 2002's *Murder Mysteries*, Gaiman has also been active in various other media, including poetry, songwriting, prose, television, and film. He scripted the 1996 BBC fantasy television series *Neverwhere*, about an alternate city lurking beneath the sewer tunnels and abandoned subway stations of London, and turned it into a bestselling novel the following year. Also in 1996, he adapted his 1992 graphic novel *Signal to Noise* (about a dying filmmaker) into a BBC radio drama. In 1998 the Hayao Miyazaki animated film *Princess Mononoke* was released in the United States, with a Nebula Award–nominated English language script by Neil Gaiman. His 2001 *New York Times* bestselling novel *American Gods* won the 2002 Hugo Award, one of the most prestigious prizes in the science fiction and fantasy community, in addition to winning the Nebula, Bram Stoker, and

Locus Awards. His 2002 children's novel *Coraline* was also a bestseller, and the recipient of the Hugo, as well as many other awards.

And perhaps most importantly, in 2005 the film *MirrorMask*, directed by Dave McKean from a screenplay by Neil Gaiman, made its premiere at the Sundance Film Festival. The film, about a young female circus performer lost in a fantasy realm based on her own drawings, has been favorably compared to such fantasy film classics as Jim Henson's *Labyrinth*. Both an illustrated *MirrorMask* screenplay for adults and a *MirrorMask* children's book (each by the team of Gaiman and McKean) have been published to herald the official theatrical release of the film.

WAKING UP

Neil Gaiman rapidly emerged from obscurity to become the go-to guy for two genres that had been left for dead in comics: horror stories and fantasy tales, which he resuscitated by merging them in *Sandman*, infusing them with his own personal sense of wit and irony, and raising the bar for anyone spinning scary new yarns about monsters or retelling fanciful old stories about gods. He almost single-handedly created the need for DC's Vertigo imprint, establishing that there was a demand for mature fantasy titles that didn't necessarily involve superheroes, titles that laid claim to a more cinematic sense of pacing, realistic form of character development, and naturalistic flair for dialogue than mainstream comics generally offered.

With the increasing success of *Sandman*, Gaiman gave mainstream comics a critical acclaim they'd rarely enjoyed, and elevated the writer from second-class citizen in the comic book hierarchy to a superstar of equal importance with the penciler of any given book. In doing so he became (with the possible exception of Alan Moore) the most important comic book writer since Stan Lee, influencing the next generation of comics scribes such as Warren Ellis (*The Authority*) and Brad Meltzer (*Identity Crisis*), both of whom can thank Gaiman for the status they currently enjoy as contemporary comic book writers. By any standard, Neil Gaiman has far exceeded the expectations of even the most accomplished comics scribe of years past. In using his leverage as one of America's foremost comics writers to spawn a second career as a bestselling novelist, screenwriter, and television writer, Gaiman has shown both readers and aspiring comics scribes just what one can do in this industry by keeping creative compromises to a minimum and setting standards high.

In short, he's taught his readers how to achieve their Dreams.

DWAYNE McDUFFIE

PORTRAIT OF DWAYNE McDUFFIE BY HIS FREQUENT COLLABORATOR DENYS COWAN.

"I always wanted to be a writer, like Toni Morrison. But I'm only fifteen. I never had nothing to write about. Nothing had ever happened to me before. At least before this."

—From *Icon* #1, 1993

F or an industry that has flourished on the backs of mutants, monsters, aliens, and other "outsider" characters, the comic book biz has never been a bastion of ethnic diversity. Most comic book characters—especially in the all-too-dominant superhero genre—are as lily-white as they come: Superman, Spider-Man, Captain America, Wonder Woman. Of course, there are exceptions, such as Black Panther, Storm, Black Lightning, Vixen, and Luke Cage, but the vast majority of superheroes are of the vanilla persuasion. In 1993, a consortium of industry professionals banded together to do something about this. It was called Milestone, and Dwayne McDuffie was its cofounder, editor in chief, and the writer and cocreator of many of its titles.

Milestone didn't last long, publishing its last comic book in 1997. However, through Milestone, McDuffie helped to change the industry's view of minority superheroes, making readers see them as heroes who *happened* to be black, rather than black versions of white superheroes. Dwayne McDuffie brought multicultural awareness to comics. Today, in addition to the comics projects he's spearheading, he's a prolific writer-producer of children's half-hour animated adventure shows, most of which feature inventive, adult-friendly revampings of popular DC supergroups like the Justice League and the Teen Titans.

But a mere half-decade before he founded Milestone, McDuffie was just another comics workhorse struggling to make a name for himself.

INFLICTING DAMAGE

Dwayne McDuffie was born in Detroit, Michigan. One day during the late 1960s, when he was no more than a toddler, he wandered into a candy store with his father and picked out a comic book—and a lifelong obsession was ignited. From then on, every time he went into a candy store, McDuffie would head straight for the comic book rack. Soon he would encounter a black superhero for the first time, and his world would never be the same. "I remember those comics really well," he recalls. "Probably the biggest thing for me was the Black Panther. Don McGregor did a Black Panther series. And I was fascinated with it. I didn't understand why at the time, but the reason was because I had never seen a bunch of people who looked like me and they were the heroes. They were the heroes and the villains and the streetsweepers and the doctors, and all of a sudden I could be anything, I didn't have to be a sidekick. You know, I didn't have to be Luke Cage, the blaxploitation guy. I could be king!" In those days, writer MacGregor's Black Panther series was titled *Jungle Action*. "Yeah, and I had no sense of irony about that," McDuffie laughs. "I didn't get it. You know I look back on it, and I'm like, 'I'm glad I saw it when I saw it, because a year later I would have never picked it up.'"

McDuffie first attended the University of Michigan, before studying film at New York University's Tisch School of the Arts. At NYU he met future comics scribes Greg Wright and Dan Chichester. After he left NYU's hallowed halls, his equally comics-obsessed college buddies would help him get his first job in the industry.

By age twenty-one, McDuffie found himself working as a copy editor for a financial magazine called *Investment Dealers Digest*. "Oh yeah, it was exciting," he jokes. "I hated it." It was here that his NYU contacts came into play. "I was complaining to Greg Wright about working for a financial magazine," McDuffie recalls. "And he said, 'You know, Marvel's looking for an editor.' So I applied for the job, and unaccountably, they gave it to me, and that's kind of how I got into it." Starting in 1987, McDuffie served as assistant editor on several Marvel titles, many of them adaptations of licensed properties from other media such as *Indiana Jones and the Last Crusade*, *Who Framed Roger Rabbit*, and *Nightmare on Elm Street*. "I took kind of a huge pay cut to go to Marvel, but I was grateful," he explains. "And I started writing, to kind of pick up some of the slack financially. I sold a couple stories with me and Greg cowriting, and I sold a series called *Damage Control*, which was a comedy."

Damage Control, the first comics series that McDuffie cocreated (with *Amethyst* and *Richie Rich* artist Ernie Colon), was a satirical comic book about the clean-up crew that repairs the property damage left behind after superheroes and their archenemies wreck the city during their superpowered smackdowns. When McDuffie originally made his pitch to Marvel proposing the 1989 series, he described it as a sitcom set in the Marvel Universe, comparing it to ensemble shows like *Cheers*, *Taxi*, and *The Mary Tyler Moore Show*. Like those series, *Damage Control* would focus on a funny, unique group of characters who have an unusual job and the odd-ball people the job brings them in contact with. Only in this case, the "job" was using construction equipment to continuously rebuild New York City, and the "oddball people" were the Avengers, the X-Men, and other denizens of Marveldom. The idea came to McDuffie when he realized that no matter how much of a pummeling New York City takes in every issue of, say, *Spider-Man*, by the very next issue, everything looks good as new. *Someone* had to be on clean-up duty! Death rays nuked the Empire State Building? Giant robots left giant crater-sized footprints up and down Broadway? No problem! Damage Control is here!

The first *Damage Control* miniseries in 1989 was followed by two other four-issue miniseries over the next couple of years. The Damage Control team would also occasionally pop up in the pages of any Marvel annual McDuffie happened to be editing at the time. While it's still remembered as a beloved cult classic, *Damage Control* never won over a large enough audience to warrant regular series status. McDuffie has a theory as to why there haven't been more series like *Damage Control* since then. "I think we don't see them in the larger companies because the people who are reading [superhero] stuff have a lot to invest in it and they don't have a big sense of humor about it," he shrugs. "It was even felt by many people on staff when I was at Marvel—this was late eighties—that *Damage Control* existing undercut their characters, which, by the way, I don't agree with. I don't agree that it undercut them, but I do agree that some undercutting is a good thing every once in a while. You just don't want the stuff to be so ponderous. There's humor in life, there ought to be humor in fiction as well."

COLOR-BLIND HEROES

In the late eighties McDuffie was promoted from assistant editor to editor. He was now faced with a dilemma: what did he want to do more, write or edit? McDuffie welcomed the 1990s by quitting his editing post to embrace the full-time freelance writing life. "A lot of it was I seemed to hit my ceiling at Marvel," he says. "I wasn't going to get promoted as an editor, and I wasn't getting the writing assignments I wanted as a freelancer, so I figured if I wasn't on staff at Marvel, it would open other markets for me." He plunged into the freelance world with gusto, the highlight being his celebrated run on Marvel's *Deathlok* series. McDuffie, cowriter Greg Wright, and artist Jackson "Butch" Guice completely revamped the 1970s-era character of Deathlok, basically keeping the cyborg's retro-cool armor, a couple of character names, and little else. For one thing, this Deathlok was black, while the previous one was white. "Well, the first incarnation [of Deathlok] that I read as a kid, the hero was a guy named Luther Manning from Detroit," McDuffie recalls. "And his face was all gray and torn up. But me and all my friends, we decided he was black, 'cause his name was Luther Manning from Detroit. Also his wife was black. I found out years later that he was white, but we were sure he was black. When me and Greg Wright were gonna to do a new Deathlok, we liked the old stuff so much that I didn't want to do the old character and mess him up. So we just said, 'OK, another guy gets in there, let's make him a black guy!' Which [we thought] he was supposed to be!"

Deathlok wasn't the only superhero that was popular with black audiences. Characters who were metaphors for "outsiders" tended to be favorites with minority readers, who saw themselves in them. "Greg Wright and I also thought Thor and Hulk were black," he jokes. "Like Larry Bird; basically, any of the good ones, we'd just take. [Prince Namor] the Sub-Mariner, obviously. I've got in trouble with this before, because somebody asked me why black people like the Sub-Mariner so much, and I said, 'Because he wants to kill whitey.' And thematically, that was his thing. And we were behind that. That was like, 'Yeah!' Black comic book fans my age and a little bit younger, and certainly older—you ask them which Marvel comics they like, they're gonna say the Thing, they're gonna say Luke Cage, they're all gonna say Sub-Mariner. Namor is kind of obvious. He doesn't fit in at home, he doesn't fit in in the larger world, he's got royal blood, but it's hard to prove it, and everybody thinks he's a criminal. He's short tempered, he has impatience for the folks in the power structure, there's a whole bunch of stuff in that."

The fact that some black (and white) superheroes had a built-in black fanbase started discussions between McDuffie and some of his comics industry colleagues, which led to the development of an idea for a new comic book company. Soon, Milestone Media would emerge on the scene, and neither the comics industry nor Dwayne McDuffie would be the same again.

A MILESTONE ON PAPER

In the early 1990s, a group of black comic book professionals would meet after hours to eat dinner and discuss the pros and cons of the industry. In 1992, four of them—Dwayne McDuffie, Denys Cowan, Derek Dingle, and Michael Davis—created a business plan for a new comic book company, Milestone Media. Milestone would be a truly multicultural comics publisher, with characters that represented nearly every ethnicity. Throughout 1992, various media outlets—including *MTV News*, the *New York Times*, NBC's *Today Show*, and *Newsweek*—aired or published a barrage of stories on this bold new player in the comics biz.

The four principals (Editor in Chief Dwayne McDuffie, Creative Director Denys Cowan, President Derek Dingle, and Director of Talent Michael Davis) created a massive "bible" of character bios, story ideas, and conceptual drawings. Using the business model of an independent film company or record label as a paradigm, the Milestone founders produced their various titles independently, while using DC Comics as a distributor in order to get their books in as many stores as possible. This was also the model created during the 1930s when so-called "shops" like Eisner & Iger would write, draw, edit, and design an entire line of comic books and get a major company to print and distribute them. And if Milestone can be compared to an old-school comics company, Dwayne McDuffie, as the company's editor in chief / de facto head writer, can also be seen as Milestone's Stan Lee.

In February 1993, Milestone officially launched, and quickly became the most successful black-owned comic book publisher in American history. "There are two threads that led to Milestone," McDuffie reveals. "One of them is obviously the racial identity stuff. It was fairly common for blacks in the business to get together to talk about the kinds of stories they wanted to do but they couldn't do. Either because it didn't make sense in the [Marvel or DC] universe, or because the people who were in power there just didn't get it. The other thread is just the general freelancer [complaint of], 'Man, the editor won't let me do this! If I ran things, here's the kind of stuff I would do.' Guys like Ron Wilson, Keith Pollard, Arvell Jones, a bunch of guys tried to do this [in the 1970s], years before us. And they just couldn't pull it off because of the way the business was set up then. We were fortunate enough that it was the early nineties, people needed material—badly. The companies were competing mainly by putting out more books, and trying to push each other and the competitors off the stands, so they needed material. And everything was kind of selling, and all of the conditions were right so that the four of us could get together and say, 'Hey, we wanna do these books, under these conditions.' And pretty much Marvel said yeah, DC said yeah. DC's deal was a little better, so we went with DC."

Unfortunately, the very fact that Milestone Media, an independent comic book company, chose the ultramainstream DC Comics as their distributor caused controversy in some circles. This controversy was largely sparked by another black-owned comic book company, ANIA. ANIA was actually a consortium of four small-press companies—Africa Rising, UP Comics, Afrocentric Comic Books, and Dark Zulu Lies. They often accused Milestone of Uncle Tom–ism in the press for their alliance with white-owned DC. For their part, Milestone's founders chose not to sink to ANIA's level, and refused to publicly answer the criticism. This only made the ANIA spokespeople that much more vocal in the press throughout 1992 and into 1993, when the Milestone books were actually launched. Eventually, Milestone had to answer their accusers, which they only did as a matter of last resort.

McDuffie prefers to forget this ugly incident. "We did not launch Milestone as a black company," he explains. "Four black people owned it, but it was a completely multicultural operation, in terms of the characters we created, in terms of the people who worked on them, in terms of the people on the business side. If I had wanted to do black comics, I would have said, 'black comics.' Our main goal was to control our creative content and to present a wider range of characters both ethnically, racially, culturally, than we had seen in comics before. [ANIA] was a group of four black publishers, and between the four publishers, they had precisely three issues in print at that point. After we announced [Milestone], they announced that we had gone into business to put *them* out of business! They actually took ads out, in *The Comics Journal*—full page ads—saying, 'We suspect these black people who are actually all employees of Warner Brothers! They're Uncle Toms who've been hired to force us out of the business.'

"Well, the fact of the matter is Marvel and DC didn't actually know any of these [ANIA] guys existed. None of them were doing numbers in the direct market, I don't think any of them had actually offered a book through the direct market yet. Nobody knew about them. So this got them a lot of publicity, which is fine. But what it did to us was, from that point on we were playing defense. Instead of talking about comics, I was doing interviews explaining what the difference between black and multicultural was, and how we weren't out to hurt these guys, et cetera. It was very damaging to us. It had the potential to help them, but frankly, they didn't put any books out."

McDuffie sees ANIA's trash talking of Milestone as a Machiavellian tactic of self-preservation, but one that was ridiculously unprofessional on ANIA's part. "[Although] there were some talented people involved in ANIA," he concedes, "none of them were ready [to go pro] yet. And that's OK, because that's what a lot of self-publishers do. You do that stuff, and you get good, and then you either take it to the next level and own it yourself and keep doing that, or you trade off and you go and do a book for one of the majors. All that stuff is OK to do, I just feel really bad that a lot of it was on our back. Because when the [indie publisher] Malibu Comics guys started, there weren't a bunch of white guys saying, 'You guys aren't really white. You're gonna ruin white comics for all the white people!' "

THE DAKOTA UNIVERSE

Milestone Media's first batch of titles hit comic book specialty stores and chain bookstores in February 1993 (according to McDuffie, the fact that their launch date was during February—Black History Month—is simply a happy accident). All the Milestone characters live in the fictional city of Dakota, giving them a shared universe in which they could appear in each other's books at a moment's notice. Milestone Media's comics were famous for their emphasis on characterization, and most of the characters in the first wave of Milestone titles—those released in 1993—were cocreated by Dwayne McDuffie. The Kirby to McDuffie's Lee was artist Denys Cowan, who was the initial illustrator and cocreator of many of Milestone's titles.

The first Milestone book to hit newsstands was *Hardware*. A character often compared to Marvel's Iron Man, Hardware is in reality genius inventor Curtis Metcalf. As Hardware, he fights organized crime with the help of high-tech gadgets (laser cannons, microrockets, jetpacks), many of which are hardwired into the cybernetic battle suit he wears. However, an important distinction between Hardware and Iron Man is that Iron Man's suit covers up his face; Hardware's does not and therefore, you can tell that a black man is wearing this costume. Hardware's archnemesis Edwin Alva was a respected white businessman who employed Metcalf and had a father-son relationship with the young inventor. He discovers that Alva's been exploiting his genius and that the corporate titan sees him as a mere cog in the machine of Alva Industries—and, worse, that Alva's company is a front for his illicit activities as Dakota's leading crime boss. Metcalf decides to strike back—as Hardware. To quote Hardware: "A cog in the corporate machine is going to strip some gears!"

Many critics saw this depiction of the young underappreciated black inventor striking out on his own as a metaphor for McDuffie's own decision to leave Marvel. McDuffie confirms this: "For me, I felt like I was a pretty talented, useful guy, who had absolutely smashed up against a glass ceiling, who wasn't going anywhere, that I wouldn't get the opportunities that other people got. And it was a very 'comic book-y' way of externalizing my own anger. Hardware's not a likable guy, which I thought was important. He was a guy who had been wronged, but who was fixated on that, and let that completely rule his actions. He's incredibly smug, he's incredibly self-centered. I thought it would be interesting in *Hardware* to start with a guy who's pretty selfish, who had a spark of some good stuff in him, but who had never even drawn on those resources at all. And put him [into] a series of situations that forces him to rethink himself. The intention was to remake him into a hero over time."

Hardware's "angry young man" persona makes him commit various morally ambiguous acts, such as when he takes a life in the first issue. This is something that even your typical costumed antiheroes (think Batman) are loathe to do. This is a real person, with layers and plausible emotions. "He kills one person in the first issue," McDuffie explains. "And he suffers for it for the remainder of the series. He's not the Punisher. He thinks about the guy all the time, he has all these mental conversations with the guy he killed, he realizes that there were better ways to handle that."

The next Milestone book that was released was the atypical group title *Blood Syndicate*, whose members got their powers because of the most fundamental event of the Milestone Universe, "The Big Bang." The Big Bang was a highly anticipated turf war between all the gangs on Dakota's worst section, Paris Island. The police knew about the impending Big Bang, and they decided to make it work in their favor by firing an experimental radioactive "tear gas" into the fray. Ideally, the gas would act as a marker and allow them to identify and arrest any gang members present at the megatussle. However, they didn't anticipate the side effects of the gas, which killed hundreds of gang members and left the few survivors with superhuman abilities. These "bang babies" came together to form the Blood Syndicate, the most unstoppable gang ever!

The members of Blood Syndicate include Flashback, a woman who can rewind time for a few seconds to disorient her opponents; Fade, Flashback's brother, a phantomlike figure we later find out is HIV positive; Wise Son, whose ultradense molecular structure makes him well-nigh invulnerable; Masquerade, who can assume whatever shape she desires; DMZ, a mysterious masked character with superhuman strength and the power of flight; Third Rail, who takes on the power of any energy source he touches; the monstrous Boogeyman, who wields talonlike fingertips that would give Wolverine pause; and Brick House, a woman who was fused with a brick wall during the Big Bang, and as a result, has become a walking pile of bricks not unlike the Fantastic Four's Ben Grimm. Part of Dwayne McDuffie's plan for *Blood Syndicate* was to create a truly multi-cultural supergroup, and the membership of this uncanny cadre consists of black, white, and Hispanic superhumans, some of them heterosexual, some homosexual. As with other Milestone books, part of the agenda was to have *Blood Syndicate* address various social issues. We see the characters deal with Fade's sexual orientation (he's one of the few openly gay super-heroes in mainstream comics) and Flashback's drug addiction. And we see the group develop from a bunch of mismatched gang members who can't stand each other and who are thrown together by circumstances beyond their control into a surrogate, constantly bickering, dysfunctional family.

McDuffie sees the harsh reality of gang life as something that should have been portrayed sooner in the mainstream comics world. "First of all, everybody's the hero in their own life," he explains. "More importantly, these are all people with talents and abilities that society didn't allow them to exploit. A successful drug dealer could probably sell financial packages. He could sell cars. He could run a small business. And it's probably a hell of a lot easier if no one's trying to kill you. People find the life that's available to them. I'm thinking a lot of these guys are in these situations because they did the best they could out of the possibilities that were presented to them. So thematically, a lot of *Blood Syndicate* was about what happens when you get some perspective. You can't see what's out there unless you can stand on something. The higher you're standing, the more of the world you can see. If you stand at the bottom of the hill, you can see your block. So these guys, their thought is, 'I'm gonna control the entire block.' And these are guys that have dealt with the possibilities they had and all of a sudden, they've got power, and still a very limited perspective of the world. And that book is about them learning more about the world and more about the opportu-nities their powers allow for them. And some guys [in Blood Syndicate] go, 'Oh great, I'm really strong, now I can rip bank machines out of the wall!' And other guys are thinking, 'I'm really strong, I can go shake down the mayor and make him put more money into the school system.'"

The fourth Milestone title to be released was also the story of a "bang baby." This was *Static*, cocreated by Dwayne McDuffie and Denys Cowan. When smart-ass teenager Virgil Hawkins sneaks over to the notoriously dangerous Paris Island on the night of the Big Bang to impress his friends, he's sprayed by the same radioactive gas as the members of Blood Syndicate, and he finds that he now has electrical powers. He can manipulate electromagnetic currents, generate lightning bolts, and even surf through the air on electrically charged metal discs (like garbage can lids) to simulate flight. If Hardware is the Iron Man of the Milestone Universe, Static is definitely its Spider-Man, the neurotic adolescent suffering through a never-ending torrent of girl problems, homework problems, and money problems.

Not that *Static* was averse to dealing with serious social issues as well. On the cover of 1995's *Static* #25, set for release during Valentine's Day, Virgil and his girlfriend Daisy were kissing beside a box of condoms and a safe sex manual. Or at least, that was the plan. This image, meant to promote safe sex awareness, erupted into Milestone's only serious tussle with DC over content.

"Here's what happened," McDuffie reveals. "The cover was kind of charming. It was the two of them, Virgil and his girlfriend, making out on the couch. There were socks, and a jacket, and a pack of condoms [in the background] on the cover. I wanted the condoms there because Virgil is a very responsible kid; he would wear condoms. DC didn't want to do that cover. They never mentioned the condoms until about the third argument. I actually said, 'OK, I'll take the condoms off the cover. As long as the condom's in the book, I've got no problem with it.' They said, 'No, no, DC doesn't use sex to sell its books.' And I was absolutely incensed. I pulled a pile of DC comics, including an issue I remember really well of *Legion of Super-Heroes* that month, which was a shot of [LSH member] Dream Girl's ass and her looking over her shoulder, saying, 'I'm back.' And I said, 'You do too use sex to sell covers!' I think I said something like, 'So when did this policy start? This week?' And I had a huge argument with [DC's management], and [they were] very offended. And what we did was say, 'OK, we'll run the cover as intended on the inside front cover.' When you open it up, it's the cover as we handed it in. I still really disagree with DC on this. I think they weren't uncomfortable with sexuality, they were uncomfortable with *black* sexuality. That's my feeling, based on conversations we had."

But for the most part *Static*'s content was largely uncensored by distributor DC. Nor was *Static* Milestone's most popular title. That slot would be reserved for its third title, the aptly named *Icon*.

ICONTROVERSY

Created by McDuffie (writer) and Mark Bright (artist), the character Icon was originally an alien on an intergalactic cruise who crash-landed in the American south in 1839. Rescued by a slave woman and assuming the shape of the dominant species, the alien was raised as the slave Augustus Freeman. Since he doesn't age past a certain point in adulthood, Augustus periodically poses as his own son. Now known as the wealthy conservative businessman Augustus Freeman IV, he hides his powers from the outside world.

One night Augustus's mansion is burgled by a group of wannabe-criminal teenagers, one of whom, Raquel Ervin, is goaded by the others into coming along. The kids figure that they'll get away scot-free since the cops will all be over at Paris Island taking care of the Big Bang. However, none of them counts on the mansion's owner being invulnerable. Augustus scares the kids away with his superpowers, which include flight and superhuman strength. He gives them a Booker T. Washington–style speech about pulling themselves up by their bootstraps before mercifully shooing them off his premises. Most of the kids don't get anything out of the experience, but for Raquel, this is a life-changing event. She visits Augustus the next day, proposing that he become a crimefighter and that she be his sidekick. After much soul-searching and realizing that there are people who need his help, Augustus Freeman agrees to adopt the persona of Icon, and he takes on Raquel as his sidekick, Rocket. He imbues her with gadgets that allow her to fly, and to absorb an opponent's force and throw it back at them.

BLOOD SYNDICATE WAS A RARITY IN COMICS, A SYMPATHETIC DEPICTION OF GANG LIFE.

However, the realities of life as a black man in America are not lost, even on one as powerful as a superhero. The first time that Icon and Rocket fly down to help the police, the cops surround them and tell them to keep their hands in the air. Rocket can only say, "I bet this never happens to Superman." Here we see that, as with all his other Milestone characters, McDuffie has kept one foot in the world of fantasy and one foot in the real world. In an America where black men are routinely pulled over by police for the crime of being black, McDuffie muses, the same thing would doubtless happen to a superhero.

Icon and Rocket had a unique relationship. They were often at odds, Icon's Booker T. Washington self-reliance philosophy clashing with Rocket's W. E. B. DuBois–inspired philosophy of helping the downtrodden. At one point, Icon and Rocket lock horns over his decision to support an amuse-ment park that is being built on Paris Island, thus making many of its residents homeless. More importantly, when she found out she was pregnant, Raquel clashed with Augustus over her decision to keep the child. This made her the first superhero who was an unwed teenage mother, and predictably, it also sparked controversy.

"That was really conscious," McDuffie points out. "There were a couple of things going on in the culture at the time that really annoyed me. One was the demonization of unwed mothers. It was just this idea that they were bad people who were trying to get over on the rest of us by

ICON AND ROCKET. ICON WAS MILESTONE'S FLAGSHIP CHARACTER, ALTHOUGH MCDUFFIE HAS OFTEN CONSIDERED ROCKET TO BE THE REAL PROTAGONIST OF THE SERIES.

taking all that juicy welfare money, because you know, that's a *great* life. And the fact of the matter is, we all know unwed mothers. A lot of us love people who were unwed mothers. So what I thought I'd do was, I would create this character, I would make people like her, and then I would reveal that she was this stereotype that they dismiss so easily."

McDuffie says that the character of Rocket was even more important than Icon in some ways; the story is often told through her eyes, and she comes up with the original idea for her and Augustus to put on colorful costumes and be superheroes. "To me, *Icon* was always [Rocket's] book," he admits. "She was the protagonist. Icon was her idea. She was the most interesting thing to me about the book." When Rocket discovers that she's pregnant and decides to keep the baby, it fueled a healthy debate among readers on both sides of the abortion issue, which was exactly what McDuffie had in mind when he and his colleagues were developing Milestone: comic books that fueled intelligent social discourse.

THE LAST MILE

In 1994, thanks to the companywide Milestone crossover event called "The Shadow War," in which the government conspiracy behind the Big Bang was uncovered, the second wave of Milestone books was launched. Many of these Milestone books were written or created, or both, by McDuffie, who continued to edit much of the Milestone line. These "second wave" books continued to bear out his dictum that Milestone be a multicultural comic book universe. The group book *Shadow Cabinet*, for example, was led by the omniscient East Indian mystic Dharma, and its

ROCKET WAS THE FIRST SUPERHERO WHO WAS AN UNWED TEENAGE MOTHER. PREDICTABLY, THIS SPARKED CONTROVERSY.

membership included Iranian superhero Iron Butterfly (she can bend any metal like silly putty), as well as black hippie shape-shifter Sideshow, and the lesbian couple Donner and Blitzen (the former has superstrength, the latter superspeed). *Xombi*, meanwhile, is one of McDuffie's more existential, surreal concepts. When Korean American research scientist Dr. David Kim is accidentally injected with his own microscopic nanotechnology, he discovers that he can regenerate lost limbs and, in effect, can never die.

The prolific McDuffie also edited various Milestone comics such as the *Blood Syndicate* spin-off miniseries *Wise Son: The White Wolf*, written and illustrated by Ho Che Anderson. And Milestone introduced the comics world to a wide array of exciting new writing and cartooning talent, such as *Ghost Rider* scribe Ivan Velez (*Blood Syndicate*) and *Earth X* artist John Paul Leon (*Static*).

Yet despite such diverse offerings Milestone saw a rapid decline in sales. Titles were quickly dropped from its roster, until only three titles remained: *Icon*, *Hardware*, and *Static*. Early in 1997, Milestone stopped publishing. Several possible reasons have been given for Milestone's lack of sales success: a largely white, emotionally immature superhero comics readership that saw black superheroes as "a black thing" and therefore wanted nothing to do with them; comics shop retailers who refused to stock enough copies of the books, assuming that said white audiences wouldn't buy them; the misperception that the books were overtly political, separatist "activist literature," the sort of thing Malcolm X would create if he was a comic book writer (Malcolm X-Men?).

What cannot be disputed is that, although acclaimed by both media critics and fellow comics pros alike, Milestone had the misfortune to arrive in the midst of the early-nineties comics glut. This "glut period" saw the demise of fellow indie comics companies Comico and Eclipse, and the coronation of the upstart Image Comics, a line started by a group of Marvel's star artists who'd jumped ship to make it on their own. With Image hogging the spotlight and DC and Marvel instituting sales gimmicks ("Death of Superman," anyone?), Milestone's product often got lost in the shuffle. According to McDuffie, Milestone Media stopped publishing because he and the other founding partners saw the writing on the wall, and they knew that the end was near.

This was particularly heartbreaking for McDuffie, who'd been the principal writer/cocreator for all three of Milestone's last surviving series, and who didn't have time plotwise to adequately tie up all the loose ends and give each title a proper send-off. In many cases, the series' *intended* final issues were written and even somewhat illustrated, but never completed, and certainly never published. McDuffie had also long planned to do a special "wrap up" issue to put a cap on the Milestone universe that would serve as a grand series finale to his characters. This too was written but hasn't been drawn yet. "It would have tied up all the loose story ends," he explains. "It would have been a complete story for people who've never read it before. It's like, from a reader's point of view, here's what happens to everybody. It was actually going to be called *Milestone Ultimate*. I pitched it to [DC] several times since then, but I don't think they really want to go down that road again."

So, what is the future of Milestone Media? Milestone does still exist as a licensing company, and occasionally there is interest in bringing back the comic book line, starting with fan favorites like *Icon*. Recently, Milestone Media was involved in the *Static Shock* animated series that ran on the WB network (as part of the Kids WB programming block) from 2000 to 2004. The series was an adaptation of the Milestone series *Static*, and Dwayne McDuffie was the show's story editor. He also wrote many episodes of the four-time Emmy-nominated series, and the character's cocreator Denys Cowan directed various episodes. In terms of the comic books, however, McDuffie says, "I'm sure one of these days [we'll do something]. Everything comes back. The epigraph to the unpublished final Milestone book was Eudora Welty saying, 'Never think you've seen the last of anything.'"

ANIMANIA

The *Static Shock* cartoon gave McDuffie entrée into the world of animation, a world where he fits in quite well. Today, McDuffie is one of the most sought-after writer/producers in the television animation business, penning episodes of *Scooby-Doo*, *Teen Titans*, *Justice League*, and its more recent incarnation, *Justice League Unlimited*. With the two *Justice League* series, McDuffie, along with fellow writer/producers like Bruce Timm, Rich Fogel, and Paul Dini, has brought a depth and complexity to these characters that was certainly missing from 1970s-era superhero shows like *Challenge of the Super-Friends*. The character-driven writing on the show continues to surpass many of the live-action dramas currently on television, a testament to McDuffie and Co.'s love for the superhero genre. And many of the McDuffie-scripted episodes of *JLU* have shone the spotlight on DC's African American superheroes, such as Green Lantern John Stewart (voiced by Phil LaMarr) and Vixen (voiced by Gina Torres), giving the show a more multicultural bent than previous animated offerings.

And in the midst of all this animania, Dwayne McDuffie still finds time for the occasional comic book writing assignment. This includes his pet project, a graphic novel entitled *The Road to Hell*, cowritten by McDuffie and his Milestone associate editor Matt Wayne. They originally wrote it as a screenplay—it was even optioned by a major production company—but when nothing came of it, the script reverted back to them, and they decided to develop it as a graphic novel. McDuffie describes *The Road to Hell* as a romantic comedy, but with a faustian twist. "It's about a female scientist who has built a machine to go to hell," he explains. "Literally. And her assistant has an unrequited crush on her. The IRS comes to take the ship away because they owe back taxes, so they make a run for it and end up in hell. Satan falls in love with her, so there's a love triangle between her, Satan, and the assistant." *The Road to Hell* is illustrated by the versatile Rick Parker, who was McDuffie's letterer on *Damage Control*. McDuffie will be self-publishing the graphic novel in the near future (as of this writing).

NEVER THINK YOU'VE SEEN THE LAST

Dwayne McDuffie did what millions of disgruntled Americans would love to do: he struck out on his own and went into business for himself, creating and controlling his own product through Milestone Media. People who were usually not given a second look in other comics—black and Asian characters, gang members, gay and lesbian characters, drug addicts, pregnant teens—were here given the spotlight, and superpowers to boot! Through Milestone's distribution deal with DC, McDuffie and the company's other founders were free to develop a line of titles which would be seen by the largest number of people possible, making the company the most successful black-owned comic book company ever. Milestone may have lasted for just five years as a comic book publisher, but Milestone Media is still a viable business, and there's always the chance that they'll make a triumphant return to the comics game. And for one brief, shining moment, Milestone Media waved the banner of comic book multiculturalism, and succeeded where so many others had failed.

Today there are more minority superheroes in the comics mainstream than ever, from DC's *Steel* (a character based in part on Dwayne McDuffie himself) to acknowledged Milestone fan (and *House Party* director) Reginald Hudlin's successful recent run writing Marvel's *Black Panther*. Storm is one of Marvel's most popular *X-Men* characters, and DC's current Firestorm is black, as is Green Lantern John Stewart. There's still much work to be done in terms of making superhero comics as representative of the America in which they live, but Milestone led the way and inspired plenty of others, who are now continuing their work. The Milestone universe lives on in the hearts and minds of millions of wide-eyed, cereal-slurping children as they plop down in front of the television to watch the oft-rerun *Static Shock* animated series, created by McDuffie. And McDuffie himself has continued to bring a multicultural sensibility to animated shows like *Justice League*, creating black characters with dignity and integrity.

By any standard, he's reached a creative milestone.

HO CHE ANDERSON

SELF-PORTRAIT.

"The church was what made him. The church was who he was. It gave his whole world order, gave it balance. It made him special—he was the reverend's boy. The reverend's boy wasn't allowed to feel anger."

—From *King: Volume 1*, 1993

We know comic books are good at telling tales of costume-clad superheroes, intergalactic space explorers, and mysterious, ebony-robed vigilantes. We also know that comics are a good medium for delivering stories about awkward, giddy teenagers; zany, anthropomorphic talking animals; stalwart cowboys bravely manning the frontier; and goopy, slime-dripping radioactive monsters. And recently, there's a slew of talented cartoonists telling stories about their own everyday lives, in a stark, brutally honest autobiographical manner. However, one important genre that's often ignored in books about comics history is the nonfiction biography. Max Gaines, who invented the comic book with *Famous Funnies* in 1934, pioneered the comics biography through his Educational Comics, which published titles like *Picture Stories From World History* in the 1940s. More recently, efforts such as 1994's graphic novel *Introducing Kafka* (by Robert Crumb and David Zane Mairowitz) and Chester Brown's 1999–2003 series *Louis Riel* (about the nineteenth, century Canadian revolutionary) have eschewed the sugarcoated *Classics Illustrated* approach to historical biographies that Gaines insisted upon.

But perhaps the most well-known of the recent spate of comics biographies comes from Brown's fellow Canadian cartoonist, Ho Che Anderson. Anderson's *King*, a massively ambitious, three-volume series of graphic novels chronicling the life and death of the Reverend Doctor Martin Luther King, Jr., was published by Fantagraphics Books intermittently over the course of ten years (1993–2003). One of the things that made *King* such an important undertaking is that Anderson forsook the oft-accepted portrayal of Dr. King as a one-dimensional angelic martyr, painting an unflinchingly honest, warts-and-all portrait of his subject. The *King* trilogy firmly established Ho Che

Anderson as an artist to watch. Unsurprisingly, Anderson's take on this beloved national icon also sparked quite a bit of controversy.

Of course, as anyone familiar with his other work knows, being provocative is nothing new to Anderson. Whether he's chronicling the adventures of superheroes or real-life heroes, one look at the rest of his oeuvre will tell the reader that this is one artist who tells it like it is. . . .

THE ALTERNATIVE SCENE

Ho Che Anderson was born in 1969 in London, England, to a Guyanese mother and a Jamaican father. He was named for the revolutionaries Ho Chi Minh and Che Guevara, perhaps signaling the overtly political path his life would take. In March 1975, the family moved to Toronto, Canada. From the beginning, Anderson had a fascination with words and pictures. "I've been interested in comic books pretty much my whole life," he admits. "I read them when I was a kid and I knew from the time I was a kid that I wanted to be an artist; I wasn't sure in what form, but I knew I wanted to draw in some capacity, and I also knew pretty early on I wanted to write as well. By the time I became a teenager I think I'd already put it together in my mind that doing comic books would be a pretty good place to practice both disciplines. I don't know if there was ever a point where I said, 'OK, I'm going to do comics,' it just seemed to be the direction I was going in and there was nobody around to say this wasn't the right thing, so I just kept doing it."

Once he discovered comic books, he started worshipping at the altar of Mighty Marvel. "Influences when I was a kid were all the Marvel Comics guys," he nods. "You know, guys like Steve Ditko, Don Heck, Jack Kirby, Stan Lee obviously, all those guys in the fifties and sixties who were kicking ass back then. I didn't get into anything beyond Marvel Comics until I was like nineteen, in my late teens. By that time my interest in the whole superhero thing was beginning to wane considerably in favor of girls, and in favor of stuff that I'd guess you'd call more of the alternative scene at this point." Though he'd abandoned Kirby and company for underground cartoonists such as Robert Crumb, the shadow of Kirby's influence is still present in Anderson's bulky, powerful figures, larger-than-life behemoths who seem to be made of solid granite.

During high school, Anderson started sending out samples to various comic book companies. "I stocked up an impressive array of rejection letters [from] Marvel and DC," he recalls. Then there was Comico, the now-defunct independent comics publisher, which was most known in the 1980s for publishing artist/writer Matt Wagner's *Grendel* (now published by Dark Horse), the chronicles of a masked assassin and crime lord consumed by the spirit of vengeance. Ho Che Anderson's first paid gig in comics was as an illustrator in the anthology title *Grendel: Black, White, and Red* in 1988. It would sit on the shelves for ten years before seeing print. (Later, he would illustrate another story for Wagner in 1990's *Grendel Tales Preview*.)

But Anderson's career jump-started in 1989, when he started doing work for Gary Groth's Fantagraphics Books, publishers of such unique comics as Stan Sakai's *Usagi Yojimbo* (literally, 'Samurai Rabbit') and the Hernandez Brothers' *Love & Rockets*. "I'd sent some samples of some stuff out to them [Fantagraphics] as part of that whole group of people I was sending stuff out to back when I was a teenager," Anderson recalls. "What happened was, one day I got a package and letter in the mail, from the people who were beginning Eros Comix [Fantagraphics's erotica division], kind of a call for submissions. I sent something again, and lo and behold a couple of weeks later Gary Groth called me back and said, 'You know, Eros is actually Fantagraphics, *I'm* actually Fantagraphics, I'm interested in your work. Are you interested in doing something for us?' What do you do, say 'No'? This is what I'd been trying for many years, so this was my first chance to actually write and draw my own material! No way I was going to turn that down! So I did my first book with them, *I Want to Be Your Dog* [published in 1990]. I finished that and I went directly to *King*, so I couldn't have been more than nineteen or twenty when I went on to *King*."

Anderson notes that "it was quite a transition" going from *I Want to Be Your Dog*—a graphic novel about sadomasochism—to a serious historical drama like *King*. He shrugs; "Why not? Why should people be pigeon-holed? I think everyone is schizophrenic to a certain extent. I mean, I like [erotica], but I also like things that are serious, so why can't I express them both? That's one of the things I appreciate about comics. You can do both."

In retrospect, *I Want to Be Your Dog* was just Gary Groth's way of getting Ho Che Anderson's feet wet as a writer/artist before he moved him on to bigger and better things. Groth had always wanted Fantagraphics to publish a graphic novel about Martin Luther King. With Ho Che Anderson, he knew he had found just the man for the job. "I think it was during that first conversation, actually, that [Groth] talked to me about *King*, which I was only too happy to take on," Anderson recalls. "Apparently, it was a gamble on his part because he didn't know what he was getting into. I mean, he didn't know, really, if I was any good or not, [if I was] able to handle a project like that. I suspect me being one of the few black cartoonists out there, and him having a big interest in telling the story of Martin Luther King, was probably [the main reason.]"

Regardless of the reason, Gary Groth now had his artist-writer for his *King* project, and Anderson was hungry to prove himself. But the *King* project proved to be an even more massive undertaking than either man imagined.

RESEARCH AND DEVELOPMENT

In creating *King*, Ho Che Anderson's first task—and it was a mammoth one—was to research the life, death, and career of one of the most frequently discussed public figures in American history, the Reverend Doctor Martin Luther King, Jr. Ho Che Anderson may have had his first preliminary discussions about *King* with Gary Groth in 1989, but due to all the research involved, the first volume of *King* didn't appear on bookshelves until 1993. "It took about a year and a half of research, and then writing, and then drawing, for that first book to actually come out," Anderson explains.

When researching *King*, Anderson relied on a myriad of books and documentaries to thoroughly immerse himself in the subject, becoming a bona fide MLK authority in the process. "Basically, whatever I could find over the

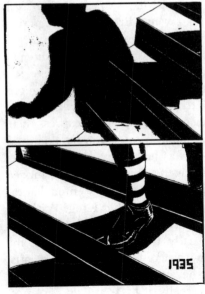 

ANDERSON SHOWS US THE TIMID YOUNG "ML," WHO HAS MILES TO GO BEFORE HE BECOMES THE DR. KING WE'VE COME TO KNOW.

ANDERSON'S DYNAMIC RE-CREATION OF THE LEGENDARY "I HAVE A DREAM" SPEECH HAS AN EPIC QUALITY NOT UNLIKE THAT FOUND IN ANCIENT GREEK TRAGEDIES.

years that would help, that would aid in the story, I gathered and I examined and took copious notes from," he says. "I saw documentaries like *Eyes on the Prize* and read quite a few books, like *And the Walls Came Tumbling Down* by Ralph David Abernathy. I spent about six or seven months doing nothing but reading, initially to write the first draft of the script, and then over the years I continued to research and weave more and more stuff into the story."

Anderson made sure to include scenes from King's life that were very much open to the public record, such as King's "I Have a Dream" speech in Washington DC. But he also took dramatic liberties to create scenes that no one could possibly have been privy to, such as King's rose garden meeting with President John F. Kennedy, during which no reporters were allowed. The only two people who knew what really went on during that meeting were Dr. King and President Kennedy, and neither of them was spilling the beans any time soon. So Anderson took an educated guess. In his version of the meeting, King urged the President to take a firmer stance against segregation and to more openly declare his allegiance with King's cause. "Now, something like the rose garden speech—I'm reasonably certain that that's the kind of thing they would have spoken about," Anderson notes. "Whether it was presented in that exact form no one will ever know, because both those people are dead. I'm sure there were some photographers running around, but I doubt there were very many sound guys sitting there recording their every word. So, you keep it within certain parameters and go from there. You research the hell out of it, then you just trust your abilities as a writer and as an artist, and that's the best you can do. Like I said, I never made any claims that this is a kind of documentary. I said that right from the start, I said it was a primer: this is one man's riff on what might have happened, so if somebody feels that what I've presented is inaccurate, please just go out and do your own research, and tell me where I've messed up."

Also in this scene, the two men commiserated on the subject of infidelity, something they both knew a little something about. "I don't know if Kennedy actually mouthed those words, but I'd be surprised if somewhere in their conversation, something similar didn't pop up," Anderson explains. "They're both intelligent guys, they knew what was going on. Who were they fooling? I mean, that was standard then. Guys could do whatever they wanted back then, it was not that big of a deal. I mean, I'm sure it was a big deal to their wives, but I'm also sure it was more or less accepted and part of the 'privileges of being a man.' I don't necessarily condone it, but I'm not going to judge them for it either."

IN KING, HO CHE ANDERSON SHOWED AN ALL-TOO-HUMAN MARTIN LUTHER KING, A DEPICTION THAT ANGERED SOME READERS.

This is an issue that the *King* books have been criticized for: their frank depictions of Martin Luther King's extramarital affairs. Though well-documented (and reportedly, Coretta Scott King knew of them as well), many readers felt that this aspect of Dr. King's life was inappropriate in a graphic novel about such a universally admired and respected man. The *King* books also depict Dr. King as all-too-human, someone who, although immensely charismatic and good-hearted, was also fallible and occasionally exploded in anger at his staff members. This was Anderson's way of steering the audience away from the commonly held image of Dr. King, that of a one-dimensional saint, and toward someone more readily accessible and fleshed-out, someone we can all relate to. Although, again, that's not how some readers saw it.

"Why should I portray some kind of saintlike figure that's simply not who he was?" Anderson asks. "In [King's] own words, 'I'm not a saint, I'm a sinner just like all God's children.' He said this himself. He knew his own limitations. I feel like it'd be a disservice, a dishonor too, if I tried to portray him as a person who he wasn't; that just seems silly to me. Also, first of all, for a story, where's the story? Where's the drama if all that's just sweet? It's not interesting to read, and also I think, like I said, it's a dishonor to who he was. If he was able to rise above his limitations, isn't that an impressive feat? Isn't that an incredible thing? Where's the test if everything comes easy to him? Saints just are not interesting."

Anderson is also keen to point out that he didn't simply fashion Dr. King's womanizing out of thin air. "Oh, that's a fact," he nods. "You read Abernathy's book, he's pretty frank about King's escapades on the road. And, you know, there's a famous incident where [FBI director] J. Edgar Hoover audiotaped a bunch of his escapades while he was away from home, compiled them on a tape, sent them to King's wife with a note that King should kill himself lest this stuff could become public knowledge. I mean, say what you want about Hoover, he didn't have to make this stuff up, he was recording King doing what he did, so that's a fact. My feeling is, I didn't give that stuff any more weight in the book than anything else. I think this stuff is presented as just simply one facet of a very complicated man's life, and it gives a certain amount of weight within the greater scope of the story, but we don't dwell on it, we move on."

Did Anderson ever worry about the negative reaction he might provoke by showing the dark side of a national hero? "No, I just don't care about that stuff," he shrugs. "People have attacked me for that kind of thing. They go crazy. That's not going to stop me from telling the story I want to tell or conducting my life. No matter what you do, you can't do anything that's not going to piss *somebody* off, that's not going to offend *somebody*, so why even worry about it? If I had told the story in a completely reverential tone, it wouldn't have been reverential *enough* to some people, but I'm not going to worry about that stuff, rest assured. If somebody wants to put a bullet in my head over that kind of thing, they're going to do it whether I want them to or not, and that's going to be the story of me. I don't worry about it."

STYLE AND INFLUENCE

Another often-cited aspect of the *King* books is their cinematic flair; *VIBE* magazine compared Ho Che Anderson to Orson Welles in terms of his "mastery of shadows and moods." It's evident that Anderson had been studying old movies when one notices the film noir–style use of black and white, the virtuoso camera angles, and the confident, rhythmic sense of pacing throughout *King*. Consider a scene in which Dr. King and a colleague get on a bus and sit in the back minding their own business, when a little old white lady gets on, looking saintly and frail as she smiles to the bus driver. She takes one look at Dr. King and scowls, muttering, "Niggers." The disappointed look on Dr. King's face says it all. The scene is completely visual, dripping with chiaroscuro ambience, and its staging is directly indebted to filmmaking stylists such as Welles or Scorsese. The recurring use of testimonial interviews with people who knew King is a device that was also used in Welles's masterpiece *Citizen Kane*, and this is most likely not a mere coincidence.

Theater has also influenced *King*, in scenes such as the two-character, monologue-heavy rose garden scene. "God, I'm more influenced by theater and film than I am by comic books!" Anderson exclaims. "It's my dream to eventually wind up in the cinema in one form or another, as a screenwriter, as a director, however I can claw my way in. I love comic books, comic books and movies are my great loves. I'm not sorry I chose to go down the road of comic books, but I also have regrets that I hadn't started [working in] film around the same time, because cinema especially has huge, huge, huge influences on me. I love visuals, and the kind of kinetic energy of the cinema and comic books, so I guess my heart will always go more toward celluloid than the stage. The work of Oliver Stone, Martin Scorsese, Spike Lee, people like that influenced *King* tremendously."

However, the theatrical influence is still there, specifically in the clipped language of *Volume 1*. The overlapping dialogue of many scenes recalls not only directors like Robert Altman, but playwrights like David

Mamet. "The funny thing is, I love Mamet, and he's definitely been an influence, but when I wrote [*King: Volume 1*], that was coming strictly out of my head," Anderson reveals. "I discovered Mamet a couple years after that, and I remember reading *Speed-the-Plow*, and I was like, 'Holy fuck! We're writing the exact same way!' I felt like I was reading a kindred spirit once I started actually reading his plays. But by that point, it just felt too artificial to me, I wanted more of a flow than a stutter."

In 2004, when Anderson had the opportunity to collect all three volumes of *King* into one mammoth edition (with an introduction by noted scholar Stanley Crouch), he achieved the "flow" he sought by largely excising the fragmented, staccato dialogue of *Volume 1* and replacing it with less stylized chit-chat. Consider the scene early on in which a college-age Dr. King is talking to a condescending yet well-meaning white woman. In the original version, King's dialogue reads: "I mean, I—a gathering like this where I'm from with Whites and Blacks sharing ideas, um, talking . . . like *we're* talking . . . No. *No.*" In the revised, collected edition, the dialogue now reads, "Where I'm from, something like this, with Blacks and Whites mingling so easily and sharing ideas—it just wouldn't happen."

Anderson points out that making the dialogue for *Volumes 2* and *3* less stylized than those for *Volume 1* wasn't so much a choice as a necessity. "I mean, I couldn't have gone back to [the style of] *Volume 1* whether I wanted to or not, it's just wasn't where I was anymore," he explains. After all, *Volumes 2* and *3* were written when Anderson was almost a decade older than he was during the creation of *Volume 1*, and by this time, he was a more mature man with a different writing style. But he was never concerned that the fact that parts two and three weren't as stylistically written would make *King* seem tonally inconsistent. "I knew I was going to go back and try to smooth out [*Volume 1*] as much as I could when I did the collection," he reveals. "The thing is, sometimes I'm an audience member myself, so I have respect for how an audience feels, and part of me feels kind of bad if a reader appreciates something and it's been changed. There's kind of a trust you get into with the reader and I don't want to violate that, but at the same time, I only care up to a certain point. Like I said, I'm not getting paid big money for this, so I guess I've got to be the audience for the most part, and I don't get a lot of fan letters from people telling me 'I love this, don't change it.' If I got that, maybe I'd be more reverential for the old stuff, but I don't have those kind of readers. For me, I've always got to please myself, quite frankly. If it's inconsistent, I can't live with it."

Writing and illustrating *King* was also an emotional undertaking for Anderson, as it altered his feelings about the man and his legacy. "It's interesting," he muses. "Before I started the book I didn't really give King much thought one way or the other. That might make me the worst person to write the book, or the best person to write the book. I'm not really sure. I didn't go in with any preconceived notions, with any expectations, with any axe to grind, or with any kind of mandate to make him good, bad, or whatever. I simply went in with curiosity, wanting to learn as much about him as I could and to let what I'd learned dictate the kind of story I was going to tell, so any extent that I gave any thought to King's legacy before taking this project on was, well, he got up and he gave the incredible 'I Have a Dream' speech and then his life . . . that was pretty much it for him. It was a fateful stop. Learning and doing the research, I learned that he was no saint. He was a man of incredible achievement, but, you know, hey, he was a sinner just like the rest of us, flawed just like the rest of us, *yet* with the ability to rise above those flaws, to rise above the limitations fixed by many of us, and to make a pretty substantial impact on the culture, at least on the popular culture."

And if creating *King* didn't start out as a labor of love for Ho Che Anderson, it certainly was by the time he'd finished it. So what changed? "By then, I'd realized that this guy kicked ass! He was an incredible man. Able to talk to the people in the street and the people in the boardrooms, able to talk to power players and the brothers and sisters on the street. That's a rare gift, you know? I developed an incredible sense of love and appreciation for the guy. I'm not reverential toward the man, it's more that I have incredible respect for him. You can't tell somebody's life story without developing some kind of love for who they were. I just don't think it's possible."

ENDING AN EPIC

King: Volume 1 follows Dr. Martin Luther King from his childhood to his involvement in the Montgomery, Alabama, bus boycotts, and it ends on a cliffhanger in 1960, when King is abruptly stabbed by a crazy woman while promoting a book chronicling said boycotts. *Volume 2* begins with his recovery, and chronicles his growing political influence (and with it, the accompanying threats to his life and safety), and his attempts to help the embattled Freedom Riders in the South. It ends on a note of hope, with his 1963 March on Washington and his "I Have a Dream" speech.

But those of us who know anything about King's life know the worst is yet to come in *Volume 3*, by far the darkest chapter, which opens with King losing a strong ally, the slain President Kennedy. We see King making a valiant effort to reach out to black street gangs, while being criticized by everyone, from the media to young black militants. The FBI is shadowing him. Things are starting to look bleak, and a 1968 Memphis sanitation workers' strike ends in chaos and violence. Shortly thereafter, King is assassinated in the Lorraine Motel. But a story this epic needs an epilogue, and that's where Ho Che Anderson was of two minds. In the original version of *Volume 3*, the epilogue consisted of a four-page spread in which we see a slew of vignettes, snippets of the continued race wars played out in the present day: A black woman is falsely accused of shoplifting by an Asian woman. White cops cruelly stare down a group of young black men as though they were criminals, completely ignoring the neo-Nazis right beside them. Has anything really changed since Dr. King's day? The struggle goes on.

In the collected edition of *King: Volume 3*, Anderson decided to change this epilogue. It now ends with a reprise of the same sequence we see at the collected edition's prologue: a young Martin Luther King listening to the radio as Nat King Cole's "Sweet Lorraine" wafts over the airwaves. He drapes his necklace over a crucifix, an iconic scene, and one that reminds us of King's dream, his struggle, his hope for the future. It's a bittersweet, dreamlike image, but it's less cynical than the "present day" epilogue Anderson had previously chosen. "The contemporary stuff at the ending was dropped, and the reason I did that," he explains, "was because looking at the book, the three volumes as a whole, I realized that the ending was such a downer and was kind of a slap in the face to all the work that these people had done! Because what it said was, despite of all their struggle, they hadn't made much impact. Essentially, it continued on the way it always has. In some ways, I think that's true, but in other ways I don't think that's true. I think their work did have an impact, and I just wanted an ending that was a little bit more reflective of that. Not just more reflective, but a little bit more hopeful."

A WISE JOURNEY

Ho Che Anderson, faced with the Herculean task of documenting the life of a true American legend, understandably took his time developing *Volumes 2* and *3*. But as he figured out a way to continue the saga after *Volume 1* was published in 1993, he still had to pay the bills. So he embarked on a number of other comics projects: he was a frequent contributor to the Dark Horse comics magazine *Deadline USA*; he illustrated a children's book, *Steel Drums and Ice Skates*; he wrote and illustrated a young adult novel, *The No-Boys Club*;

A RARE MAINSTREAM OUTING FROM ANDERSON, WISE SON SHOWCASES THE KING CARTOONIST'S UNIQUE TAKE ON THE SUPERHERO GENRE.

and he cocreated the 1999–2001 Fantagraphics comic book series *Pop Life*, which he wrote (it was illustrated by frequent collaborator Wilfred Santiago), about struggling musicians in his hometown of Toronto. But the most striking of these projects was also one that on the surface might seem an odd choice of material for someone who'd established himself as a serious artist. That project was the superhero title *Wise Son: The White Wolf*.

Wise Son, which Anderson wrote and illustrated, was a four-issue miniseries published by Milestone Media during 1996 and 1997. Wise Son was a member of the multicultural superhero group Blood Syndicate, a street gang that had acquired superpowers in the wake of "The Big Bang," an explosion that had granted extraordinary abilities to various citizens throughout the fictional city of Dakota. The *Wise Son* miniseries takes place in the slum district of Paris Island, forever known as "the bad part of town." But this miniseries has about as much to do with typical superhero fare as pro golf has to do with miniature golf. And it's where Ho Che Anderson was truly able to spread his creative wings.

This was Ho Che Anderson's first full-fledged foray into the superhero genre. Wise Son, a.k.a. Hannibal White, is a classic antihero in the mold of *The X-Men*'s Wolverine or *Buffy the Vampire Slayer*'s Angel. He's a tough guy loner with a sensitive side, he's nigh-invulnerable, and he's constantly waging an inner battle with his own dark side. True to the antihero mold, Wise Son's story is one of redemption. Hannibal White starts out the series as a drunken failure, only looking out for number one. Soon he finds a mentor, who sees his inner goodness. He comes to recognize his own inner strength as well, and use it to save the people he loves from the rising racial tensions on Paris Island.

Anderson says that he was given quite a bit of creative leeway with the material. "Milestone had certain parameters," he explains. "They knew that they wanted him to be away from his group, and they wanted to have kind of an old man character that guides Wise Son toward Islam—that was the whole thing, he was an Islamic character. So they gave me these parameters and said, pretty much, 'Do whatever you want, within reason.' So I created this story in which the character is about to turn twenty years old. And he's deeply disturbed by who he is, and what his life has become, and he decides just when [the Blood Syndicate is] going to throw this big birthday party for him, that he's going to exit. He's going to go out on his own, and there's this two- or three-week odyssey that he goes on. He starts shacking up with women, just kind of fucking them for their money and for their hotel rooms, and he meets this old man who recognizes him as being this undisciplined kind of character but with a lot of heart, and takes him under his wing. At the same time there's this neo-Nazi group, the Children of the Ivory Fist, and they've been going around killing these Muslim ministers. So, these events collide, and they start to threaten the old man, and by this point Wise has decided that the old man is under his protection. So it kind of comes to a head one night."

Here Anderson was using the superhero genre to tell an intimate story about one man's personal journey, without any of the cartoon derring-do or kung-fu fisticuffs one would expect from a superhero comic. The violence in this book is real, and it is jarring. When a character is shot or stabbed, they die, and there's rarely anyone there to help them. And this makes Wise's position that much more dire: although no one can hurt *him*, he's cursed to watch everyone around him die. And there's only one of him, hardly enough to stop the violence, to curb the evil. The reader feels a palpable sense of Wise's frustration, his tension and his helplessness. This is as far as one can get from "Truth, Justice, and the American Way."

SCREAM FOR TOMORROW

In the wake of *King*'s success (*Volume 1* alone was Fantagraphics's most successful title of the year when it hit in 1993), Ho Che Anderson has seen the book become a frequently cited academic resource in schools and libraries all over North America. All of which strikes him as a bit surreal. In fact, while he was writing *King*, Anderson couldn't have imagined it would have the impact or acclaim that it's earned since then. Why does this surprise him so? "I don't know, [when I first developed *King*] I was just staying in my room, basically," he explains. "When I started out, you know, there's no way for a kid to know that people will take him this seriously. I did the best I could, but I guess I just never really thought that it would have the kind of impact that a bunch of academics would want to latch on to; so, it surprised me then, it surprises me now. I mean, I think it's a well-researched book, and I certainly wrote the shit out of it, but I guess it's some sort of inferiority complex on my part."

This "inferiority complex" certainly hasn't kept Anderson's productivity levels down. Since he finished *King*, he's been working furiously on a handful of comic book projects. One of those projects recently saw fruition as the Fantagraphics graphic novel *Scream Queen*, a chilling story of revenge and betrayal. "*Scream Queen* is a ghost story focusing on two characters," Anderson reveals. "One [is] named Avril, whose car has broken down in the desert when she's picked up by a mysterious unnamed woman who takes her to her job. [It's in the] dead of night, middle of the desert. We learn a little bit about who both of these women are, before suddenly, the woman who dropped Avril off at her job suddenly has to take off, and that's when we take a little bit of a twist and realize we're dealing with something other than a nice little story between two women! I've always loved ghost stories and their depiction, so this is kind of my attempt to navigate those waters." The woman turns out to be the living dead, come to take her ex-lover to the other side. She follows in the literary tradition of scorned women who exact revenge, a tradition seen everywhere from Greek tragedies such as *Medea* to horror novels such as Stephen King's *Carrie*. In *Scream Queen*, as in *Wise Son*, Anderson shows that he's just as adept in genre fiction as he is in straight period drama. And with other projects in development such as the satirical science-fiction comic *Corporate World* ("It's got spaceships and guys with ray guns, but also the kind of stuff I've been known for a little bit more, [i.e.,] social realism."), it looks like he's just getting started.

Ho Che Anderson is, as his name indicates, an artist with a deeply felt sense of history and struggle. The man who once thought he was the "worst person for the job" of telling the life story of Dr. Martin Luther King has penned and illustrated the definitive graphic novel on the subject, a work that has become the subject of scholarly debate for its frank discussion of its subject's flaws. In doing so, he's joined the ranks of fellow cartoonists who chronicle history in comic book form, a venerable breed that includes Art Spiegelman and Sue Coe. The brilliance of his *King* trilogy has been acknowledged by academics like Stanley Crouch and major publications like the *Guardian* and the *New York Times*. And a quick glance of Anderson's post-*King* résumé points to the fact that his major comics all touch on the same topic. Whether it's a study of racial strife such as *White Wolf*, or an angry treatise on scorned women like *Scream Queen*, Anderson's art is the work of a storyteller obsessed with the theme of oppressed peoples fighting for vindication. What's ironic is that it's the same message at the heart of most mainstream superhero comics; this staunch alternative cartoonist simply took a more realistic road to get there.

MARJANE SATRAPI

SELF-PORTRAIT.

"Now that the revolution was finally over once and for all, I abandoned the dialectic imperialism of my comic strips. The only place I felt safe was in the arms of my friend."

—From *Persepolis*, 2000

In just five short years, Marjane Satrapi has catapulted to comic book stardom, largely as a result of her first major work in comics, *Persepolis*. *Persepolis* is the story of how Satrapi came of age in Iran during the Islamic Revolution of 1979, and how she and her family coped with the various political and cultural changes that ensued, such as oppressive censorship, religious fundamentalism, and the veils females were suddenly forced to wear. Her parents eventually sent her to live in Europe, where she wouldn't be forced to wear veils of any kind, literally or metaphorically.

Often compared favorably to her friend and mentor Art Spiegelman, Satrapi's autobiographical comics are infused with a refreshing frankness and honesty sometimes lacking in the more subdued works of her Western contemporaries. There's an urgency here that's apparent even in her lighter graphic novels such as *Embroideries*, a refreshingly comedic series of vignettes in which the women in her family trade stories about love, sex, and passion. Marjane Satrapi is a distinct new voice on the comics scene, a natural storyteller who fills a much-needed gap. Political without being didactic, smart without being a smart-ass, she's unshackled by the bullshit pleasantries and political correctness that hamper so many American cartoonists. And if her story is an open book, thank goodness she's chosen the medium of *comic* books to tell that story. We're all the more privileged to be her chosen audience.

THE WORMS OF DRACULA

Marjane Satrapi was born in 1969 in Rasht, Iran, the only child of outspoken Marxist parents and the great-granddaughter of one of Iran's last emperors. She grew up in Tehran, where she attended the Lycée Français, and she was not much of a comic book fan growing up. Comics were just something that she saw in toy stores around Tehran, and she regarded them more or less indifferently. The problem was, she didn't identify with the characters she was seeing on the comics page. "I don't come really from a culture of comics, I should say," she points out. "It's not that in Iran we didn't have any comics, because of course [we had] the translations of [Herge's] *Tintin*, and [Goscinny and Uderzo's] *Asterix* and these things. The problem with *Tintin* was that all the main characters are male. Plus, I thought that Tintin, he was really disgusting looking."

However, when Satrapi was about seven years old, a comic book affected her for the first time. It really got under her skin—literally. "There was this toy shop that was very close to my house that sold American comics and one of this comics was called *Dracula*," she recalls. "It was drawn in the same way as *Wonder Woman* and *Superman* and all these comic books that were [popular] in the seventies. We were very much invaded by the American culture at the time. Anyway, the Dracula comic was in English, and I had a cousin who was younger than me. He was sure that I could read everything. And so he asked me, 'Can you read that?' And I was like, 'Yeah, yeah, I can read it.' So I started translating the whole thing, and I said, 'It is written if you want to become Dracula, you have to eat raw chicken!' So the whole summer, we kept on eating raw chicken. If our parents bought some chicken, we would steal a piece and eat it raw. And the result was, we got worms at the end of the summer. With raw chicken and these things, you get worms. So that was actually my first relationship with comics. I got worms. But I was not really a comic reader, and the first time I start reading comics, I was twenty-seven or twenty-eight."

That fateful comic book was Art Spiegelman's *Maus*, and it was the first comic book that Marjane Satrapi read that got her hooked on comics as a medium. More importantly, *Maus* convinced her that comics could be a viable art form. Since leaving Iran for good at age twenty-four (she'd briefly lived in Austria during her teen years, only to return to her family in Tehran, events that are chronicled in *Persepolis 2*), she was studying art in Strasbourg, but soon relocated to Paris. "The girlfriend of [cartoonist] Christophe Blain, she was in my class when I was studying in Strasbourg," Satrapi explains. "So I met Christophe Blain, and I moved to Paris, and they had this studio. Somebody left and that was a table free. And I asked Christophe, 'Can I take this table?' 'OK sure, you can come.' And that's how I ended up in a studio with cartoonists!"

These cartoonists introduced her to the world of comic books, starting of course with Spiegelman's *Maus*, an international classic. "Before *Maus*, my idea about comics was like anybody's idea about comics," she explains. "For me [comic books] were something for retarded adolescents, and it was just bullshit stories, it was nothing interesting. When the first comic that you read is *Maus*, suddenly you're like, 'Oh, it's not exactly the way I thought.'" Satrapi didn't know much about the history of this art form, but she willingly sought out other graphic novels and voraciously, hungrily, consumed them. "I read [Chris Ware's] *Jimmy Corrigan*, I read lots of the best cartoonists. I read Joann Sfar, and Christophe Blain, and then after that I started reading this series called *Billie Holiday* that's made by Sampayo and Jose Munoz. I read *Palestine* by Joe Sacco, and then I read *David Boring* by Daniel Clowes. Then I read also the book of [Alberto] Breccia, this Argentinian cartoonist. Breccia—he's a little bit in the same side as Munoz, but it is much more abstract."

THE BIRTH OF PERSEPOLIS

At this point, Marjane Satrapi was only an observer, not a participant, preferring to read graphic novels but never trying to actually write or illustrate one herself. What made her want to cross that line and actually draw her own comics? "You know, me making comics," she reveals, "that was just a coincidence! It was absolutely not planned that I was going to make comics. What I was sure about was that I wanted to write and I wanted to draw. So first of all, I was like, 'I'm going to make children's books,' which I made, actually. The thing is, you have to be almost like a monk to be able to make comics. It's extremely long work. You have to have a scenario, you have to have dialogue, you have to compose each frame."

Still, Satrapi was sharing a studio occupied largely by cartoonists, and though she was loathe to admit it, comics seemed to be the best medium to express the stories she wanted to tell. "Christophe Blain, he made me enter into this studio where every other cartoonist of the new generation in France, they were working here! And I saw them working, and I was saying, 'Jesus Christ, what maniacs! I would never be able to do their work.' And every day we were speaking, and I was saying that in my country this, and in my country that. And these guys, they say, 'It is so interesting and I want you to make this story.' And I don't think it was so interesting for them. They just wanted me to shut up, so they say, 'Why don't you write that? Why don't you do something out of it?' So my friends actually in my studio, they pushed me, in a way, to start making comics. And I [was] sort of like, 'OK, I will try.' And also it is so important for me to say this first [comics] story [I drew], that was *Persepolis*. So I started, and really, the first page of the comic that I made, I was like, 'Oh my God, I want to do that in my life!' I *knew* it. Suddenly it became completely obvious, because it's a very particular form of narration in comics. First of all, comics is the contrary of all the other forms of illustration. The illustration in comics, they always have to have movement because you have to show the movement. It is the only medium in the world in which the images, they are the part of the narration and are not just there to illustrate the text."

Satrapi found that the medium of comics gave her immense freedom as a storyteller. "In comics, what is amazing for me is that you can write with the images," she notes. "So it is a very special language, and to understand how to use this very international and without-any-borders language, it gives you freedom! Because suddenly you can talk about extremely subtle stuff without using words. And people everywhere in the world, they understand almost the same thing from the same image. It is just amazing for me."

Persepolis probably wouldn't have evolved from a tentative artistic experiment into a series of bestselling graphic novels without the intervention of cartoonist Emile Bravo, who counseled Satrapi that her stories about growing up in the shadow of the Islamic Revolution were worth telling. He served as a mentor to her in much the same way that Christophe Blain had. "[Emile Bravo] was basically the one who really taught me everything about comics," she reveals. "He was absolutely passionate about the fact that [*Persepolis*] was a very important story, that it was a global problem, a human problem. And he was really the one who taught me how you think as a cartoonist, how you write as a cartoonist. So he followed my work from the beginning until the end. And he taught me a lot of things. The good thing was that I was surrounded by many, many very nice people, and the answer to the people that tell me, 'Oh, you're one of the only women in the comics, how do you feel, et cetera?' It felt great, I can tell you, it felt great. Because all my male colleagues, they absolutely wanted to protect me, they wanted to help me, and everybody was extremely nice. Everybody was going to the radio show or something, they were talking about my book. And then they tell you, 'Oh yes, the men, they are so macho, and they are so bad, they want us to die.' I don't believe that. So far I can tell you that in comics, basically almost everyone is a man. Rarely you see women. But experiences, at least they were great with them."

Another catalyst for Satrapi's plunging headlong into *Persepolis* was that her attempts at a children's book illustration career had met with rejection at every path. "In the world of publishing, you have to be already published to be able to get published," she explains. "And also, I really presented myself in an extremely bad way. I said, 'Oh, excuse me, I'm shit, and my project is shit,' and I didn't have any trust in myself. So of course nobody wanted to trust me either. It was like that for two years. I received about 186 'no' answers to all my projects."

Satrapi finally realized that if she self-published her own comic book, at least she'd be a published illustrator and this would give her the confidence to move on to her goal of writing and drawing other projects, such as children's books. "In 1999," she recalls, "I started making these comics with the idea that, 'OK, if nobody wants to publish it, I will just make copies and just give it to my friends. And that will be it.' And so I met this publishing house called L'Association because I knew one of the people [there]. And I presented them the project, and I said, 'Here is the first volume [of *Persepolis*].' And [editor Jean-Christophe Menu] said 'OK, we're going to publish it.' And the reason I'm very faithful to L'Association— even today I'm publishing with them—was that the day that Jean-Christophe Menu called me to say that the book is going to be published, and I told him, 'You know, *Persepolis* [is] going to be four volumes.' And he said 'OK, then we're going to publish four volumes.' And I said, 'Yes, but for example, if the first volume sells only two hundred or three hundred, what would you do?' And he said, 'I have never published any book until now in my life to make money out of it, so even if [it] sells fifty, it's not a problem. We'll publish all of them.' So these kind of things you don't hear very often nowadays. So I was really lucky."

STORIES AND STATEMENTS

Menu, good to his word, published *Persepolis* in four parts in Europe; one volume was released every year from 2000 to 2003. In the United States, it appeared in two volumes, published in 2003 and 2004 respectively. Book one of *Persepolis* (U.S. version) concerns Marjane Satrapi's childhood in the aftermath of the overthrow of the Shah's regime and the subsequent Islamic Revolution. We see how, starting in 1980, all women were forced to wear veils. Marjane's mother was harassed by fundamentalists for not dressing modestly enough. Marjane's father's friend Mohsen was mysteriously executed shortly after he was released from prison, where he'd been tortured for the better part of the 1970s. We see Marjane's Uncle Anoosh arrested as a "sworn enemy of the Republic" and then senselessly executed as a suspected Russian spy.

Perhaps most importantly, we see how confusing and traumatic all of this is to little Marjane, who's just trying to process and understand all this chaos. She has conversations with God, who appears to her as a grandfatherly, bearded friend; she starts reading a comic book titled *Dialectic Materialism*, about Descartes and Marx, which opens up her young mind to the world of ideas and philosophy; she threatens a neighbor boy with nails arranged on her hand like brass knuckles, because the boy's father was in the Shah's sadistic secret police; she tells her friend Laly, who's been told that her father Siamak was on a trip, that Siamak is really dead; and generally, young Marjane simply tries to cope. In 1984, her parents send her to Vienna, feeling that Tehran was unsafe for a young girl with a tendency to speak her thoughts.

Anger and frustration toward the Western media's portrayal of her homeland also factored into Marjane Satrapi's creation of *Persepolis*. "I heard so many strange things about my country [in the media]," Satrapi explains. "I mean this way of looking at some country, to say suddenly a whole country, they are fanatics. Or a whole country, they are like this, they are like that. I mean, we are the same people. In the seventies, Jimmy Carter was coming to our country with his wife to have lunch with the king. And about two hundred thousand Americans were living in Iran and it was not fanatics, and we were good people. So how come suddenly we became fanatics? These things that I heard about my country were so far from what I knew about my country, and I kept on saying this story forever. I went from the point of view that I was not a politician, and not a historian, and not a sociologist, but I am born in a certain time in a certain place. And I can know nothing about nothing, but something that I know *is* what I have seen and what I have heard and what I've experienced myself. So nobody can take that from me. And so I wanted to give my version of the story [to] try to make people understand that it's not exactly the way you think it is. Just listen to my point of view and maybe you will understand what has really happened."

And this also raises the rather sobering issue that since *Persepolis* is an autobiography, it features portrayals of her parents that are not always flattering. In one scene, Marjane's mother, outraged at both her daughter and the family maid for attending a revolution protesting the Shah, slaps them both across the face. Many parents would have a problem with their children airing their dirty laundry, and showing them as flawed. But Satrapi says that her parents, also portrayed in the book as open-minded intellectuals, had no problem with this portrayal. "First of all, I am very honest about them but I love them very much and I think you can feel it through the book," she notes. "These are the people that I really, really, really, really love, and they have their weak points, and they are not perfect, and nobody is perfect. And I love them more because of their imperfections. Yeah, once in a while I tease them. But I tease them in real life too. I tease them much more in real life than I do in the book."

Marjane partially attributes the fact that she was even able to take on a mammoth project such as *Persepolis* to the way she was raised by her parents. "In my family, we would always have different points of view," she

From Persepolis: The Story of a Childhood by Marjane Satrapi; translated by Mattias Ripa and Blake Ferris, translation © 2003 by L'Association, Paris, France; used by permission of Pantheon Books, a division of Random House

SATRAPI DOESN'T SUGARCOAT HER CHILDHOOD, AS IN THIS SCENE WHEN HER MOTHER HITS HER FOR DISOBEDIENCE.

reveals. "We could criticize each other, we could even shout at each other, and a day after it was over. Criticism is not something bad. It is something that I have for my education. Because you criticize also the things that you love the most because you—in a way—you have the conviction that these things have a potential of being much better. When I was in America, people they would say, 'Why do you hate so much your country?' And I would say, 'Why do you think I hate my country? I love my country. I want my country to be better. I think that we have a great potential. I have spent four years of my life trying to humanize my country, not because I hate it, because I love it!' So it is the same thing, the relationship that you have to people. Criticism, that means that you care."

REAL LIFE: THE SEQUEL

In 2004, *Persepolis 2* (a compilation of the European editions of *Persepolis 3* and *4*) was published in the United States. Just as *Persepolis* is about how frightening and confounding the world is for a small child, *Persepolis 2* is about the hard choices we make during adulthood. Here we see Marjane Satrapi's tumultuous years in Austria, where aside from having her first serious relationship with a man, she bounces around from a boarding house to her friend's house to a communal apartment to being homeless on the street. After fainting from malnutrition, she finds herself in the hospital, and with no other choice, she flies back home to Tehran, which she immediately finds stifling: the mandatory veils; the denial of all things Western (pop music, neckties, makeup); the heavy, shapeless clothing; the morbid obsession with the martyred dead. She enters art school in 1989, but this proves a farce, as the female life drawing models are draped in veils and body-length robes, and thus impossible to render with any degree of anatomical accuracy. (And since the moral code forbids women from looking at the figure of a male they're not married to, she finds drawing male models equally infuriating.) Marjane plows through art school emerging as a top student, by this time stuck in a failing marriage. By 1994, having graduated, divorced, and sick of the rampant sexism and censorship so prevalent throughout her homeland, she goes to France.

One theme that runs through *Persepolis 2* is that old chestnut "you can't go home again." This is crystallized in the scene where Marjane meets up with her old friends, who now (in the privacy of their own homes, where they can't be scrutinized) have done up their hair and makeup to resemble *90210*-ish American television stars. When it comes out that Marjane is no longer a virgin, and in fact has had more than one lover, one of her friends blurts out, "So what's the difference between you and a whore?" This makes Marjane realize that for all their attempts to mimic carefree Western ways, her friends still cling to traditional beliefs and therefore think of her as a decadent Western woman. But Satrapi harbors her friends no ill will for their rude behavior. "They were young people and they were full of hormones, like all the young people," she laughs. "And of course I did what they [would have] loved to do, so it was a matter of jealousy and envy I think. Because I was free enough in my mind to do what I wanted to do and they were not. But you know, I am still friends with all these people. I don't have this kind of deep hate for people, never. You still have the cruelty of your childhood when you are eighteen or nineteen. You say things without thinking. Only if they do something bad then I will kill them with my own hand, but you know, if you call me whore one time, OK, what the hell. It is better to be a whore than to be stupid. And that is something I have never been in my life, stupid."

Similarly, Satrapi doesn't shy away from showing her own dark side in *Persepolis 2*. In one scene, she finds herself outside of a shopping center wearing forbidden lipstick and sees the Guardians of the Revolution (the morality police) barreling through town preparing for a raid. Panicking, she decides to divert their attention away from her lipstick by directing them toward an innocent bystander, saying that he made an indecent comment to her. He is taken away by them and she is safe, until she gets home and relates the incident to her grandmother, who chastises her for her cowardice.

As Satrapi herself tells it, it wasn't particularly painful relating these events in the *Persepolis* books. "I don't have this Judeo-Christian bad conscience, you know," she explains. "I don't feel guilty and I don't write these things to feel better in my life. This is not the point. The point is to say even for someone who is as aware as myself, or who says what she feels, et cetera, the fear makes you completely paralyzed and when you are fearful, you can't do anything. It was to underline what I have always said, it's not that people suddenly become crazy. It is that when you make a totalitarian regime that is based on the notion of terror, of fear, they paralyze your brain, and then you don't think anymore because whatever you do is because of your fear. So this episode, that was to say, even me who has never denounced anyone, in a situation when I was scared, I did the same thing. So you know, this superhero story, I mean Superman is nice and everything, but who believes in Superman? If you just show how nice and how clean you are, [what's the point]? I want one person who can present he has never done anything bad in his life. I haven't met them, and that is also part of my charm. Bad things I have done. That is my experiences. I don't deny them, and I can't even say that I regret them. Because if I didn't do them, I wouldn't know how bad they were. So now I have this notion of myself, of what I really don't like in my life, and that is because of the knowledge I have by doing them. So it's part of the reality. Everybody is complex and yes I show myself as a cute little intelligent child, [but also] a little bit cruel."

Another major theme which strongly pervades both volumes of *Persepolis* is that of religious hypocrisy. Throughout both books, we see several self-proclaimed spiritual people (e.g., the Guardians of the Revolution) committing violence toward innocents and simply behaving in a cowardly, self-serving manner. However, Satrapi is not condemning religion, nor is she denouncing spirituality. She's merely pointing out that some people are so corrupt that they'll use anything to further their own bestial ends, including the tools that are meant to bring them closer to God. And Satrapi also shows us the inverse of this, the good people who really are men and women of God, the rare ones who haven't been corrupted by the hypocrisy and cowardice that runs rampant in any culture.

For example, there's the scene where Marjane is taking an "ideological test," which is mandatory for entrance into the local university. The mullah who's testing her values her honesty and her fearlessness; later, he is the reason she's not expelled for speaking her mind against the confining veils and robes she and her fellow female students are forced to wear in art class. She considers this mullah a "true religious man," and here we see that her perspective on religion is anything but one-sided.

"First of all, the problem with religion is not the religion itself," she explains. "If the religion is kept at a very personal level because everybody believes in something in one way or in another, it's fine for me. People, if they want to have the longest beard in their life, if they want to cover themselves as they like, this is their problem. I don't have any judgments about that. People can believe and behave the way that they want. The problem when dictatorship goes with the religion is that in religion, something that you lose is the notion of doubt. In any ideology that is made by human beings, like fascism, Nazism, you have a human being behind it, so you can always doubt about it. When it comes to religion, they say God has said so. And God's a very abstract notion. And you can say anything and then say God said it. Why the hell is the religious person going to be closer to the God than myself? If there is a God, it is close to all of us. He is in all of us. All of us are a little bit of the God. So this is the problem. So the person who says, 'I am the voice of God,' in a way he puts himself as being the

elite. 'I am the best, I am closer to God.' I don't believe in any sort of hierarchy and nobody's closer. That's why I don't like these people. Because
they take the most profound feeling in human beings—the need of God,
the need of knowing why we are here, why we have to die and all of that.
Can you imagine that we die for the same reason that a worm dies? The
cells, they stop reproducing themselves just because, well, we have to make
the next generation stronger and all of that. Nobody knows why the cells
stop reproducing. And with that, it is for the same reason why the cat and
dog and chicken dies. The only problem is that we are conscious about that.
So it is a complete mess. So of course we need God and religion. Of course
we need all of that. But then, you know some people they will tell you, 'Oh
I have a very special relationship with that.' So that is something that I
refuse. The hypocrisy, the abuse of power. And people today they say, 'Oh,
this is Islam.' Can you believe they are talking about one religion? One single religion that has been mixed by politics and it has given a good result?
What about the Inquisition? What about the Middle Ages?"

THE VAGARIES OF MEN

In 2003, as a change of pace between the two *Persepolis* books, Marjane
Satrapi released the light, funny, episodic graphic novel *Embroideries*, a collection of anecdotes about the sex lives of Iranian women. As Marjane and
her mother gather together with the other women in her family and some
family friends to drink tea, they inevitably start telling stories: about the
woman who tried to use a razor on her wedding night to pretend she was
a virgin, but ended up slicing her husband's testicle; about the thirteen-
year-old girl who found herself engaged to a sixty-nine-year-old general,
who then refused to grant the child a divorce; and about the pleasures of
being a mistress, the one woman in a married man's life who doesn't have
to put up with his bullshit. The very title *Embroideries* refers to the medical procedure of "sewing up" a woman's vagina so that it appears that she's
a virgin. This procedure, practiced frequently in decades past but not so
common anymore, is emblematic of the sociological changes that have
taken place in Iran, where in the past, a woman was expected to be a virgin on her wedding night. As in the West, that's simply not the case anymore. Even in Satrapi's lightest book, she sneaks in sly social commentary.

The very concept of *Embroideries* caught some off guard; although the
book was originally conceived as a sort of intermission between the two *Persepolis* volumes, publishers in other countries didn't always understand this. "The
thing is [in Europe], *Embroideries* came between *Persepolis 1* and *Persepolis 2*,"

Satrapi explains. "And in America it came after *Persepolis 2*, which makes a big difference. In the first *Persepolis* book I wrote so much about the torture and the war and the dead people and the blood and all of that, that I suddenly realized that there is all this cute and nice and humorous things that I don't have the space [for], and this is not the sort of place to talk about. And I wanted to make this book as a breather.

"And I also wanted to test another form of narration, because the form of *Embroideries* is extremely different from *Persepolis*. For me, *Persepolis* is a book in which I try to make people understand. That's why you have all these frames,

A MORE LIGHTHEARTED EFFORT THAN THE PERSEPOLIS BOOKS, EMBROIDERIES FOCUSED ON THE SEX LIVES OF IRANIAN WOMEN.

it's extremely mathematically made—everything is extremely clean. You cannot lose yourself. But for me, each story has its own narration. The way you make the layout cannot be the same, the format cannot be same, nothing can be the same. For me, the challenge is that [*Embroideries*] is about 140 pages and it happens in a living room. How am I going to make it attractive enough that after ten pages, you are not bored. So each page, I have to [think], 'OK, how am I going to compose the page that is not going to [just] be five women sitting in a living room?' So, I have to find a new way. And I was like, 'OK, it's a conversation. The conversation is open.' In a conversation, you enter when you want and you get out exactly when you want. It's a very open form. So I could not have any frames, because the book has to look like a conversation. And it is so exciting to me to do something that I have never done. And I get extremely bored to do something that I had already done."

And for her blunt honesty in telling the sometimes embarrassing or humbling stories of her female relatives, Satrapi doesn't feel she's incurred any anger or resentment on their part. "My mother read it," Satrapi recalls. "And she said, 'Wow! For this country to change, we need women like you.' You know Azar Nafisi, the writer of *Reading Lolita in Tehran*? She is a big hit in America. She's a teacher of literature and all of that, she told me it was the first time she heard an Iranian talking about eroticism—she loved the book. I had very many good feedback. My father said if anybody criticized me, he will hit them in the face. I'm surrounded by people that are not offended by this sort of thing. As in [*Persepolis*], all the faces and all the names have been changed. So nobody can recognize themselves, because I'm completely aware they are very very intimate stories. These are not the real people. The stories are as I really heard them, but you know the lady in the story for example, who has four kids and this and that, in reality, that is not her name at all. She doesn't have four kids, but only one. But of course some people, they are scandalized. I don't care. Sex to me is a very sweet subject to talk about. I don't know why we can make all these cooking books and everything about eating and all of that, and another pleasure, we cannot talk about it without being immoral. It comes from the feeling of guilt, the church says that sex is bad because Jesus was born and he died a virgin, and Mary was a virgin and all of that. This is amazing that we're sitting here in 2005 and they still believe in the same thing!"

PLUM, GRAD, FILM

Marjane Satrapi has seen her talent as a cartoonist grow and mature rapidly over the past several years. "Oh, it has changed, naturally it changed," she nods. "I have learned to draw better, I have learned to write better. It is much more important for me to be able to surprise myself than publishing something that the market wants me to publish. There are so many things that we can make in comics. Everything is possible. It's an amazing medium."

Satrapi considers her new graphic novel *Chicken and Plum* (published in 2005 in Europe) to be her greatest accomplishment in the comics medium. "The book is about this musician, and his instrument gets broken," she explains. "And you understand later that it's his wife who breaks it one day out of anger. And he tries to buy a new one, and he buys about four or five of them, and none of them makes the noise, the sound that he likes, and he can't bear it, and he decides to die. And he lies down in his bed, and eight days after, he dies. The story is about the eight days. And through whatever he thinks, the flashback to the past, what is going to be in the future, you completely understand why this story happens and you're surprised by the motive of this very slow suicide. I really wanted to write about death. It's because my relationship in my culture toward death is not same relationship as in the West. Because in the West, you are young and performing and then you are not there anymore. You don't become old, you don't lose your power, you don't die. But in my culture, you talk about dying all the time, you go to the cemetery. I use a lot of Persian poetry. But you will see that this is the book that I prefer. Maybe the next story that I write will be the book that I prefer again. But until the latest book that I make, this is the book that I prefer the most. I think it's good. If I make a book and say, 'Oh Jesus, the book that I made before was much better,' then I will stop making books."

Her next graphic novel will be called *The Eleventh Graduate*, and will see print in America in 2007. "It is the story of my other grandmother from my father's side because she was the eleventh woman who graduated from high school in Iran in her village," she reveals, taking pains to explain that this is *not* her matriarchal grandmother, who is depicted in the *Persepolis* books and *Embroideries*. "This is a woman with a very incredible story! She escaped from her parents' house dressed as a man, in order to be able to marry my grandfather. They made six children together because she absolutely wanted to have a daughter and God gave her six sons. My grandfather at the same time was a great gambler, he was gambling all the time and he was a teacher at the same time. So, this is the story of this woman, the story of this man, the story of the love, the way they met, the way they got separated. And also my grandmother, she was a very mean person, a real witch. A very intelligent witch, but a real witch. And also to try to understand through all this gambling and all these things, how this woman, she lost her innocence and she lost her humanity and lost her humor. From being ironic, she became sarcastic, and from being sarcastic she became cynical, and from being cynical she became a complete nihilist, and from then she had complete hate of humanity. They are the two stories that go in parallel. For me, a big love affair that finished, and a big hate. I love those kinds of stories. I love the kind of thing that are not very fashionable today [in most autobiographical comics]. Mostly better to talk about the pimple on your face or that you need some butter in your fridge and this absolutely kind of nonsense stuff. You know, I love this big saga of things that are not as beautiful as a film with Elizabeth Taylor and Richard Burton, but they are more real. And exactly because they are more real, they are more romantic and more dirty. So this is what I want to try to say all of that in the same book. So, I will see how I will manage to do that."

And as she manages to tell one family story in comics, Satrapi is hard at work trying to tell another true-life saga on celluloid. She's adapting

IN PERSEPOLIS 2, SATRAPI LENT CREDENCE TO THE OLD CHESTNUT "YOU CAN'T GO HOME AGAIN."

the two volumes of *Persepolis* as a black-and-white animated film, with a tentative release date of 2007. "I cowrote it and am codirecting it with a friend of mine whose name is Vincent Paronnaud," she reveals. "We have never directed a movie, but we try. So if in 2007 if you hear about an animated movie of *Persepolis*, that means that we have done it. If you don't hear about it, that means that our producer has hanged himself. So it's either one or the other. It's [produced by] 2-4-7 Productions. The thing is that we don't have so much experience, but we're extremely motivated, we're very enthusiastic, and we work with a very great team of animators. And actually, I know that even Americans are involved in investing into the project!" Her exuberance in telling the story of *Persepolis* on the page makes its film adaptation one of the more eagerly awaited animated projects of 2007, one that's sure to expose her story to an even wider audience.

THE STORY OF A RETURN

In just a few short years, Marjane Satrapi has risen to the top of the autobiographical comics pantheon, eschewing the usual subject matter of day-to-day minutiae and dysfunctional families for bigger themes like war, true love, life, and death. And all the while, in books like *Persepolis* and *Embroideries*, she's given us a more balanced, humanized view of Iranian life than CNN could ever hope to conjure.

Her career is chock-full of the kind of ironies that success brings; the children's books editors deemed "unpublishable" when she first started trying to sell them are now sought after by major publishers. Her childhood, at turns wondrous and confusing, has made excellent fodder for a series of graphic novels and a forthcoming animated feature film. But most ironic of all is the fact that the outspoken girl who was never interested in comic books—after all, the one childhood memory she associated with it was a case of worms—found that comics were the perfect medium to tell the sort of stories she was interested in telling. And with books like *Chicken and Plum*, it's obvious Marjane Satrapi isn't content with simply returning to her childhood again and again for source material; she's intent on telling new and different types of stories each and every time, growing as an artist. Truly, the comic book industry sorely needs more voices like hers, at once angry, passionate, and hilarious.

INDEX

Numbers in italics denote illustrations.

Wise Son: The White Wolf, 212, *231, 232–33,* 234
"The Woman Who Couldn't," 86
Women and the Comics, 89, 91
The Womenation, 85
Wonder Warthog, 83
Wonder Woman, 79, 81, 90–91, *90*
Wonder Woman: The Once and Future Story, 91
Wood, Wally, 10, 64
Wow, What a Magazine!, 4
Wright, Greg, 200, 202
Wrightson, Berni, 83, 150, 175
Wyatt Wingfoot, 56

X

X-Men, 30, 58–59
X-Men, 47, 58–59, 172
X-Men #1, 58
X-Men (movie, 2000), 67
Xombi, 212

Y

Yeah!, 144
Yosemite Sam, x
You Are Here, 160–62, 168
Yronwode, Catherine, 89, 91

Z

Zap, 12, 83
Zulli, Michael, 186
Zwigoff, Terry, 105